Transportation and economic stagnation in Spain

David R. Ringrose: *Transportation and economic stagnation in Spain, 1750–1850*

Durham, N. C.

Duke University Press

1 9 7 0

PRINTED IN THE UNITED STATES OF
AMERICA BY THE SEEMAN PRINTERY

Preface

By about 1800, Spain was caught in a serious and perhaps insoluble dilemma by the fact that the traditional transport system of the interior had reached the limits of its capacity. "Modern" European technology at the time offered as alternatives both macadamized roads traveled by freight wagons and barge canals. These were experimented with and proved inappropriate because of the amounts of capital required to install them and the inflexible nature of the services they provided. The resulting bottleneck in the supply of transportation created social and economic stagnation in the interior for half a century. Beyond the scope of this study, one could hazard the suggestion that railroads, introduced into Spain after 1850, also proved incapable of sustaining long-term economic growth in the interior. They appear to have raised the level of internal urbanization, population, and regional specialization in monocultures, but left the economy of the interior stagnant once again in the last decades of the nineteenth century.[1]

It is reasonable and thought provoking to remove the locational elements from the situation and emphasize the problem in the abstract. This suggests that a backward region can develop a technically primitive transport system which meets the needs of a slowly evolving society, only to discover that beyond a given point the system is incapable of continued expansion. The alternatives then become stagnation or the introduction of new transport techniques. A region or society faced with such a dilemma may find that the techniques offered by the "advanced" world are inappropriate, or, once installed, achieve only a part of their apparent potential. The only possible outcome is economic stagnation until further alternatives appear.

If such a dilemma could confront Spain, an essentially European

1. Such an implication can be drawn from a review of Jaime Vicens Vives, *Manual de Historia Económica de España* (Barcelona: Editorial Vicens Vives, 1964), graphs of volume of imports and exports, p. 629, cotton imports, p. 608, numbers of livestock, p. 593, and population growth, p. 562. The decline of the interior is illustrated by Vicens Vives, *Historia de España y América* (5 vols.; Barcelona: Editorial Vicens Vives, 1961), V, 19, table of population shifts by province. Some of the problems of introducing the railroads are given by Rondo Cameron, *France and the Economic Development of Europe, 1800-1914* (2nd ed.; Chicago: Rand McNally & Co., 1965), pp. 160-172.

country, at the edge of but nevertheless within the European economy, it is plausible that European transport technology at given times was inappropriate to many underdeveloped areas, and for that reason they remained backward. A random and perhaps extreme example of this is the portion of Peru located across the Andes in the upper Amazon Basin. At first glance, it appears that the area could have been opened with railroads. Yet a preliminary cost analysis in 1960 showed that rail transport would in fact have cost from 50 percent to 430 per cent more per ton/mile than a modern trucking system.[2] The choice was obvious, but in the era before highway transport was well developed, there passed some sixty or more years during which the railroad was the most "modern" alternative, and conceivably a quite impractical one.

In Peru the extreme backwardness of the area being developed made the primary considerations the cost of installation and maintenance. In an old and complex society, this is complicated by other "costs" in the form of social and institutional change. One would not have to search far to find other samples which suggest that one must examine carefully the failure of particular regions at various times to respond as expected to borrowed technology.

The implications of an inelastic supply of a particular type of transport and the lack of an alternative can also be applied to situations in sixteenth- and seventeenth-century Europe. A concrete example is the city of Venice, with its increasingly difficult problem of finding adequate supplies of ship-building materials. This hampered the city's ship-building industry, made the supply of shipping inelastic, and contributed to the stagnation of the commerce and naval power which were the bases of Venetian properity.[3]

Returning to land transport, and using a wider frame of reference, an inelasticity of transport supply may well be related to the crises of the seventeenth century. The 1600's marked the final, clear-cut economic supremacy of the North Sea countries over those of the Mediterranean, and this was probably associated with the failure of the technology and organization of land transport to develop at the same pace as maritime technology. Medieval land transport was based on pack animals, carts, wagons, and roads which were little more than customary rights-of-way between towns, providing a great number of alternate routes.[4] By the

2. John B. Lansing, *Transportation and Economic Policy* (New York: Free Press, 1966), p. 156.
3. Frederick C. Lane, *Venetian Ships and Shipbuilders of the Renaissance* (Baltimore: Johns Hopkins University Press, 1934).
4. Robert S. Lopez, "Evolution of Land Transport in the Middle Ages," *Past and Present*, No. 9 (1956), 23-28.

thirteenth century the elaboration of transport based on this system provided wagon transport over long distances which was on occasion actually cheaper per unit/distance than coastal shipping.[5] There is little to suggest more than marginal improvements in overland transport until the development of canals with modern-style locks and turnpikes with all-weather surfaces in the eighteenth century.[6] Braudel, however, suggests that land transport was able to compete against the perils of sea transport until about 1600. Thereafter the growing relative superiority of sea transport lowered shipping costs enough to cause the decline of areas in the Balkans, Alps, and Spain which could not use this alternative.[7] Here again, the alternative offered by the "modern" technology of the time was inappropriate or impractical to a number of areas, especially in southern Europe, and the only alternative was commercial and industrial stagnation.

Yet another application of this study is possible. In a recent article on "new" and "traditional" approaches to economic history,[8] Fritz Redlich discusses Robert Fogel's attempt to determine the net social benefits which railroads brought by analyzing and theoretically reconstructing United States growth as it might have occurred if railroads had not been invented. Redlich raises the question, "At what point would economic development, under way by 1800, have become an arrested development [in France, England, or the United States] for lack of adequate transportation?"[9] This study answers the question with regard to Spain. It does not, however, do this with the elaborate theoretical and "counterfactual" apparatus which Fogel recommends,[10] but rather with a more traditional approach based on careful use of many kinds of sources, including statistical data where possible. The content and findings of the work invite comparison with the role of transport in other countries.

Despite the use of an institutional approach and detailed concern with non-economic factors, an attempt has been made to minimize the haziness of theoretical assumptions which Fogel warns against. This was done by basing the work on a rudimentary but sound framework of

5. *Ibid.*
6. Charles Singer, *et al.*, eds., *A History of Technology*, Vol. III, *1500-1750* (Oxford: The Clarendon Press, 1957), pp. 139-48.
7. Fernan Braudel, *La Méditerranée et le monde méditerranéen à l'époque de Philippe II* (Paris: Colin, 1949), pp. 244-49.
8. Fritz Redlich, "'New' and Traditional Approaches to Economic History and Their Interdependence," *Journal of Economic History*, XXV (1965), 480-95.
9. Redlich, p. 487.
10. Robert Fogel, "The New Economic History: I. Its Findings and Methods," *Economic History Review*, 2nd ser., XIX (1966), 642-56.

supply and demand, analyzing the components of both sides of the equation and the imperfections in the transport market, especially on the crucial supply side.

The result does not answer a question such as Fogel asks: "Can we measure the effect of something by reconstructing the world as though that thing had not occurred?" Rather, it asks the more traditional questions: "What happened, and why; what did not happen, and why not?" These questions are mirror images of the one suggested by Fogel, since they imply that under alternate circumstances a different outcome would result.[11] Nevertheless, I would agree with the substance of Redlich's argument that, from the historian's point of view, an answer to the second question must be attempted before experimenting with the first.

Implicit in all of the preceding, and in the study which follows, is the premise that economic growth and development are impossible without a ready supply of specialized transport. Specialization here implies transport that is divorced from the seasonal manpower requirements of agriculture, can ignore all but the worst limitations imposed by weather, can handle a considerable volume of goods, and can surmount obstacles of terrain and distance with relative effectiveness. The validity of the premise needs little theoretical justification—it is contained implicitly or explicitly in most discussions of economic development.[12] One has only to point out that no commodity—food, raw material, or finished product—is more than potentially marketable or usable until it is transported to the consumer.

In basic economic terms, therefore, transport is a factor of production, and its cost is a cost of production.[13] If the supply of this factor of production is inelastic, beyond a certain point its increasing scarcity will cause the cost of production in general to rise sharply, limiting markets for goods produced, and thus stifling further expansion of output.

Transport services, however, are also a product, and therefore are influenced by a complex pattern of factors of production. These factors are both economic and social, and include the level of existing technology, the appropriateness of newer innovations to the given context, the availability of capital for installing technology, and the socio-eco-

11. Fogel, p. 655.

12. As random examples, see: Phyllis Deane, *The First Industrial Revolution* (Cambridge: The University Press, 1965), chap. v; Hla Myint, *The Economics of the Developing Countries* (New York: Praeger, 1965), pp. 29, 41, 96-97; W. W. Rostow, *The Stages of Economic Growth* (Cambridge: The University Press, 1960), pp. 24-26.

13. Harold J. Barnett and Chandler Morse, *Scarcity and Growth: The Economics of Natural Resource Availability* (Baltimore: Johns Hopkins University Press, 1965), pp. 143-45.

nomic institutions which determine how available resources and technology are to be used. All of these must be examined in detail in assessing the impact of alternative transport techniques and the limitations of existing ones.

At the level of observed examples, this study illustrates how transport limitations contributed to Spanish economic stagnation as the eighteenth century ended and the nineteenth century began. At a more general level, it suggests by example that the factors which shape and limit the existing transport system of a backward country are very complex and intimately connected with the social, economic, and political arrangements in the society concerned. It also illustrates how institutions and resource endowment in such an area may preclude the introduction or successful use of ostensibly superior techniques, with the resulting legacy of long-term stagnation.

In making a study such as this, one invariably accumulates a long list of obligations which deserve acknowledgment. Among my American acquaintances, I am grateful to Professor Earl J. Hamilton for initial encouragement on the project, and to Professor Julian Bishko for suggestions and advice after reading an advanced version of the manuscript. My colleagues in the Rutgers Department of History have made similar contributions and criticisms, most particularly Professors Herbert Rowen, Carter Jefferson, Trian Stoianovich, Henry Winkler, and Harold Poor.

The study would have been impossible without the generous assistance of numerous Spanish scholars, archivists, and officials. First among these is Don José Tudela de la Orden, now retired from the Archivo Histórico Nacional in Madrid, who began the study of the carters and was most generous in assisting my work. Another such person was Don Antonio Matilla Tascón, of the Archivo de la Hacienda, who directed me to several valuable sources. Also deserving more recognition than they generally get are the staffs of the Archivo Histórico Nacional, the Archivo General de Simancas, and the Archivo de la Real Chancillería de Granada. Similar recognition is due to present and past archivists in Seville, Málaga, Granada, Murcia, Madrid, Burgos, Palencia, Alcalá de Henares, and Toledo, whose efforts have made those collections usable. Finally, recognition is due to a most conscientious young lady from Valladolid, Ana María Hurtado, who spent many dreary hours in the archives at Simancas.

The later stages of revision and preparation were facilitated by grants-in-aid and a Summer Fellowship from the Research Council of Rutgers, The State University. The research itself was made possible by twenty-one months of support in the form of a student grant under the Fulbright-Hayes Program, and by a Fellowship from the Vilas Foundation of the University of Wisconsin. The help of the Director of the Fulbright Office in Madrid, Don Ramón Bela, was invaluable, and the warmth, kindness, and generosity of the Assistant Director, Doña Mathilde Medina, will never be forgotten.

The three most important acknowledgments, however, are due closer individuals. Foremost among these is recognition of the time which my wife, Kathryn, contributed—many long hours in cold, dusty archives, and many dreary hours drawing maps and making lists with no clear purpose in view. I also wish to acknowledge the time and care that Professor Domenico Sella devoted to studying and criticizing the early drafts of the study. Dr. Sella acted as my thesis adviser, and most of his suggestions for revision have been accepted with gratitude. Lastly, I wish to thank Professor Rondo Cameron, who was my adviser during much of my graduate work. It was through him that I was drawn to economic history, and it was his advice and assistance which made the research possible and financially feasible.

Table of Contents

List of Tables

List of maps

Abbreviations

Actas   *Actas de las Cortes de Castilla*

AGS   Archivo General de Simancas
    Catastro   Materials from the *Catastro* of the Marqués of Ensenada
    Guerra   *Secretaría de Guerra*
    Hacienda   *Secretaría de Hacienda*
    Sello   *Régistro de Sello*

AHN   Archivo Histórico Nacional (Madrid)
    Clero   *Sección de Clero*
    Códices   *Sección de Códices*
    Con.   *Sección de Consejos Suprimidos*
    CRC   *Colección de Reales Cédulas*
    Hac.   *Sección del Consejo de Hacienda*
    Osuna   *Sección de los Osuna*
    SID   *Servicio de Información Documental*

AHP   Archivo Histórico Provincial
AA   *Archivo del Ayuntamiento* (town council)
A Medinaceli   Archives of the Medinaceli family (Seville)
ARCG   Archivo de la Real Chancillería de Granada
doc.   document
fol.   folio
leg.   *legajo* (bundle)
lib.   *libro* (book)
NR   *Novísima Recopilación de las Leyes de Castilla* (1804-1807)
tit.   *titulo* (title)

Introduction

Lack of an adequate transportation system in the Spanish interior was a primary cause of the political and economic stagnation of the country in the nineteenth century. In the early eighteenth century Spain began a demographic, economic, and political recovery which steadily increased the demand for transport services. As the rural population grew, it required an increasing volume of interregional transfers of subsistence commodities. At the same time, there was a gradual expansion of the urban population, especially in Madrid. This required ever more supplies, brought over increasing distances. The central government grew steadily, expanding its functions and rebuilding the army and navy. In the process it hired increasing amounts of transport away from the private sector. Finally, the government engaged in a widespread effort to expand exports and stimulate new industry in the interior. To the extent that this increased the tempo of internal trade, it brought a demand for transport to service new economic activities.

Through much of the century the transport system, based on animal power and primitive roads, met these demands with some success, although the economy of the interior continued to lag behind that of the coastal provinces. By the 1790's, however, the supply of transport was falling behind the demand, and in the years preceding the Napoleonic invasion the lack of transport was becoming critical. The result was a bottleneck which limited economic growth in the Castilian plains and mountains until it was finally broken by railroad technology after 1850. The older transport system was unable to provide the cheap and flexible transportation needed to reach the scattered markets of the interior. Despite the relative prosperity of the eighteenth century, therefore, the central areas developed little industry of their own, nor could they provide an elastic market for the industry of the coastal regions.

To a large extent, the transport system was limited by its backward environment. The availability of resources, their geographical distribution, patterns of land ownership and control, the attitudes of high-income groups, the effectiveness of government, and the willingness and ability to use available technology all effect economic growth. In Spain many of these factors worked to limit the transportation system.

At the same time, however, the social and economic structure of an activity such as transportation acquires a degree of autonomy from the economy as a whole. If this autonomous structure remains flexible and able to adapt new technology to local conditions, it will encourage economic growth. If it becomes rigid, its ability to supply the specialized transportation required by a developing economy remains limited. It becomes impossible to overcome the obstacles to economic growth. The interaction of transport with other factors and its crucial importance are made obvious by a brief comparison of developments in Spain and England.

In the eighteenth century some of the peripheral regions of Spain, notably Catalonia, began to exploit ocean transport to gain access to overseas raw materials and markets. The royal government's conscious reform of commercial, naval, and colonial administration contributed greatly to these advances. Such policies, coupled with a local tradition of commerce and industry, created a small industrial complex in Catalonia resembling that of England. But unlike England, there was little parallel development in the Spanish interior and little interaction between the central regions and the progressive coast.

In England there had been a rapid development of import-export trade beginning in the late seventeenth century, creating both capital and markets for British industry.[1] Equally important, however, was England's substantial domestic market, generated by the agrarian revolution. England by 1750 had the highest per capita income in Europe, matched only by the Netherlands, while France, the third wealthiest country, was noticeably poorer. Moreover, English wealth was distributed widely enough to generate mass buying power for manufactured goods. A critical factor allowing the exploitation of this potential market was England's small size and many navigable rivers. With a modest investment in connecting canals and roads, producers could reach a large part of the interior market at reasonable transport costs.[2]

No comparable estimate of per capita income in Spain has been constructed, but the level was well below that of France, as illustrated by comparative grain yields in the 1840's. The average yield in the Netherlands was 14 hectolitres of grain per hectare, in Great Britain it was

---

1. Ralph Davis, "English Foreign Trade, 1660-1700," *Economic History Review*, 2nd ser., VII (1954), 150-66; Deane, chap. iii; A. H. John, "Aspects of English Economic Growth in the First Half of the Eighteenth Century," *Economica*, XXVIII (1961), 176-190.

2. Deane, pp. 6-8, and chap v.

13.2, in France 9.3, and in Spain 6.2, one of the lowest in Europe.[3] In a country which was nearly 95 per cent rural, the figure for Spain implies an extremely low average income. With a poor and dispersed population, the absence of a cheap and flexible means of transportation combined with the relatively large size of Spain to keep the interior market extremely small and static.

Since land transport was not available, the only outlets for Catalan manufactures were the Spanish coastal towns and Spanish America. Spain's only modern industry had to rely upon the possession and political control of a distant empire for its markets. The fragility of this arrangement was made painfully clear during the French Wars when the American market was permanently lost and Catalan development retarded for fifty years. The nature of the transport system in the Spanish interior was a crucial factor in the inability of Catalonia to develop alternative markets for its manufactures in Spain proper.

This suggests a high degree of local and regional isolation in the interior; yet other evidence indicates that a substantial amount of transport activity took place. This requires careful examination, since it is easy to explain stagnation when transport is not available, but more difficult to explain it when transport does exist but cannot be used for development.

Among the conditions suggesting local isolation were widely dispersed markets and producers, poor or nonexistent roads, long distances, a lack of usable waterways, and low incomes. Some writers, noting these conditions, have concluded that little transport activity existed. Yet Earl J. Hamilton comments at one point on the regularity with which prices in distant regions experienced parallel fluctuations, even though price levels varied considerably.[4] Only a variety and substantial volume of goods regularly moving between regions can explain such parallel price movements.

Although regional specialization and differences in price levels helped generate trade and transportation, much of the explanation of the paradox comes from the organization of transport itself. If transport was more widely available than is supposed, why was it so difficult to

3. Jerome Blum, *Lord and Peasant in Russia from the Ninth to the Nineteenth Century* (New York: Atheneum, 1965), p. 330.

4. Earl J. Hamilton, *American Treasure and the Price Revolution in Spain, 1500-1650* (Cambridge, Mass.: Harvard University Press, 1934), pp. 203, 221. In 1799 wheat was 22 *reales* the *fanega* in Salamanca, 55 in Guadalajara, 60 in Toledo. Olive oil was 30 *reales* the *arroba* in Seville and Jaén, 69 in Toledo, and 80 in Granada. *Censo de la riqueza territorial e industrial de España en el año 1799, formado de orden superior* (Madrid: Ministerio de Hacienda, 1960).

promote factories and economic development? Such efforts found collection of raw materials and distribution of products major obstacles.[5] It appears that transport was available for some purposes, but not for others.

Despite considerable complexity and the presence of a large body of professional carters, the traditional organization of transport in the Spanish interior was severely limited in its ability to respond to economic change. The same problems of population dispersion, topography, and lack of capital which shaped the old transport system also hindered the effective use of better means of transport. The government, as the principal innovator in eighteenth-century Spain, lacked the resources to install the canals and paved highways which European technology had made available. Such facilities were not, in any case, easily adapted to the rugged and dry conditions of Castile. Traffic on most routes was slight; there were many connections required between small groups of consumers and producers and long distances to be covered. This called for a widespread network of improved local roads tied to a few modest canals, not the grandiose highways and canals which the Spanish planners copied from the French.

Transportation thus remained restricted to pack animals and relatively crude but sturdy ox-drawn carts. Pack animals constituted some 90 per cent of the transport pool. Such transport relied heavily on farm animals and manpower and was bound up with a vital pattern of transfers of food and other necessities imposed by the poor quality and unpredictability of Castilian agriculture. It therefore was not available to support new types of economic activity.

The carting industry, by contrast, was highly professionalized, but was equally restricted in its ability to support economic growth, partly because the carters' services were effectively monopolized by the government, which had to meet the needs of its bureaucracy and of Madrid, the administrative center. The carters were also hampered by their dependence on town commons for pasture while in transit and by their need for extensive winter pastures. The steady population growth after about 1750 brought increasing pressure for enclosure of open land just when the carters needed more grazing areas in order to expand their carrying capacity. As a result, the carters were unable to keep up with the demands put upon them. The supply of Madrid became increasingly precarious, and the government had to divert ever more of these pro-

5. James Clayburn La Force, Jr., *The Development of the Spanish Textile Industry, 1750-1800* (Berkeley: University of California Press, 1965), pp. 49-50.

fessionals to hauling supplies to the capital. This immediately curtailed the supply of professional transport for other uses.

The traditional transport system was thus proving inadequate for the needs of expanding urban life. The small proportion of the transport pool specialized enough to be flexible had to be diverted from other economic activities to supply the capital. Vital to the rural subsistence economy, seasonal pack-animal transport could not be drawn from the countryside. The cost of improved transit facilities and bad planning prevented the introduction of new means of transport. As a result, the supply of specialized transportation fell behind the demand, and a transport crisis developed which could only heighten the economic stagnation in the interior by choking off such progress as the eighteenth century had achieved.

The problem was not merely an economic one. In the Spain of the Old Regime, transportation was an activity deeply imbedded in a complex of social, legal, and political institutions. It is correspondingly difficult to talk about a general market for transport services, although within particular segments of the market the supply and demand mechanism of classical economics can be observed. Most carters, and a few muleteers, as professional carriers, belonged to brotherhoods which exercised some control over members and often engaged in collective bargaining to obtain contracts. As with the Mesta of the sheepherders and the more typical urban-based guilds of the Old Regime, the carting brotherhoods possessed certain unique privileges. In some situations therefore, they were subject to the general law of the land, while in others their own privileges took precedence.

These special privileges and exemptions were granted by the Crown of Castile over a period of three hundred years. At first they were intended to free the carters from localized restrictions, but gradually they became a device for subsidizing the carters with special pastures, tax exemptions, draft exemptions, and rent controls. Such subsidies guaranteed that transport would be available to the government when needed. Once accustomed to the privileges, the carters were left dependent on the government to enforce them. As a result the crown could easily assert a priority for government demands above all others in the economy.

To maintain this relationship, the crown gradually developed a bureaucratic arm which supervised the carters and acted as a system of special courts with exclusive jurisdiction over infringements of the carters' privileges. Every time the government used legal coercion to aid or control carting, it added to the imperfections in the market for transport services. Indeed, many of the privileges amounted to a form of disguised taxation imposed on municipal and private landowners. It is necessary, therefore, to examine the relationship between transportation and the government, as well as the institutional, legal, and political aspects of transport itself.

In a wider perspective, it is apparent that a policy of subsidizing transport with special privileges led the crown into contradictory policies for internal economic development. The government attempted to cope with population pressure by encouraging land enclosures designed to create an independent peasantry. It thus found itself in the position of encouraging enclosures on the one hand, while on the other its special courts were trying to maintain open grazing for the carters. Land hunger and the resultant enclosures help to explain why carting could not expand at the end of the century.

Basically the transportation problem concerned all of Spain, but since most of the interior provinces were under the old Crown of Castile, the focus of this study is on Castilian institutions and sources. The non-Castilian coastal areas, while economically important in their own right, were centered on seaports and had relatively little need for extensive land transport systems. The lack of cohesion of Spain was heightened by rugged terrain which hindered access from Portugal, Catalonia, and Valencia to Castile. Moreover, these areas long were administered separately, had distinct monetary systems, and were set apart from Castile by customs barriers. Only after the middle 1700's did the separation begin to break down, but even then internal trade remained much the same.

The most obvious change was the mid-century reform of the customs which removed the tariff barrier between Castile and the Crown of Aragón and equalized duties at most Spanish entry points. Parallel to this there appeared signs of Catalan penetration into the economic life of Castile and some growth of interregional trade. Nevertheless, there were no significant modifications in the pattern of Castilian transport before 1850. At the most there was a partial reorientation of long distance transport towards eastern, rather than northern, Spain, with no fundamental changes in the basic mechanisms of transport.[6] That it was the nature of transport itself which choked the development of internal trade is shown by the relative ineffectiveness of such reforms.

In discussing transportation, an important clarification must be made. Most descriptions of Spanish overland transportation deal primarily

6. José Muñoz Pérez, "Mapa aduanero del XVIII español," *Estudios Geográficos*, núm. 61 (1955), pp. 747-98; Raymond Carr, *Spain, 1808-1939* (London: Oxford University Press, 1966), p. 202.

with communications facilities. Communication involves carrying messages, orders, mail, and people between population centers, using postal systems and, before the railroad, stagecoaches. Such transport is of great political importance because it makes possible effective government and rapid troop movements. The facilities involved, however, are often of little use to the basic problem of moving food and resources within a country or region. Only exceptionally do roads designed for communication coincide with the transport needs of a preindustrial society. In eighteenth-century Spain this was not a common coincidence. Roads were laid out with communications in mind and were not well suited to the types of transport available and the economic needs of the country as a whole.[7]

The Spanish transportation crisis was clearly present before the catastrophe of the Napoleonic invasions, and it remained a bottleneck which hampered economic growth long after. This crisis is part of the explanation for the general retardation of Spanish economic, social, and political growth. Lack of transportation long reduced the interaction between the peripheral areas such as Vizcaya and Catalonia, which have shown themselves able to respond to technological and economic developments in Europe, and the large land mass of the Spanish interior, which has proved remarkably resistant to those same changes. The result has been an underlying dichotomy in Spanish politics and economics in which the economically progressive areas have been politically dominated by the conservative interior.

7. Carr, *Spain*, p. 198.

Transportation and economic stagnation in Spain

Chapter one. *The setting*

A. *The geography and demography of Spain*

Transportation in the Iberian Peninsula has always faced serious difficulties.[1] The peninsula is a large land mass, and its important centers are separated by considerable distances. It is 600 miles from Bilbao in the North to Seville in the South. Madrid, the economic center of the Castilian interior, is 200 to 400 miles from the sea and the important peripheral towns. Not only are the distances long, but, except for the lower reaches of the Guadalquivir and Ebro, there are no navigable rivers. Before the railroad, therefore, virtually all internal transportation was by road—and in few places in Spain can one travel more than fifty miles without having to climb a mountain.

The highest mountains in the country are the Pyrenees in the Northeast, reaching heights of 11,000 feet, and the Sierra Nevada in the Southeast, which includes one of the highest mountains in Europe, the 14,424-foot Mount Mulhacén. Connecting these two east-west ranges is a broad belt of lesser mountains and highlands—rugged, dry, and infertile—which separates the Mediterranean areas of Catalonia and Valencia from Castile. This mountainous belt, with peaks higher than 8,000 feet, forms the geological backbone of the Iberian Peninsula, most of which slopes south and westward to the Atlantic. The continental divide runs roughly from the western end of the Pyrenees south toward the eastern end of the Sierra Nevada. From this backbone five bands of mountains and highlands

1. Ruth Way, *A Geography of Spain and Portugal* (London: Methuen & Co., 1962), provides a convenient and recent summary of the subject of Spanish topography. Any other information in Chapter I which is not supported by direct citations may be found in such general accounts as Richard Herr, *The Eighteenth-century Revolution in Spain* (Princeton: Princeton University Press, 1958); Jean Sarrailh, *L'Espagne eclairée* (Paris, 1954), also available in Spanish as *La España ilustrada* (Mexico City: Fondo de Cultura Económica); and Jaime Vicens Vives, *Historia de España y América*, Vol. IV (Barcelona: Editorial Vicens Vives, 1961).

run west into the Atlantic, following the basic slope of the peninsula. In the North, along the coast, the Cantabrian Mountains form
a continuation of the Pyrenees. This range constitutes a continuous
and pronounced barrier between the interior and the sea. To the
west this range broadens into a confusing tangle of ridges and valleys which covers all of Galicia and reaches into northern Portugal.
South of the Cantabrian range is the westward sloping plain of Old
Castile, a large basin about 120 miles wide and 150 miles from east
to west. It is drained by the Duero River system, but cut off from
the Atlantic by the highlands of Galicia and Portugal. Separating
this plain from Madrid and the region of New Castile is a mountain
system which runs from the northeast towards the southwest, beginning in Aragon, passing north of Madrid, and extending into Portugal where it tapers into the ocean west of Lisbon. The system is
known east to west as the Sierra de Guadarrama, Sierra de Gredos,
Sierra de Gata, and in Portugal as the Sierra de Estrela. Some of
its peaks exceed 8,500 feet. The southern plain, called New Castile
around Madrid and Extremadura in the West, contains the Tajo
(Tagus) and Guadiana rivers. These are separated by the third
mountainous belt, a range of rugged hills named the Montes de
Toledo and farther west the Sierra de Guadalupe. This ridge turns
southward in Portugal, diverting the Guadiana south while the Tajo
continues westward to Lisbon. The New Castile-Extremadura region is bounded on the south by the barren mountains of the Sierra
Morena, a range which runs roughly east-west from the spine of
the peninsula to reach the Atlantic in the Spanish province of
Huelva. To the south, these mountains drop off sharply into the
relatively fertile valleys of Andalucía, with its famous centers at
Córdoba, Seville, and Cádiz. Andalucía is bounded on the south
by the previously mentioned Sierra Nevada, a wide band of mountains running from Murcia to the hinterland of Cádiz. Rising
abruptly out of the sea, they follow the southern coast of Spain from
Almería to Gibraltar. Along the Mediterranean coast from Cartagena to Barcelona is a narrow and fertile litoral, which, joined with
the Ebro valley extending inland south of the Pyrenees, is the heart
of the old Crown of Aragón.

   In the eighteenth century Spain was thinly populated.[2] The

2. The most recent and complete discussions of the population of Spain in the

earliest usable figures for the period put the total population at between 6,750,000 and 7,000,000 in 1708-1717. At the time of the *Catastro* (1748), the population was estimated at 7,500,000 and a census in 1768 yielded the figure 9,300,000. A more careful census in 1787 counted 10,300,000 persons, while that of 1797 found 10,-500,000, a figure which may be low because of inefficient administration. Allowing for the dubious reliability of some of these figures, the population expanded throughout the century, with the fastest growth between 1748 and 1768. This was a period of relative peace and prosperity within the country and was followed by a noticeable slackening in the population growth rate toward the end of the century. For the eighty years 1717-1797, the figures suggest an average annual increase of .6 per cent, a reasonable rate for a pre-industrial society without modern medicine.[3] For the shorter period 1748-1797 the average was .8 per cent, and for the twenty years 1748-1768, the average annual increase may have been as high as 1.2 per cent. The precision of such data can be questioned, but there is no doubt that the population increased markedly in the last half of the eighteenth century. It also appears that by the decade of the 1790's the rate of increase had fallen considerably.

The slight urbanization as late as 1800 implies that most of the population increase was in the countryside. At the end of the century there were only 40 towns in all of Spain with more than 10,000 people, and 17 of them were in Andalucía. In that region large towns were not a sign of true urbanization because the latifundia system forced many farm laborers to live in large communities which were essentially oversized farm villages. Madrid, with about 170,000 people, was the only town of more than 50,000 which

eighteenth century are found in the work of Jorge Nadal, *La población española* (Barcelona, Ed. Ariel, 1966) and in three publications by Antonio Domínguez Ortiz: "La Población española a lo largo de la historia," *Boletín de la Real Sociedad Geográfica*, LXXXVI (1950), 250-85; *La Sociedad española en el siglo XVII, I* (Madrid: Consejo Superior de Investigaciones Científicas, 1963), 101-60; *La Sociedad española en el siglo XVIII* (Madrid: C.S.I.C., 1955), pp. 55-76. A less detailed review of the subject is found in two works by Jaime Vicens Vives: *Historia*, IV, 8-16; and *Manual* pp. 440-42.

The lack of population shift to the towns as the total population grew is demonstrated by María Dolores Mateos for the province of Salamanca in *La España del antiguo régimen: estudios históricos*, ed. Miguel Artola, No. 0, *Salamanca* (Salamanca: Universidad de Salamanca, 1966).

3. Deane, p. 21.

was not a seaport. Table 1 lists the size of some of the important
towns as of 1800, when substantially less than 10 per cent of all
Spaniards lived in towns of more than 5,000. In the Castilian provinces, the percentage was below 5 per cent.

Table 1. *Population of important towns in Spain about 1800*

Interior towns	Inhabitants	Seaports	Inhabitants
Madrid	167,000	Barcelona	115,000
Murcia	40,000	Seville	96,000
Granada	40,000	Valencia	80,000
Zaragoza	40,000	Cádiz	70,000
Toledo	25,000	Málaga	50,000
Valladolid	21,000		
Burgos	9,000		

SOURCE: Jaime Vicens Vives, *Historia de España y América*, Vol. IV, *Burguesía,
Industrialización, Obrerismo* (Barcelona: Editorial Vicens Vives, 1961), pp. 8-10.

Not only did the interior have few large towns, but the over-all
population density was low. In most of the interior provinces it
was less than twenty persons per square kilometer. (See Table 2
and Map 2.) Given the size of Spain and the nature of the terrain,
such a dispersion of the population implies that what market potential existed in the interior was very difficult to exploit. Yet, relative to the total population, the thinly populated interior regions
included a major part of the inhabitants. Excluding the more dense-
ly populated coastal areas of Catalonia, Valencia, Galicia, Asturias,
and the Basque Provinces, the interior and southern provinces contained 63 per cent of the population. Even excluding the area
around Seville and Cádiz, the figure is still over 50 per cent.[4]

Clearly, the collection of food and raw materials and the distribution of any product not available locally in Castile had to
overcome serious obstacles: distance, terrain, and dispersion of producers and consumers. There were, however, geographic factors
which encouraged the development of transport in the interior.
These included the towns, regional differences in resources, and regional irregularity in the annual rainfall.

4. Vicens Vives, *Historia*, V, 19-20.

The role of the interior urban centers in the long-distance transport network is not clear. Such towns were religious and civil administrative centers and attracted the locally important landlords and nobility as residents. This created a small market for non-essentials and supported groups of merchants, artisans, and domestics who satisfied the regular demand for manufactures and goods not produced locally. The volume of such commerce was small. The towns also generated a demand for staple foods and fuel, com-

Table 2. *Population densities in the provinces of Spain, 1800*

Interior provinces		Peripheral provinces	
Region / Province	*Inhab. / km²*	*Region / Province*	*Inhab. / km²*
Old Castile-León		Northern Coast	
Avila	18	Alava	30-40
Burgos	24	Guipúzcoa	67
León	16	Vizcaya	35
Palencia	27	Santander	(*see* Burgos)
Salamanca	15	Asturias	39
Segovia	19	Galicia	62
Soria	19	Crown of Aragón and Navarre	
Toro	20	Aragón	18
Valladolid	23	Catalonia	28
Zamora	18	Navarre	36
New Castile-Extremadura		Valencia	43
Cuenca	10	Andalucía	
Extremadura	12	Córdoba	24
Guadalajara	25	Granada	28
La Mancha	11	Jaén	29
Madrid	18ᵃ	Seville	33
Murcia	19		
Toledo	17		

a. The population density of the province of Madrid exclusive of the city of Madrid.
SOURCES: José Canga Argüelles, *Diccionario de hacienda* (5 vols.; London, 1826-27), IV, 350-54, article "Poblacion," as quoted in Richard Herr, *The Eighteenth-Century Revolution in Spain* (1958; 2nd printing, Princeton: Princeton University Press, 1965), p. 94. Vicens Vives, *Historia*, IV, 8-14, appears to have reworked the original census figures and suggests slightly higher figures for a few provinces, but does not supply a complete list of provinces. In any case, the differences from Canga Argüelles appear uniform, so that the relative magnitudes above remain valid.

modities usually available from the nearby countryside. Only wine
and olive oil were staples which sometimes came from more distant
sources. Some towns, such as Segovia and Ávila, also had the ves-
tiges of handicraft textile industries which had flourished in the
sixteenth century. By 1800 most such industry had long since disappeared or had migrated to the countryside because of stultifying
guild control.[5] Only Valladolid and Salamanca in Old Castile and
Granada and Córdoba in the South were inland centers with more
than local economic importance and populations of over twenty
thousand. These provincial towns did not greatly influence the
over-all pattern of demand for transport as reconstructed from the
sources.

Only the city of Madrid constituted a significant, concentrated
market in the interior. Supported by the central government and
the resources the government could command, Madrid played a
major role in shaping the transport pattern.

Substantial regional differences within eighteenth-century Castile created possibilities for the mutual exchange of various products. The northern fishing villages and seaports supplied fish and
European imports, the latter apparently in small volume. Old Castile provided wheat for much of the interior, especially Madrid.
New Castile grew some grain, produced large quantities of wine,
and together with Extremadura raised livestock for wool, hides, and
urban meat supplies. Parts of the provinces of Cuenca, Soria, Ávila,
and Granada produced wood products, and certain districts in Extremadura, Toledo, and Cuenca had the necessary clays for manufacturing pottery and cooking utensils. Andalucía, though relatively
distant from the center of the country, contributed large quantities
of olive oil, quality wines, sugar, and some fruit, and also was the
point of entry for colonial products. The areas around Murcia and
Valencia produced citrus fruit and rice, while Cartagena and Alicante were the seaports for the most convenient route from the
Mediterranean to the interior, via Murcia and Albacete. Finally,
several regions scattered throughout Castile specialized in providing
transport service itself. Residents of such areas, unable to live on

5. Vicens Vives, *Manual*, pp. 485-86; José Gentil Da Silva, *En Espagne, développement économique, subsistance, déclin* (Paris: Mouton, 1965), pp. 125-36; J. H. Elliott,
Imperial Spain, 1469-1716 (London: Edward Arnold, 1963), pp. 111-12.

local resources, only seasonally employed in agriculture or producing a commodity for some distant market, frequently engaged in transportation to supplement their incomes.

Such regional specialization was by no means as general in the eighteenth century as it became after the introduction of railroads. Nevertheless, it was well established before 1800 and may be attributed to the variations in soil quality, patterns of landholding, and the availability of transport.[6] Spain is a dry country and only the Cantabrian coast and Galicia receive more than 40 inches of rain each year. The fringes of Old Castile, northern Extremadura, and the Guadalquivir valley in Andalucia average 20 to 40 inches, but the central basin of Old Castile and most of New Castile average only 12 to 20 inches per year. A large region around Cartagena, Murcia, and Almeria receives less than 12 inches of rain per year. This rainfall pattern obviously favors cultivation in some areas over others. The generally low rainfall is aggravated by its irregularity from year to year. Most of the agricultural regions experience drought or near drought one year in three or four.

Soil quality is also uneven, and only a few coastal regions such as Valencia and lower Andalucía have deposits of rich alluvial soil. The rest of Spain is covered with infertile mountains or a thin layer of moderately fertile soil deposited by forests which were cut down long ago. Under dry conditions such soil is prone to erosion, especially when grazed by sheep and goats or when cultivated only in alternate years, as was the custom until recently. The fields, when fallow, were ploughed to conserve moisture, thus exposing them to wind erosion and to gullying during the occasional heavy rains.[7] Rain and soil conditions thus left farmers with little margin for error and encouraged them to concentrate on crops which were the most likely to survive.

Patterns of landholding also caused regional specialization. In much of New Castle, Extremadura, and Andalucía large latifundia operated with day labor were common, and the land was often used for livestock or cash crops such as olives. Since the peasant had no

6. For a theoretical elaboration of this idea, see Mitchell Harwitz, "Regional Development Policy," in *Transport and Economic Development*, ed. Gary Fromm (Washington, D. C.: Brookings Institution, 1965), pp. 146-47.

7. Way, pp. 61-62.

control over the land he worked, he could not use it to raise the grain he needed. In effect, he was forced to bear the cost of transporting such basic necessities from distant sources. The reverse was the case in Old Castile and parts of New Castile, where renting, sharecropping, and leasing of farm plots were more common practices. The peasant could force town governments to distribute municipally owned lands and concentrate on wheat and vines. The result was a trend to those crops in the northern and central plains. This latent pressure for opening land to agriculture was demonstrated when monastic and municipal lands were sold off after 1836. A large amount of land, much of it marginal, was put to the plow in a short time. This was the culmination of a trend which began with government encouragement under Charles III in the late eighteenth century.[8]

The marked tendency for various districts to concentrate on one or two crops suggests that transport was making possible the interregional transfers which specialization implies. These exchanges were obviously basic to the rural economy.

In addition to the need for regular transfers of subsistence commodities, periodic regional droughts created irregular but urgent demands for transport. While it was rare for the crops to fail in all parts of Castile in any given year, it was quite common for the rains to skip one region or another, creating localized scarcity. The result was abnormal increases in the demand for transport to move vital commodities. The problem of survival then forced the peasant to become a transporter. These increases in transport services, however, were oriented to specific and urgent local needs and brought little addition to the transport available to supply Madrid in bad years. To find transport for that purpose, the central government had to mobilize the specialized elements of the transport industry.

B. *The economy of Castile*

As the distribution of population implies, the economy of Castile in the eighteenth century was rural and agrarian.[9] Large land

8. Vicens Vives, *Manual*, pp. 567-75, 587-88; Carr, *Spain*, p. 23.
9. A more complete summary of recent interpretations on this topic may be found in Vicens Vives, *Historia*, IV, 158-225.

holdings predominated, though often the peasant farmer share-cropped or rented the land. Agrarian yields, severely limited by poor soil and primitive technology, were among the lowest in Europe. The Roman-style plough was used extensively, and work animals were relatively scarce. In Old and New Castile, a normal harvest yielded about three times the amount of seed sown, a very good harvest about five times the seed. Three-fourths of the arable land was devoted to wheat, barley, and rye, although rice production was expanding in Valencia, and maize had become an important crop in the extreme north by 1800. Despite the concentration on cereals, there were frequent grain shortages, and as early as 1756-1773 imports averaged 1,200,000 bushels per year.[10]

The agrarian sector, involving 95 per cent of the population of Castile, supported the Spanish nobility, and the fortunes of this class were definitely improving after 1750. Food prices were rising with the total population and the expanding money supply, and were rising faster than prices for other types of goods. Rents exacted by landowners increased accordingly, as new leases were imposed on tenants.[11] As rents rose, there was growing pressure for enclosure of grazing land and many landowners and communal councils were putting large parts of their holdings under the plough. This agrarian prosperity had its negative side, since the enclosures undermined the position of livestock raisers, particularly the wool producers of the Mesta. The Mesta had received royal support before 1750, but thereafter it faced enclosure of grazing land and removal of rent controls on sheep pastures. The Mesta was also deprived of its special legal jurisdiction, and was confronted with a new export tariff on wool, intended to divert that raw material to Catalonia.

Similarly, sugar and cotton, important products in southern Spain during the sixteenth century, were reduced to only local significance by competition from the Spanish colonies. The same fate

10. By way of comparison, B. H. Slicher van Bath lists the average eighteenth-century wheat/seed ratios in fifty-nine locations throughout Europe. Eight of these averaged 3.5/1 or less, while in thirty-three cases they exceeded 6.0/1. B. H. Slicher van Bath, *The Agrarian History of Western Europe, A.D. 500-1850*, trans. Olive Ordish (London: Edward Arnold, 1963), pp. 330-33. To compare imports with total production in a very rough way, a total of 90,000,000 bushels of grains were produced in Spain in 1797. Vicens Vives, *Historia*, IV, 163.

11. Raymond Carr, "Spain," in Albert Goodwin, ed., *The European Nobility in the Eighteenth Century* (London: A. C. Black, Ltd., 1953), p. 51.

hit the silk industry of Toledo as it was swamped by French and Valencian competition. In the North, competition from France, Flan-
ders, and the Netherlands was depressing domestic flax production.

Even the increasing wheat and wine production faced serious
limitations. Since farmers in much of the central area worked on
relatively short leases which allowed the landlord to raise rents if
the tenant increased his production by improving the farm, there
was little incentive for the peasant farmer to make improvements.
The increases in production came from opening new farm lands
rather than through increased per acre yields. Also, growing concentration on single crops destroyed much of the grazing in such
monoculture areas and restricted the number of animals the farmer
could maintain. This in turn reduced the amounts of fertilizing
manure available per cultivated acre and hastened the decline of
the soil.

There was very little non-agrarian production in eighteenth-
century Castile beyond local handicraft activities. A few mining
centers were active throughout the century, including the Riotinto
copper mines and the Almadén mercury mines, but the lead mines
of Linares were in decay as were the Basque iron industry and the
silver mines at Guadalcanal. In the 1790's a few coal mines were
opened in Asturias as the charcoal supply dwindled, but Vicens
Vives is convinced that Castilian metallurgical activity was lower
in the eighteenth century than in the sixteenth.

Considerable quantities of low-quality woolens were produced
in the interior for domestic use, but most of them were made on
old, outmoded looms in cottages. These activities were concentrated
around Palencia, Segovia, Toledo, and Cuenca. In this connection
the Spanish government made a considerable effort to develop a
modernized textile industry in Castile. In the last half of the eighteenth century more than a dozen large factories for the production
of quality woolens, silks, and cottons were opened. Modern machinery and foreign technicians were imported at great expense.
These experiments invariably failed as a result of archaic bookkeep-
ing, oversized bureaucracy, unrealistic assessments of the market,
poor marketing techniques, and high transportation costs.[12]

12. La Force, *Textile Industry*; see also his "Royal Textile Factories in Spain, 1700-
1800," *Journal of Economic History*, XXIV (1964), pp. 337-60.

It is clear that the central provinces of Spain in the 1700's were little more than producers of raw materials and foodstuffs and imported the small volume of luxuries and industrial products demanded by the slight urban population. Only in the peripheral areas of Catalonia and Valencia can any economic growth and development be seen outside of the agricultural sector. In Catalonia the eighteenth century saw the development of a substantial cotton and woolen textile industry using modern machinery and capitalist organization. There are some signs of a developing penetration by Catalan business into Castile. Catalans were to be found taking over the Galician fisheries, pushing their way into the commercial monopolies of the Five Greater Guilds of Madrid, and increasingly participating in a direct trade with America, especially after this trade was liberalized in 1778. Yet despite the vigor of Catalan development, there are very few examples of regular commodity transfers between Catalonia and Castile compared with the volume of traffic of various sorts present within the interior.

Castile was a land with a small urban sector, great variations in regional specialization, and limited commercial organization. It required transportation to move basic necessities from one region to another and to support its towns, especially Madrid. The population was spread thinly throughout the area, but was expanding after 1750 and converting land from grazing to arable. Some peripheral areas, notably Catalonia, were experiencing vigorous economic development. This, however, was based on the availability of the American market and had had, by 1808, little success in developing markets in the Spanish interior.

C. *Roads and waterways*

One of the most important reasons that the peripheral industries could not develop markets in the interior was the lack of roads and waterways for the use of boats, barges, and freight wagons. The alternative means of transport which eighteenth-century technology offered were coastal shipping, river transport, paved highways, canals, and the paths and trails which met local needs. The first two of these can be passed over quickly when dealing with the interior. Coastal shipping helped to integrate economic activity among the peripheral regions, and Pierre Vilar has found that such traffic was increasing steadily throughout the eighteenth century, much of it carried on by Catalans.[13] By 1840, in fact, most large coastal towns were connected with regular steamer service.[14] Such developments, however, had little effect on the interior.

River transport had equally little impact, since most Spanish rivers are small and vary in size from season to season. The only navigable stretch was from the Atlantic to Seville, and for small boats as far as Córdoba.[15] In the sixteenth century attempts were made to canalize the Ebro under Charles V and the Tajo (Tagus) to Toledo under Philip II, but neither project was able to overcome the engineering problems involved.[16] The Ebro project was revived in the eighteenth century as part of the projected canal system of that period.

For the interior, therefore, the most promising transport innovations were paved highways and canals, and major attempts were made to introduce both. The government began construction of a highway system in the last half of the eighteenth century, but the network was designed to connect Madrid with the periphery, rather than to open up the large and thinly populated interior.[17] These royal highways took the most direct routes from Madrid to their peripheral destinations, Irun, Barcelona, Cartagena, Cádiz, Badajoz, and La Coruña, and often bypassed important cities such as Toledo and Valladolid. Such highways were designed for efficient communications and had little impact on the vast areas between them.[18]

The royal roads equaled anything in Europe for size, capacity, cost, and slowness of construction. They were thirty to sixty feet wide, built with the latest techniques on carefully constructed lime-

13. Pierre Vilar, *Catalogne dans l'Espagne moderne* (Paris, 1965), III, 192-93, 206-207, 236-37.

14. Richard Ford, *Handbook for Spain, 1845* (London: Centaur, 1966), I, 116-18, 309, 345. First published in 1845.

15. Way, p. 37.

16. Elliott, *Imperial Spain*, p. 291. In a letter Dr. Elliott gives the source as Jerónimo López de Ayala, Conde de Cedillo, *Toledo en el siglo XVI* (Madrid, 1901), pp. 59-63.

17. Gonzalo Menéndez Pidal, *Los Caminos en la histoiria de España* (Madrid: Instituto de Cultura Hispánica, 1951), reviews some aspects of the topic, with roadmaps based on old guidebooks.

18. Ford, *Handbook*, I, 77, says the royal roads were "drawn in a straight line . . . with many of the most ancient cities . . . left out. The wide extent of the country is most indifferently provided with public means of inter-communication. . . ."

stone foundations under a domed surface of small rock, and flanked by extensive retaining walls. These highways were often driven straight through mountains and swamps at great expense, even though they could have skirted them more cheaply. Frequently construction was delayed by the lack of a huge bridge or causeway which was to keep the road level through a valley, when a mild gradient would have served just as well.[19] As one traveler observed, "Road building is so slow, because of the number of bridges needed and the tendency of engineers to emphasize straightness and levelness, that the first sections of a road are already falling into decay before the road itself is finished."[20]

Slowness of construction, plus the devastation of the Napoleonic wars and subsequent neglect, meant that as late as 1840 important parts of this radial system were still incomplete. Early nineteenth-century observers such as Mackenzie and Ford, while noting occasional use of large modern wagons, imply that the royal roads were unable to generate much improvement in the transport system.[21]

In only two cases did these highways coincide with economic needs closely enough to influence economic patterns in the interior. One example involves the highway from the port of Santander to Reinosa and Alar del Rey on the Castilian plateau. This allowed wheeled traffic to reach the coast, brought about a pronounced change in the long-haul traffic pattern of northern Spain, and even fostered a degree of economic development in the immediate area.[22] The only other "modern" road which had any observable impact was the royal highway from Madrid through the Guadarrama Mountains. Built in the 1750's to allow easy access to the royal palaces of El Escorial and San Ildefonso, this road also facilitated cart traffic between Old and New Castile, easing the problem of supplying Madrid.

Similar observations and conclusions apply to the attempts to build a canal system. By the end of the 1780's three major projects

19. Joseph Townsend, *A Journey through Spain, 1786-1787* (Dublin, 1792), II, 31-33, III, 223, 296, 315-16; Arthur Young, *Travels in France in 1787, 1788, 1789, and a Tour into Spain* (Dublin, 1793), pp. 627, 629.

20. Henry Swineburne, *Travels Through Spain, 1775-1776* (London, 1779), p. 71.

21. Ford, I, 28-29, 32, 52-53, 59, 362, II, 488-93, 787, 914, 966, III, 1289; Alexander MacKenzie, *A Year in Spain by a Young American* (Boston, 1829), pp. 72-73, 174-75.

22. On this subject see Vicente Palacio Atard, *El Comercio de Castilla y el puerto de Santander en el siglo XVIII* (Madrid: C.S.I.C., 1960), and sec. B of chap. ii below.

were underway, the Canal of Aragón, the Canal of Castile, and the
Guadalquivir Canal. The first was to run from the Mediterranean
Sea up the Ebro River to the area north of Burgos. From there it
was to cut through the Cantabrian Mountains to the Bay of Biscay,
dropping nearly three thousand feet in a few miles. The Canal of
Castile was to run from the westernmost point on the Canal of Aragón past the city of Palencia to Valladolid. From there one branch
was to reach west to Zamora, and another south to Segovia, just
across the Guadarrama Mountains from Madrid. The third canal
was to follow the Guadalquivir River up into Andalucía and then
extend north through La Mancha and New Castile to Madrid.[23]

The northern canals received the most attention. The Canal of
Aragón was based on the sixteenth-century project of Charles V and
was revived in 1768 with a contract to a French construction company. The company soon failed and the project languished until
1779 when the government stepped in with large subsidies. Construction on the Canal of Castile, begun in 1753, went on intermit-
tantly until 1779, when it was suspended pending further construction on the Canal of Aragón to their point of juncture. Work
on the southern canal project did not begin until 1788 and only a
few miles were ever completed.[24]

The routes of the canals probably were closer to what was needed
to create a national market in the Spanish interior than the planned
road system, but they suffered even more than the latter from the
disparity between ends and means. In rugged, arid Spain, the plans
called for several hundred miles of canals with standard specifications that included a nine-foot depth, a bottom width of twenty
feet, and a top width of fifty-six feet. Such canals required aque-
ducts, embankments, and cuttings on a grandiose and expensive
scale.[25] As an acute English observer noted in the 1780's, canals on
a more modest scale would have served the potential traffic just as
well and been much easier to build.[26] Although some two hundred

23. Townsend, I, 209-15, 366-70; Herr, map facing p. 130.
24. Antonio Ballesteros y Beretta, *Historia de España y su influencia en la historia
universal* (Barcelona: Salvat, 1932), VI, 184-85; Swineburne, p. 85; Ford, II, 955.
25. Comte Alexander de Laborde, *Voyage Pittoresque et Historique de l'Espagne,*
published in *Revue Hispanique*, LXIII (1928), 1-572 and LXIV (1929), 1-224; see
vol. LXIII, 172; Townsend, I, 209-15, 366-70.
26. Townsend, I, 209-15, 366-70.

miles of these canals were eventually built, and construction was revived in 1830 after a twenty-two-year lapse, none of the critical junctions was ever made, with the result that for economic purposes the canals began nowhere and ended nowhere. By 1840 only two stretches appear to have been in use, with steam packets traveling from Valladolid to Palencia and from Zaragoza to Tudela.[27]

Serving the vast spaces between the magnificent but often incomplete highway and canal projects of the eighteenth century was an elaborate network of primitive local trails. These were the *caminos* (roadways or trails) of general use, as opposed to the *carretera* or *calzada* (highway). The latter is a constructed road, and one gets the sensation that it was an outside intrusion into the local community. The *camino* was and is basically an untended right-of-way established by custom for local purposes. Under Spanish conditions such roads are more useful than appears at first glance. Once the winter rains have stopped and the ground has dried, such roads or trails acquire a stone-hard surface which demands little care. In areas which had sandy soil, there existed a variation called the *carril*. This was an ordinary *camino* or trail with two narrow bands of stone paving to carry cart wheels. On level terrain such roadways allow the use of carts and today tractors and even automobiles. In the frequent rough areas, the *camino* generally degenerated into a path or track suitable only for pack animals.

Since such primitive roadways were necessary to local residents, a certain amount of local maintenance was provided out of self-interest—repair of bridges, bypassing of washouts, etc. Such maintenance was theoretically required by law from the days of Ferdinand and Isabella, but outside the urban centers it was probably fortunate that these requirements coincided with local necessity.

For practical purposes, then, the rural economy of the interior was served by a network of primitive roadways and trails which crisscrossed the country in all directions, connecting most towns, reaching into every valley, and crossing every mountain pass. A system of improved wagon roads could conceivably have encouraged some economic growth in the interior, but the government's plans concentrated on communications between Madrid and the periphery. The canals were better oriented to the economic

27. Ford, II, 954-55, III, 1430-31.

needs of the interior, but were hampered by unrealistic planning, exemplified by the project for a canal through the Cantabrian Mountains. In both cases these limitations were aggravated by the grandiose scale of construction chosen by the government. Such an approach multiplied costs in a capital-poor land and slowed construction so that the capital invested remained inactive indefinitely and in some cases was permanently lost.

The economic development of the interior, therefore, remained dependent on the ability of the traditional transport system to use the primitive local roads in meeting new demands as they arose. The bulk of the goods moving overland continued to travel over the network of trails and paths which grew up to meet local needs. There is little indication that any real improvement in these conditions occurred before 1850.[28]

28. Vicens Vives, *Manual*, pp. 615-16; Carr, *Spain*, pp. 202, 256.

Chapter two. *The demand for transportation*

Three types of demand shaped the transportation system of eighteenth-century Spain. The largest of these was the demand for cheap, seasonal transport to carry subsistence commodities over distances ranging from a few miles to over two hundred. These interregional exchanges were required by local and regional variations in resources. Another demand for transportation was created by the trade in raw materials, manufactures, and imported merchandise. In contrast to the subsistence exchanges, this involved a small volume of valuable goods. Only one or two raw materials in this category were handled in moderately large quantities. This merchandise was carried relatively long distances since the potential consumers were scattered in small pockets throughout the country. The third distinctive type of demand was that created by the Spanish state. The government needed transport services for the army, for naval supplies, for the salt tax, and above all for the supply of Madrid. All three of these demands, in fact, had two components, one being the needs of the country as a whole, the other being the needs of Madrid, the largest concentrated market in the country.

It is very difficult to judge the relative importance of these various demand patterns. Most of the sources which would permit a close analysis are scattered in dozens of local archives, and many have disappeared. Some specific figures for parts of the demand, especially in connection with Madrid, are available. These suggest that Madrid was the largest single market in the interior, but was far from obscuring the elaborate network of transport services which spread throughout the country. Included in this network were several regular patterns of exchange between regions. This kind of exchange involved subsistence goods and was bound to the subsistence economy of the countryside.

Reconstructing these transport patterns really amounts to reconstructing the trade patterns of the country. The volume of this trade in turn reflects the volume of demand for transport, if only at the point where the demand curve crosses the supply curve under existing circumstances. It is the demand at that point which is described below. For the most part, the trade-transportation pattern was observed through an extensive study of transporter activity registered in the replies to the *Catastro* of the early 1750's. The *Catastro*, explained more fully in Appendix A, was based on a list of forty-two questions which was sent to every community in Castile. Question 32 dealt with the service occupations of the area and any income received by residents for transport services was to be recorded in the reply. It is likely that the activities of many carriers went unrecorded, and when they were listed, frequently it was with little or no detail. A review of the replies from about 3,000 towns which showed transport activity yielded some 500 examples of transportation wherein the origin, destination, and cargo were listed in detail.[1] The maps that follow are based largely on these data, which are discussed in the appendices. The *Catastro* data have been supplemented with 250 similar references extracted from various other eighteenth- and early nineteenth-century sources.

A. *Movements of food and fuel*

The greatest volume of transport activity was that which serviced the interregional exchanges of subsistence commodities and the delivery of such goods to Madrid. The patterns of transport/ trade involved are illustrated on maps three through seven. The commodities in question were undeniably of vital importance to the countryside: wine, olive oil, fish and preserved meat, grain, fuel, and salt. The maps show clearly that there existed an elaborate network of interregional trade and transport connecting widely separated rural areas with complementary specialization.

Map 3 illustrates the numerous transfers of wine from the river bottom areas in Old Castile to the towns on both sides of the Cantabrian Mountains along the north coast. In the center of the country, wine came from the provinces of Toledo, Guadalajara, and the historic region of La Mancha, now partially in the provinces of Ciudad Real and Cuenca. In the South, wine traveled from the

1. AHN, *Hac., Libros Resúmenes del Catastro.* See also the appendices to this study.

area around Seville to the mountains, and from the Jeréz region to Cádiz for export.

The few transfers of olive oil which are clearly described followed analogous patterns. The movements are invariably from south to north or northeast. From the provinces of Córdoba and Seville olive oil was carried to Madrid and to various towns in Cuenca province. From there it was taken by other transporters to Valencia, where it was exchanged for rice. Some olive oil was also produced in New Castile—Extremadura. This was carried from the province of Toledo to Madrid and to the province of Valladolid in the heart of Old Castile. From Old Castile other carriers transported it up into the Cantabrian region. Salamanca and probably Zamora were similarly supplied with olive oil carried from Extremadura.

The trade in fish (Map 4) involved primarily the import of dried codfish from various coastal towns in the north, especially Bilbao. Cod and sardines were carried from the coast inland through the mountains to numerous points in Old Castile and to Madrid. Madrid also received some of its fish from the Mediterranean port of Cartagena. The mountainous regions inland from Valencia drew supplies from that port, while the inland city of Granada imported fish from Málaga and other southern ports.

The commodity which appeared most frequently in this pattern of subsistence exchanges was grain, especially wheat. The great majority of such transfers originated in the plain of Old Castile, always the breadbasket of Spain (Map 5). From the regions around Salamanca and Valladolid substantial quantities of wheat were carried to the northern towns along the coast and in the Cantabrian mountains, to the towns of the central mountain belt, and to Madrid. In one case, probably exceptional, wheat was shipped all the way from Salamanca to Seville. A second pattern connected Andalucía and Valencia. Carriers from Cuenca took wheat to Valencia and Valencian rice to Andalucía, and returned to Cuenca with olive oil. The area around Seville should have shown grain movements, and some towns indicated that their carriers handled wheat, but did not specify source or destination. Both Seville and Cádiz were big enough to draw grain from considerable distances.

Madrid, of course, stands out as a major market for the internal grain trade, using more than a million bushels of wheat a year.

Most of it came from Old Castile although the city had some regular New Castilian sources, and in time of drought grain was imported overland from Santander and Murcia.

Charcoal and firewood are not foodstuffs, but since they were the universal fuels for cooking and heating, they must be counted among the important commodities of the subsistence economy. Charcoal was produced in the mountain valleys bordering the plain of Old Castile, and was one of the items which were exchanged for the wheat and wine of the plateau (Map 6). More striking, however, is the concentration of charcoal at Madrid. The commodity often came from places well over fifty miles from the city, although its transport offered little promise of return cargoes, and annual consumption was about 12,500 tons.[2]

The distribution of salt (Map 7) was supervised by the crown and administered through eleven district administrations, each of which in turn supplied a number of lesser salt depôts (*alfolies*) scattered through the district.[3] The professional carters often found the salt trade in Old Castile very convenient, since it involved cargoes which moved from east to west—from the salt deposits at Poza near Burgos, or the area between Guadalajara and Soria to the cities of Valladolid, Ávila, Salamanca, and León. This provided a paying cargo on the trip between the delivery points for wool and wood and the pickup points for grain and charcoal bound for Madrid.[4]

Certain points are clear concerning the demand for transport for the movement of basic necessities. The maps and the tables cited in Appendix B suggest that the provincial towns of ten to twenty thousand rarely acted as centers or markets in the transport/trade pattern of the countryside. This may be due to an insufficient sample of transfers, but it is equally possible that most of their needs were met locally. It is certain that a carrier would avoid the inevitable local taxes in such towns if his real destination were beyond it.[5] It appears that the patterns of demand were regular enough for

2. AGS, *Hacienda, Dirección General de Rentas, 2ª Remesa*, leg. 4894.
3. *Actas, 1563-1713*, XVII, 424. This is the organizational decree of the salt-tax in the 1590's.
4. AHN, *Con.*, leg. 2425.
5. Writing in the early nineteenth century, Richard Ford observed that many towns had inns and stopping places outside the walls for the carters and muleteers, allowing them to avoid gate duties if only passing by. Ford, I, 389.

trade to function between rural districts without the need of central markets to act as go-betweens. The observed fact is that a high proportion of transportation which did not service Madrid consisted of transfers from one rural area to another.

Among the interregional patterns of subsistence transfer, two in particular stand out. In the first, the plain of Old Castile, the mountains to the south, and the mountain and coastal region to the north maintained a substantial trade pattern based on fish, dried foods, fruit, wood, charcoal, and olive oil, all carried into the plain, and grain and wine, which were taken back to the areas around the valley. The frequency with which this pattern appears and the number of provinces involved suggest that not only was regional demand effective over a considerable distance, but that the volume of goods moved was substantial. Another well-defined exchange pattern existed with its center in the province of Cuenca. The transporters of that province were drawn as far as Valencia with wood, wheat, and olive oil, to Andalucia with Valencian rice, and to Madrid with wine, wood, and olive oil. Other such patterns undoubtedly existed in Andalucía, but the lack of detail from the area precludes generalization.

One of the most notable things about the maps is the obvious importance of Madrid in the Castilian transport-trade pattern. The capital drew upon a large part of the interior for its needs, attracting subsistence commodities from long distances, despite rough terrain. A sizable proportion of all commodities transported anywhere in Castile ended up on the Madrid market. Yet the capital was almost never the source of goods of any sort; it was not a center of trade, but one of consumption. Production for such an urban market represents economic activity more complex than subsistence agriculture, but in Castile, where subsistence included widespread exchanges of goods, sale of surplus production in Madrid was but an additional complication of the subsistence pattern. If a surplus of wheat appeared in the villages of Guadalajara, for example, it might be sold for cash in Madrid, but the cash was then used to buy charcoal or wine directly from the nearest regions which produced them.

In general, therefore, there was a widespread system of exchanges of basic subsistence commodities, some of it concentrated on Madrid, much of it involving trade between rural areas. This was done with little reliance on marketing centers. Such centers were replaced by two substitutes: the great predictability of the demands of the various interior regions, and a flexible system of seasonal transport in which the carrier often acted both as transporter and trader.

B. *Indirect-consumption commodities*

In contrast with the preceding section, this one is designed to illustrate the movements of commodities which were connected with economic activity more complex than the exchange of goods for direct consumption. Salient differences here are that the network for distributing such non-subsistence goods was more elaborate and widespread, but that the volume of traffic was relatively small compared with that of subsistence commodities.

The numerous references to individual commodities have been grouped into six categories, as shown in Table 3, and transfers of five of the groupings have been plotted on maps. In the sixth group, the number of complete descriptions of transfers was insufficient to warrant a map. In all categories there were many incomplete descriptions of transfers, and the towns of the transporters involved are indicated where possible.

In addition, a number of transporters were found who did not or could not specify particular commodities as their accustomed cargo, but who did give specific origins and destinations for the transfers they made. One group of these, called *arrieros ordinarios*, specialized in visiting urban centers on a regular basis to make purchases on special order, much like the commission merchants of medieval Europe. These transfers are shown on Map 12. The other group consists of a number of carriers who specified where they went, but either did not describe their cargoes or simply used the term *mercancias* (merchandise).

The movements of raw wool shown on Map 8 present a very clear pattern for the major part of the wool trade. Most wool was clipped in Segovia or Soria and shipped north to the area around Burgos. There it was cleaned and prepared for export, then hauled to the ports at Bilbao and Santander. In the early part of the century, the wool export trade concentrated in Bilbao, but after mid-century, Santander attracted an increasing share of the business.

Table 3. *Indirect-consumption commodities transported*

I. *Raw fibers*
  Wool
  Flax
  Hemp
  Esparto

II. *Textiles, Fiber Products*
  Linen
  Wool cloth
  Canvas
  Hemp cloth
  Silk
  Plaited esparto
  Clothes
  Blankets
  Rough flannel
  Stockings (wool)
  Coarse woolens
  Garters
  Hats
  Haberdashery
  Esparto products
  Rope (esparto)
  Heavy cording

III. *Metals, metal products, and pottery*
  Iron
  Copper
  Lead
  Mercury
  Worked metal
  Hardware
  Hatchets
  Pots
  Clay pottery
  Glazed pottery
  China or porcelain

IV. *Building materials*
  Lumber
  Sawn planks
  Ship timber
  Imported woods
  Stone columns
  Building stone
  Whitewash
  Marble
  Lime
  Tiles
  Bricks

V. *Spices and other specialties*
  Beeswax
  Potash
  Soap
  Paper
  Candles
  Cacao
  Sugar
  Resin
  Honey
  Saffron
  Tobacco
  "Spices"
  "Drugs"
  Candy
  Chocolate
  Cinnamon

VI. *Hides and leather goods*
  Hides
  Skins and pelts
  Tanned hides
  Leather
  Cordoban
  Shoe sole leather

Most of this wool was carried in oxcarts and the wool export trade represents the principal non-governmental activity of the organized carters.

There were proportionately fewer references to fibers other than wool, probably because they did not figure as important exports. The movements on Map 8 from the north coast represent the transport of flax to the interior as part of the general pattern of exchanges between Old Castile and the coastal area. There are indications of flax converging on Palencia, which was a traditional textile center. In the South, hemp and esparto, for rough cloth and rope, traveled from Granada and Andalucía as far as Cartagena, and flax was carried from Granada to La Mancha.

Textiles were probably the type of manufacture in greatest demand, although the examples encountered have a somewhat random appearance. (See Map 9). Most of these movements involved domestic products, although there are references to imports via Valencia and Alicante. Madrid was a major market for textile products, drawing woolens from Cuenca, silk from Valencia, imported cloth and clothes from Alicante and Murcia, and hats from Barcelona. Old Castile also provided some demand for such goods, drawing rough linens into Palencia for finishing and redistribution, silk from Valencia, clothes from Murcia, and woolens from Guadalajara. At the same time, Palencia sent wool blankets to Extremadura. Muleteers from Toledo carried worsted stockings south to Andalucía and returned with woolen cloth. In the South, Seville, Córdoba, and Cádiz all drew silk from Valencia, Cádiz being the outlet to the colonies.

Transfers of metal and metal products had a similarly random appearance, but were too scarce to warrant graphic presentation. Lead moved from Linares in upper Andalucía (Jaén) to Valencia, mercury from Almadén to Seville, and copper from Rio Tinto to the mint at Segovia, all for governmental purposes. In the private sector, iron traveled from Nava del Rey in Valladolid province to western Spain, while the area near Segovia sent iron to Toledo and northern Spain. There were also several references to iron transport from the province of Cuenca, but with little detail as to its destination.

The transfers of building materials on Map 10 include wood for buildings and ship construction, a handful of examples of stone, cement, plaster, tile, and brick, and the movement of certain specialized items intended for the royal palace, under construction in Madrid between the 1730's and the 1780's. The three longest transfers are of the last type, including imported wood from Cádiz to Madrid, stone columns from Bilbao, and marble from Valencia. The transfers which end at Málaga, Seville, and Santander are examples of the government's efforts to obtain ship timber. It was often necessary to cart such timber more than a hundred miles overland to the shipyards. The remaining examples follow now familiar patterns. Building materials moved from mountain areas to important centers such as Valencia and Granada, and traveled considerable distances from the mountains into the plain of Old Castile. Many cargoes of wood and stone converged on Madrid from distances of up to fifty miles, and in one case timber was brought more than a hundred miles from the forests near Cuenca.

Despite the number of commodities included in the category "spices and specialty items," few complete transfers were recorded (Map 11). Most of these involved tobacco, which traveled under government license from the main factory in Seville by pack animal north to Madrid; from there it was distributed throughout Old Castile. It traveled in the same fashion to Málaga and probably most other cities. According to a document in the municipal archives of Murcia, the movements converging on that city represent spices, and it would be surprising if other urban centers did not receive similar shipments. Sugar and cacao were transported in substantial quantities, especially to Madrid, but only two examples of these items actually appeared, moving from Valencia and Granada to New Castile. Many of the goods in this general grouping were very small in bulk and moved as part of the mixed cargoes illustrated in Maps 13 and 14.

Map 12 illustrates the activities of a class of specialized muleteers (*arrieros ordinarios*) who traveled from their home towns to provincial capitals, seaports, or Madrid to purchase items specifically requested by local residents. They were important in connecting the towns of Old Castile with the seacoast and Madrid. In the South they provided a commercial link between the outlying communities and the major centers of Seville, Córdoba, Málaga, and Cádiz.

In a considerable number of cases, transporters indicated their

origins and destinations, but not their cargoes. Most of these transfers, which are illustrated on Map 13, were carried out by carters
and muleteers engaged in the transport of relatively valuable items.
The sources frequently refer to cargoes of *mercancias* (merchandise),
and many of the movements are either between important towns or
have one terminus at a seaport. It is probable, therefore, that these
transporters, traveling over long distances with mixed cargoes,
played a central role in the distribution of imported goods and
other expensive items throughout Castile. Madrid attracted a high
proportion of these commodities, just as it attracted a high proportion of the basic necessities available in the country. By combining
Maps 11, 12, and 13, one can obtain at least an impression of the
wide-ranging activities of the relatively few muleteers who handled
high-value trade goods for the narrow luxury markets of the interior.

In general, the indirect-consumption commodities in this section were hauled longer distances than subsistence goods, but frequently only in small quantities or with a government subsidy.
Madrid clearly attracted a large share of the goods in some categories, especially textiles, building materials, and imported merchandise. Imports and manufactures were carted and packed to
Madrid from Bilbao, Santander, Asturias, Portugal, Seville, Cádiz,
Valencia, Alicante, and Cartagena. The actual volume of this traffic
cannot even be guessed at, since the examples of transfers to Madrid
range from single packs of mixed merchandise from Asturias to at
least one entire cart train of imports from Alicante.[6]

Old Castile and Andalucía attracted considerable parts of the
internal trade in non-subsistence goods, and there was a relatively
elaborate trade pattern between Andalucía and Valencia, via Cuenca
province. In these areas, however, no examples of shipments as large
as those reaching Madrid were found. The secondary markets for
general merchandise were served by muleteers operating on a relatively small scale.

Only in the case of the export trade in the North is any precise information available concerning the demand for transportation
of indirect-consumption goods, provided by an able study of eigh-

6. Juan Masía Vilanova, "Dos épocas históricas en las comunicaciones Alicantinas,"
Galatea, núm. 1 (1954), pp. 14-17.

teenth-century Santander.[7] The royal highway from Santander to Old Castile, via Reinosa, was specifically built to allow the cart traffic of Castile to reach the coast, and was designed to connect with the projected Canal of Castile, which was to pass through Alar del Rey at the northern edge of the Castilian plain.

In earlier times transporters had moved eastward across Castile and then struggled through the mountains to Bilbao. In 1730 José Patiño suggested that a cart road to Santander would shorten the distance to the sea, permit the navy to bring ship timber from the Sorian forests, and allow commerce to avoid the customs posts on the Basque frontier.[8] The road, begun in the 1740's and opened in 1752, quickly developed a considerable flow of traffic. The government charged a moderate toll, and despite successive reductions in rates, the volume of receipts rose steadily.[9]

The new road had an immediate impact on the pattern of the wool export trade. Bilbao had monopolized this trade for centuries and in the late 1740's was exporting between 23,000 and 28,000 sacks of wool per year. Since a sack (*saca*) contained about 225 pounds of wool, this amounted to between 5.2 and 6.3 million pounds of wool per year. The total remained fairly stable through the 1760's, but the export figures for Bilbao fell to half their earlier levels, indicating that about 12,000 sacks (2.7 million pounds) of wool were being carted to Santander over the new road.

Bilbao had recovered some of her wool trade by the late 1780's, but only after a second road was built through a nearby mountain pass. This allowed Bilbao to capture some of the increase in the total volume of wool being exported. By the late eighties, the volume had risen from the *ca.* 25,000 sacks of mid-century to totals which regularly exceeded 32,000 sacks. Santander was able to retain about one-third of this considerably enlarged wool trade.

Although the road was completed in the fifties, until the 1780's there were no notable economic changes in the area other than the shift in the wool trade. Only then did other export trades develop in the region, reflecting the fact that in 1778 the crown opened the American empire to direct commerce with most Spanish ports, including Santander. The new road was thus only one of the factors

7. Palacio Atard, *Santander en el siglo XVIII*.
8. *Ibid.*, p. 62.   9. *Ibid.*, pp. 83-86.

needed to foster regional development, and only with direct access to the colonial market in the 1780's were the essentials present to generate new economic activity along the road.

The new industries in the area were flour milling and leather processing. From nothing, flour exports from Santander reached 34,000 barrels in 1787 and nearly 60,000 barrels in 1793. About 55 per cent of these totals came from the Castilian interior as wheat or flour. New water-powered flour mills appeared along the road in 1784, 1786 (two), 1787, 1796, 1801, and 1808. In years of poor harvest the flow was reversed and the road used to supply the interior.[10] There are no figures on the volume of the leather trade, but new processing establishments appeared in 1752, 1779 (two), 1795, 1797, 1800, 1804 (two), and 1805, based on raw materials brought over the new road. These developments were more than a diversion of trade from Bilbao, since they were based on the colonial trade, and Bilbao was never opened to American commerce under the Old Regime.[11]

The economic growth along the highway indicates that in the short run the transport system may have been capable of supporting moderate economic growth, given better roads in the proper places. Even this mildly favorable conclusion must be qualified, however, since the American market opened to Santander was still a protected one. Without such protection, the cost of primitive land transport would have made the development of export industries correspondingly more difficult. Furthermore, the availability of such transport was uncertain, as illustrated in the crisis of 1804-1805 when the government diverted all transport to the supply of Madrid for a considerable period.[12]

Converting the figures on wool and flour traffic to cartloads of transport capacity, the export trade required 6,000 to 7,000 loads at mid-century to move wool to the sea. By the late 1780's the total had reached 12,000 to 14,000 loads: 8,000 for wool and 4,000 to 6,000

10. *Ibid.*, pp. 142-57.   11. *Ibid.*, pp. 166-80.

12. AHN, *Con.*, leg. 49240. Gaspar de Jovellanos, writing in the 1790's, was convinced that a highway similar to the Santander road, between León and Asturias would generate similar developments in those provinces. Gaspar de Jovellanos, "Dos informes al Señor Superintendente General de Caminos: el uno sobre la carretera principal y el otro sobre dos transversales, desde Castilla a la costa de Asturias," *Biblioteca de Autores Españoles*, L (Madrid, 1918), 456-67.

for the wheat and flour which traveled to or from the interior. This is based on carts whose capacity amounted to four sacks or five barrels by weight. Four to five pack animals would have been required to replace each cartload of capacity.

*   *   *

Relative to the movement of basic necessities, the demand for any given raw material or manufacture other than wool or wood was slight. Only by combining a number of such items into one category does much activity appear. The smallness of the demand for transport for such goods is emphasized by the fact that the examples of transfers used in this section generally involved fewer men and animals than the examples of the preceding section. In some cases, moreover, mixed cargoes were itemized, so that a given shipment of merchandise sometimes appears in more than one category and map and thus inflates the apparent number of examples. The exceptions to this are the wool, building materials, and metals trades, which were usually handled in large shipments by the long-haul carters. For the other categories the transfers often took place over long distances but involved small amounts of goods.

Although the demand for non-subsistence goods was scattered, it caused the transport system to evolve a rudimentary but widespread network for distributing small amounts of such goods. This was made possible by the unspecialized nature of most transport operations. As will be shown, transporting was a marginal part of most carriers' economies, and thus they could service what small demands arose and then return to farming. Had these carriers been forced to support themselves entirely by transporting, the increased transport fees would have further restricted the market for the cargoes.

C. *The government demand for transport*

The Spanish government provided a substantial part of the overall demand for transportation in eighteenth-century Castile. It required transport for the military establishment, for routine administrative chores such as supplying the mints and royal factories and distributing salt and tobacco for government monopolies, and for

supplying Madrid with vital commodities. The government drew
upon the transport pool in various ways. It obtained the services of
professional transporters by paying competitive prices and through
a reciprocal arrangement between the crown and the organized ox-
carters of the realm. In the latter circumstance, the crown granted
special privileges and got in return an automatic priority in the use
of the carters' services. The government utilized the unorganized
peasant-transporters by means of a well-defined forced service which
was considered a form of taxation.

1. *Military uses of transport by the government.* Despite serious
efforts by the crown to modernize the Spanish army, it remained
dependent on the peasants and animals of the countryside for internal troop movements. The size of this army in peacetime fluctuated between fifty thousand and seventy-five thousand men, although it became much larger after 1793. Except for some skir-
mishes with Portugal, this force was not used within Spain until the
war with Revolutionary France (1793-1795).[13]

When an army unit moved from its billet, its commanding officer demanded one day of baggage service (*servicio de bagages*)
from as many nearby peasants as were necessary. In theory every municipality was required to have an up-to-date register of all livestock
in the area which could be used as pack animals. The officer in
charge, after reviewing these lists, assigned each town in the vicinity
a quota of animals to be provided for the next day's travel. Local
officials then distributed these quotas among the individual residents, who were obliged to appear the next morning with their
animals. All owners of animals were obligated to serve, but never
for more than one day at a time. Persons engaged in transport were
obligated for this service only in their town of legal residence and
could not be stopped on the road.

Prior to the 1790's the system aroused little comment, probably
because the demands for such services were not great. Beginning in
1793, however, Spain was forced to mobilize its military resources,
and from that date increasing use of forced transport provoked frequent complaints. Typically, the list of animals in an area was out

13. For a description of the modernization of the Spanish army in the eighteenth
century, see Domínguez Ortiz, *El Siglo XVIII*, pp. 363-88.

of date or even missing, and the town sought to delay army demands until a new list could be made.[14] More frequently, the privileged classes of the community tried to avoid being placed on the lists, citing their class standing. In theory, at least, only ecclesiastics were exempt.[15] Many protests came as the result of favoritism and use of influence in local administrations.[16]

Complaints also arose because of the casualness with which officers made and used requisitions. Lack of knowledge of an area caused officers to neglect nearby towns while making exactions from more distant ones.[17] In other cases, the officers demanded all of the transport they needed from the town they were in without bothering to spread the requirements among nearby communities.[18] On some occasions they apparently forced peasants to serve for periods longer than the legal maximum.[19] When such demands and abuses came during the ploughing and harvesting seasons, they seriously disrupted the normal economic life of the country.

Internal commerce was similarly disrupted when army units repeatedly requisitioned the services of transporters they encountered along the highways. These people had usually met their obligations in their home towns, and carried papers to prove it.[20]

The French Revolution and the Napoleonic wars apparently put a severe strain on this method of transporting troops. Dozens of protests from all over Spain concerning abuses of the system are listed in the *Libros de Matrícula* of the *Consejos* section of the Archivo Histórico Nacional. They all date from the period 1794 to 1808; the same source contains no such protests for earlier periods. Under the stress of serious mobilization the traditional baggage service system did not work well and interferred with other economic activities.

Professional carters were rarely used for routine troop movements, but when armies were actually operating in Spain, trains of carts were sometimes hired to serve as baggage trains, as in 1641

14. AHN, *Con.*, leg. 1581-2 (Seseña).
15. *Ibid.*, legs. 1703-29 (Getafe); 1677-6 (Ajalbir); 1700-21 (Daganzo de Arriba).
16. *Ibid.*, legs. 1700-20 (Domingo Pérez); 1903-36 (Antequera); 2670-23 (Calzada de Calatrava); 2657 (Baena); 1780-34.
17. *Ibid.*, leg. 1564-33 (Santa María de Nieva).
18. *Ibid.*, leg. 2062-57 (Viso del Marques).
19. *Ibid.,* leg. 2053-15.   20. *Ibid.*, leg. 2123-3.

and 1810-1813.[21] In the 1730's the army was hiring animals and wagons for the same purpose, but the specifications appear to exclude the carters of Castile. These carters, however, and professional muleteers, were used in the transportation of various kinds of munitions. When the government was anticipating war in 1737-1738, several thousand rifles, pistols, and carbines were transported from the main arsenals in the Basque Provinces and Navarre overland to Alicante, Badajoz, Seville, and Cádiz; and tons of cannonballs were moved from Badajoz to Seville and from the Basque provinces to the Mediterranean.[22]

The crown regularly used the professional carters to move ship timber for the navy. Examples of this include the transfer of wood from Granada to Málaga and Seville, from the Sorian forests to Santander (whence it went by sea to the naval base at El Ferrol), and from the mountains north of Granada to a tributary of the Guadalquivir River (so that it could be floated downstream to the arsenal at Seville).[23] This type of work had a lower priority than the supply of Madrid, but the carters preferred it because they could get backhaul cargoes at the seaports.[24]

2. *Miscellaneous uses of transport by the government.* The central government required transport for a variety of non-military purposes. One of the oldest of these demands, similar to the military baggage service (*servicio de bagages*), was employed when the royal family changed residences. The terms of this service were spelled out as early as the fifteenth century, and transport for the royal family received priority over all other business. Conscripted transporters were supposed to be paid at current prices. By the later sixteenth century this use of transport was of secondary importance, but the practice survived to the end of the eighteenth century. At that time the Spanish court regularly moved four times a year between the royal residences in El Escorial, San Ildefonso, Aranjuez, and Madrid. There is no mention of this baggage service until

21. *Ibid.*, leg. 1232-3; AA Navarredonda, *Libro de Actas*, 1641; José Tudela de la Orden, "La cabaña real de carreteros," in *Homenaje a Don Ramon Carande* (Madrid: Sociedad de Estudios y Publicaciones, 1963), pp. 354-55.
22. AGS, *Guerra*, leg. 416.
23. AA Granada, leg. 1876; AHN, *Con.*, legs. 1184-20; 2396-1.
24. AHN, *Con.*, leg. 1184-20.

late in the century, but in 1795, 1796, and 1800 complaints of abuses were filed by stable owners in Toledo and the towns of Villanueva de Bogas, Vicalbaro, and Vallecas.[25]

There is nothing to indicate how extensive these exactions were during the century. Various descriptions of the royal household suggest that it had considerable transport facilities of its own, and that the royal baggage service was quantitatively insignificant. There are numerous suggestions, however, that the size of the royal entourage increased substantially after the accession of Charles IV in 1788. This, plus growing military transport exactions, undoubtedly prompted the wave of complaints.

Muleteers were requisitioned for the royal factories, but little data was found to illustrate this. The factories were usually run by managers with government contracts, which typically included the right to requisition transport in the name of the crown, but the three examples of this provide no details.[26] In one case transporters in Segovia province protested the extensive use of their animals to provide firewood for the factory at San Ildefonso.[27] The other two examples took place during wartime and involved the requisition of transport to supply firewood for an ordnance plant.[28]

The crown maintained a monopoly over the distribution and sale of tobacco in Spain, and most tobacco entered at Seville, where it was processed in a huge government factory. To transport the tobacco inland, the crown developed a system of licenses or charters which were granted to muleteers who regularly traveled between given cities. The muleteer received a monthly fee, the tobacco was exempted from all road tolls, and the transporter was authorized to carry firearms, an otherwise illegal practice.[29] Examples of such licenses were found involving the movement of tobacco from Seville to Córdoba, Granada, and Málaga, and between the Cantabrian coast and the plateau of Castile. Another document described the way in which tobacco was shipped from Madrid to Olmedo in Old Castile and then dispersed to the cities of Valladolid, Palencia, Salamanca, and Zamora.[30]

Many of the requirements of the crown could not be easily met

25. *Ibid.*, legs. 1666-29; 1737-37; 1999-39.
26. See La Force, "Textile Factories."   28. *Ibid.*, legs. 1546-20; 1669-38.
27. AHN, *Con.*, leg. 1963-5.   29. *Ibid.*, leg. 933-4.
30. *Ibid.*, legs. 1242-19; 1813-2; AGS, *Catastro*, lib. 369—León: Llanes.

by muleteers available only in certain seasons or limited by the capacity of the animals they used. In such cases the government relied on the professional carters for transport services. The carters, in fact, provided most of the routine haulage of bulky goods demanded by the normal activities of the bureaucracy and spent most of their time working for public or semi-public agencies.

The types of work which the crown expected of the carters included road construction[31] and work on the Canal of Castile, one of the great unfinished projects in Spanish history.[32] Carts were occasionally used to move gold and silver to the mint at Seville, and trains with as many as forty-seven carts carried copper, the metal of most Castilian coinage, to the mint at Segovia.[33]

An interesting example of this kind of activity was the government's use of carters at the Almadén mercury mines. At the mine itself the government maintained a cart-train which provided a regular supply of firewood and mine timber.[34] The mercury produced at the mines was packed in leather bags containing four *arrobas* (one hundred pounds) for shipment to Seville and America. It was loaded eight to ten bags per cart. In the seventeenth century the mercury was carried by carters from as far away as Soria.[35] During the eighteenth century, the work was done on contract by the carters of Almodóvar del Pinar, near Cuenca.[36]

In addition to normal carting privileges, the carters hauling mercury had special pasturage rights within a radius of ten leagues of Almadén, and beginning in the seventeenth century, the right to take from Seville any cargo they wished for the return trip without being subjected to the usual fees and delays for weighing, measuring, and registration. The mercury traveled in large escorted convoys. In the sixteenth century the convoys left for Seville in June and December, but the December shipment was discontinued after

31. AA Navarredonda, *Libro de Acuerdos*, 1788.

32. AHN, *Con.*, leg. 2293-4.

33. *Ibid.*, legs. 2733-24; 2016-17; Ruth Pike, "Seville in the Sixteenth Century," *Hispanic American Historical Review*, XLI (Feb., 1961), 1-30.

34. AGS, *Catastro*, lib. 466—La Mancha: Almadén; Antonio Matilla Tascón, *Historia de las minas de Almadén*, I (Madrid: Ministerio de Hacienda, 1958), 76-162.

35. Matilla, *Minas de Almadén*, I, 132-33.

36. Tudela, pp. 354-55.

1615. It is not clear whether this pattern continued into the eighteenth century.[37]

The carters also handled most of the salt for the royal salt-tax agency. As illustrated earlier, this involved an elaborate pattern of relatively long transfers. It was important because the salt tax was lucrative and the salt a vital commodity, but the supply of salt did not have the element of urgency of some of the other demands made on the transport system. The demand was steady, but the volume fairly low, making it possible to keep reserves against shortages or to employ muleteers when carters were not available. As early as 1652, therefore, the Council of Castile ruled that the salt-tax farmers could not assert a government priority over carts which had cargoes under contract.[38] Carters had to leave such cargoes for other government demands.

The salt supply was thus flexible and allowed for changes in supply patterns. An example of this is provided by the carters of the Navarredonda district in the Gredos Mountains. They were required to make one trip each spring to Andalucía for salt for the salt tax in Extremadura. When the roads were damaged by floods, as in 1747, or pasture along the accustomed routes was inadequate, as in 1766, these carters were allowed the alternative of going north into Old Castile to transport salt in that area.[39]

Salt transportation was supplied largely by the professional carters, but in at least one case muleteers were regularly used. Poza, in the province of Burgos, one of the important sources of salt, listed 71 professional muleteers in the *Catastro*. Fifty-one of them, with 250 animals, worked full time carrying salt, while the remainder spent part of their time doing such work.[40]

3. *The government and the supply of Madrid.* The royal government rather than the city administration bore the responsibility for assuring Madrid's supplies of food and fuel.[41] The crown did so through the *Sala de Alcaldes y Corte*, a subcommittee of the Council of Castile originally created to arrange for the necessities of the royal family and its court. Once Madrid became the estab-

37. Matilla, *Minas de Almadén*, I, 104, 109, 135, 162, 191-93.
38. AHN, CRC, *Tomo* II, doc. 68.
39. AA Navarredonda, *Libro de Acuerdos*, 1747, 1766.
40. AGS, *Catastro*, lib. 19—Burgos: Poza.   41. AHN, *Con.*, leg. 923-31.

lished capital, the *Sala*'s function developed into that of supervising the necessities of the whole city as the seat of the court and the royal government. In doing so, the *Sala* relied heavily on the facilities of the Carters' Association to ensure adequate supplies of wheat and charcoal for the capital. The *Sala* also enforced some of the carters' special privileges concerning transit and winter pastures.[42] It worked at times through or in cooperation with other bodies, such as the Supply Council (*Junta de Abastos*), the Public Granary of Madrid (*Pósito*), and for a brief time in the 1740's through a Commission of the *Cabaña Real* of the carters, which was merged into the Supply Council after a short life.[43]

Most of these organs do not appear in the documents of the later eighteenth century, and in the 1780's the *Sala* arranged the wheat supply via the *Pósito* and the supply of charcoal and some other commodities via contracts with the Five Major Guilds (*Cinco Gremios Mayores*) of Madrid. Beginning as the five most important merchant guilds of the city, the Five Guilds developed a unified business entity which dominated the wholesale trade of eighteenth-century Madrid. By the end of the century the Five Guilds had the resources to contract for the entire charcoal and wine supplies of Madrid and the wheat supply for the Spanish army. The organization was one of the crown's few local sources of credit until the creation of the Banco de San Carlos, predecessor of the Banco de España. The Five Guilds obtained the charcoal contract for Madrid in the 1780's, made purchases from the producers in the forests, and subcontracted the transport to the professional carters, having in the original contract the power to assert the government's priority in the use of the carts.[44]

The size of the government's task in supplementing the supply of Madrid can be appreciated only through an understanding of the total volume of transport services needed for the purpose. This is especially important since the city's demands grew steadily and with them the crown's involvement in the supply process.

The population of Madrid in the early eighteenth century has been estimated at about 130,000 permanent residents, and by the

42. AHN, *Con.*, *Libros de Gobierno*, 1804, fol. 1756.
43. AHN, *Códices*, 1272b.   44. AHN, *Con.*, leg. 923-31.

last decade of the century it had reached 167,000.[45] The supply requirements of the city are given in Table 4, listing the quantities of commodities which passed through the toll gates in 1757 and 1829. The earlier figures do not include grain and charcoal, but the close parallels in other commodities suggest that the amounts of grain and charcoal for the earlier date were at least 60 per cent

Table 4. *Quantities of commodities entering Madrid*[a]

Commodity	1757	1829
Wine	500,000 *arrobas*	576,000 *arrobas*
Olive oil	96,000 "	137,000 "
Soap	33,000 "	64,000 "
Cacao and chocolate	28,000 "	29,000 "
Sugar	50,000 "	58,000 "
Meat	309,000 "	435,000 "
Bacon	17,000 "	—
Hogs	14,653 head	24,499 head
Fish	—	45,000 *arrobas*
Grain	—	759,000 *fanegas*
Charcoal	—	1,839,000 *arrobas*

a. All figures have been rounded to the nearest thousand. No figures were given for fish, grain, and charcoal for 1757, or for bacon for 1829.

SOURCES: 1757 data from Antonio Matilla Tascón, "El primer catastro de la villa de Madrid," *Revista de Archivos, Bibliotecas y Museos*, LXIX (1961), 465-66; 1829 data from AA Madrid, *Contaduría*, 3-191-4.

(to use an arbitrary and probably low figure) of the 1829 amounts. Most of the meat was driven to the city as livestock. An oxcart carried 35 to 40 *arrobas* of moderately bulky cargo or about 6 *fanegas* of grain, and large pack animals carried 8 to 10 *arrobas*.[46] On that basis, the supplies entering Madrid in 1757 would have loaded either 600,000 pack animals or 150,000 carts.

This estimate is supported by a report of 1784, which contains a "list of the carts and wagons which have entered . . . Madrid in the fifteen days indicated, not including coaches and miscellaneous

45. Domínguez Ortiz, *El siglo XVII*, pp. 134-36.
46. See the section on means of transportation in Chapter iii.

cargoes of greens, fruits, and other items for daily consumption."
Between June 23 and July 7, 1784, 10,389 carts and wagons entered
the city, an average of 693 per day, Sundays and holidays included
(June 24 was a major holiday). The report also said that on June
28, 5,068 large and small pack animals entered with the same types
of cargo and that the number "seems about the same every day."[47]
The fifteen days cited were in the busy season for transporters, but
even so it would not be hard to assume an annual volume of traffic
of the magnitude suggested in the preceding paragraph. The an-
imals/cart ratio suggested by the above, which is the only one available, implies that the 600,000 animal loads of capacity was actually
distributed between 380,000 animals and 55,000 carts.

The commodities which caused the government the most concern and which required the most frequent drafting of transport
services were charcoal and grain. In neither case does it appear that
the crown actually bought and resold more than a part of the total
supply, although all of the grain had to pass through the royal depots. To hold prices to a reasonable level, however, it was necessary
to subsidize the transport of such goods from the more distant
sources of supply when the nearer ones proved inadequate.

According to Table 4, eighteenth-century Madrid probably used
over 1,000,000 *arrobas* (12,500 tons) of charcoal per year. This is
corroborated by evidence from 1795, when 24,000 cartloads of the
fuel passed through the toll gates.[48] At about forty *arrobas* (1,000
pounds) per load, this also represents about 12,500 tons. The extent of the government's involvement in this trade is not clear, but
in 1785 the Five Guilds contracted with the crown to supply 4,000
cartloads of charcoal for the city. It is worth noting that the contractors were having trouble getting the carters to fulfill their sub-
contracts for transport because more desirable work was available
in the North. The crown supported the contractors' right to co-
erce the carters by exercising the government's priority over their
services.[49]

In the late eighteenth century Madrid required 500,000 to 600,-
000 *fanegas* (750,000-900,000 bushels) of wheat per year. All wheat

47. AHN, *Con.*, leg. 923-31.
48. AGS, *Hacienda, Dirección General de Rentas, 2ª Remesa*, leg. 4894.
49. AHN, *Con.*, leg. 1184-26.

was distributed in the city through the government grain depot, but it appears that more than half of the total arrived without government encouragement. To hold prices down and assure an adequate supply, the crown had established an elaborate collection and storage system in grain-producing areas. In this way the government was directly involved in the movement of over 150,000 *fanegas* (225,000 bushels) of wheat to the city each year. In drought years it was necessary to bring as much as half of this figure all the way from the seaports.[50] This doubled the distance which the supplies traveled and, given the slowness of oxcart transportation, reduced the capacity of the transport system, making it necessary to requisition farm animals and carts.[51] Grain transportation then took precedence over everything, to the detriment of other economic activities dependent on transport.

D. *Observations and speculations on the demand for transport*

There is no way to measure the total volume of the demand for transportation. A great deal of activity was devoted to the exchange of basic commodities in Old Castile, Andalucía, and Valencia, and a large volume of such goods was brought to Madrid. The volume of trade in non-subsistence goods was generally slight, but the distribution was widespread for the few customers who could pay the fees of professional muleteers. The largest trade in indirect-consumption goods involved the wool and flour exports of the North.

Only two elements in this demand pattern can be quantified, the northern exports at Santander and the food and fuel supply of Madrid. In 1784 some 700 carts and 5,000 pack animals entered the city each day in late June. This suggests that the over 600,000 animal loads of supplies required by the city actually arrived on 380,000 animals and 55,000 carts. The carting capacity used was in large part diverted to the supply of Madrid by the royal government and carried much of the wheat and charcoal. By comparison, the wool export trade in the North demanded 6,000 to 7,000 carts in the 1750's and 1760's.

The demand for transport grew steadily, especially for carriers

50. *Ibid.*, legs. 11452; 49248; AA Murcia, leg. 2795.
51. AHN, *Con.*, legs. 2607-2; 49328.

available regardless of the farming cycle. The population of Spain was increasing after 1750 and retaining more produce in the rural areas. This forced the crown increasingly to organize and subsidize the transport of supplies, dictating the uses of the available transport services. This was accentuated by the growth of Madrid, which increased in size over 25 per cent in the second half of the century. At the same time, the demand for transport in the North rose from 6,000-7,000 carts to 14,000 in order to service the exports of wool and flour.

In time of peace and satisfactory crops the transport system worked fairly well, but any expansion of the demand for transport of non-subsistence cargoes was confronted by periodic shortages of transportation as the government requisitioned all carriers to meet food supply crises. At such times the government had difficulty in finding transport to meet its urgent needs, especially when war and drought happened to coincide. The 1790's showed that there were limits to the amount of free transport which the countryside would provide for the army and royal household without protest. More critically, recurrent food shortages made it necessary to import increasing quantities of grain for Madrid. These imports lengthened the transport distance for such supplies and thus reduced the effective capacity of the system. Longer distances and slow transport meant fewer trips per cart per year. At the same time, drought conditions reduced the pasturage along the roads, further hampering a transport system dependent on such grazing. While the demand for transport in general was growing, and the government's erratic requirements were becoming more severe, developments were taking place in the transport system itself which limited the supply of specialized transport services.

Chapter three. *The supply of transport services, part one: technology and seasonal patterns*

Geographic conditions in the Iberian Peninsula restricted internal transport to overland techniques. The mountainous terrain and primitive roads dictated the use of pack animals, simple carts, and, occasionally, larger wagons. The agrarian and weather cycles limited the amount of time which carriers could devote to transportation. Winter weather (which made roads impassable and closed the mountain passes), planting, harvesting, and the effects of dry weather on pasturage all had to be taken into account by transporters. The technology used and the seasonal accommodations which were made are thus an important part of the supply of transport services and have major implications for the general topic of transport availability.

A. *Animals and vehicles*

Pack-animal transporters used animals of a variety of kinds and sizes, and the terminology included more than a dozen words for specific types of animals. The only distinction commonly used referred to large pack animals (*caballerías mayores*), generally mules, and small pack animals (*caballerías menores*), usually donkeys.[1] The smaller animals were rated at one-half to two-thirds the capacity of the large ones. Horses were not widely used for transport in the eighteenth century except in the area around Medina Sidonia in the province of Cádiz, and in the coastal valleys of Asturias and Galicia.[2] The use of horses as pack animals was declining. The transporters of western León used them in the sixteenth century,

1. Among the words applied to pack animals were *macho, mula, burro, burra, pollino, pollina, borrico, borrica, cabello, yegua,* and *rocín*; all refer to various sizes, strains, or hybrids of the asinine and equine species.
2. ARCG, 3-534-8; AGS, *Catastro,* lib. 378 (coastal areas of the province of León).

but by the eighteenth had converted to mules.[3] The trend away from the use of horses was probably due to the fact that they cost more to maintain than mules, but it may have been encouraged by royal policy. The crown had long attempted to reserve horses for military purposes and as late as 1709 issued a decree insisting that the old laws prohibiting the use of horses for transport be observed; mules and donkeys were specified instead. Exceptions were made for the areas where horses were widely used in transport.[4]

Table 5. *Pack-animal capacity (in U.S. pounds)*

Cargo	Relative distance and terrain	Large animal	Small animal
Straw[a]	Short distance, level terrain	300 lb.	200 lb.
Merchandise[b]	Long distance, rough terrain	200	100
Mercury[c]	Moderate distance, rough terrain	200	
Cannonballs[d]	Long distance, rough terrain	196	
Gunpowder[e]	Long distance, rough terrain	180	
Spanish Army requirements[f]		250	

a. AGS, *Catastro*, lib. 622—Toledo: Torrejón de Ardoz.
b. *Ibid.*, lib. 361—León: San Pedro de las Dueñas.
c. Matilla, *Minas de Almadén*, p. 76.
d. Michael Glover, *Peninsular Preparation* (London: Macmillan, 1961), p. 96.
e. *Ibid.*
f. AGS, *Guerra*, leg. 416.

The capacity of the animals used can be established through the occasional references to load sizes which are shown in Table 5. The figures are borne out by a road toll schedule which rated a small pack animal as carrying two-thirds the cargo of a large one

3. José Luis Martín Galindo, *Arrieros maragatos en el siglo XVIII* (Valladolid: C.S.I.C., 1956), p. 16. This study is also published as "Arrieros leoneses. Los Arrieros maragatos," *Archivos Leoneses*, X (León, 1956), 153-79.
4. AHN, *Hac., Ordenes Generales de Rentas*, doc. 236.

for toll purposes.[5] A large pack animal had a capacity of 200 to 300 United States pounds, a small one a capacity of 100 to 200 pounds. Details accompanying the examples show that longer trips and rough terrain implied smaller loads.

Three types of carts were in use in eighteenth-century Castile, but their design was so taken for granted that no careful descriptions of them are available. The three types were the *carro*, the *carreta*, and the *galera*. The term *carro* is the vaguest of the three and was applied to the light wagons used locally in most areas. They were pulled by mules and generally had two, but sometimes four, wheels.[6]

The *carreta* was the type of cart most often used for long-distance transportation. It consisted of a long, relatively narrow bed with three longitudinal timbers connected by ribs and covered with a floor. The center timber extended forward and the oxen were yoked to its end.[7] There were two common varieties of this *carreta*, both in use since the Middle Ages, and distinguished by the type of wheel used. The lighter farm cart or *churra* rode on relatively large spoked wheels, often shod with iron rims, occasionally provided with spikes or cleats to grip the soil. The heavier transport cart (*carreta puerta a puerta*) rode on smaller, nearly solid, wheels made of wood pieces and shod with a changeable wooden rim. Both were commonly pulled by a pair of oxen or occasionally by mules. Both types of wheels were at first fixed to the axle, which itself turned in its mountings. Possibly during the seventeenth century, the lighter spoked wheels began to be mounted on a fixed axle with the bearing surfaces in the wheel hubs. The heavier solid wheel was never so modified and only gradually disappeared as better roads allowed the use of larger wagons of different construction.[8] In the logging areas near Soria the solid-wheel oxcart was still used as late as the 1920's.[9]

No clear evidence was found to show that such oxcarts had much

5. AHN, *Con.*, leg. 2867-19.

6. Article "Carro," *Encyclopedia universal ilustrada europeo-americana* (165 vols.; Madrid, 1924), Vol. XI.

7. *Ibid.*; Menéndez Pidal, p. 78. The latter provides a description of the types of *carretas*, with pictures.

8. AGS, *Catastro*, lib. 14—Burgos: Palacios de la Sierra; Tudela, pp. 357-58; Menéndez Pidal, pp. 56, 76-78.

9. Documented by a photograph in the town hall of San Leonardo in the province of Soria.

advantage over pack animals in terms of lower per unit transport costs, although there is a quotation which suggests this may have been true in the 1770's. In 1773 the government had to pay fifteen to twenty *marevedis* per *fanega* per league for pack animal transport as opposed to ten to twelve for carting.[10] It is equally likely that such carts were used because they provided the only practical way of carrying certain cargoes, such as large building stones, building timbers, and ships' masts, over the primitive roads of Spain. This is suggested by the fact that the home areas of the professional carters coincided with timber-producing regions and by the continued use of oxcarts in those areas into the twentieth century. The prevalence of this type of cart was also due to the very real advantages of its simple technology. Such a cart could carry long, awkward loads; it was sturdy enough to carry heavy weights over rugged terrain; and the unshod wheels did less damage to paving than iron rims.[11] Further, a carpenter-cartmaker could easily make replacement parts of all types with a few simple tools, and replacement materials were available in the nearest woodlot.

The third type of vehicle, the *galera*, may have come into use in the late sixteenth century. The date is uncertain, since the earliest concrete reference to its use in freight transport in Spain is dated 1696.[12] The context, however, suggests that the *galera* was already well established by then, and since Philip II was using a fairly elaborate four-wheeled carriage as early as the 1560's, the *galera* probably appeared between the two dates. The *galera* was a large four-wheeled wagon, the front wheels generally smaller than the rear. It had a light cloth top and was pulled by four to eight mules.[13] This brief description indicates that it was a more sophisticated machine than the cart and was similar to the large wagons of the American West. In the seventeenth and eighteenth centuries, the use of the wagon (*galera*) was confined to the relatively open Southeast (Murcia and Cartagena) and the roads inland as far as

10. AHN, *Con.*, leg. 49240.
11. In 1785 and 1788 carts using town streets and paved royal roads were forbidden to use protruding nails to fasten iron rims to wheels and were required to have iron bands at least three inches wide. Wooden wheels were advised for highway use. AHN, *Con.*, leg. 2264-7; AA Jeréz de la Frontera, leg. 160-48; Menéndez Pidal, p. 71.
12. AA Cartagena, *Rentas*, 1696.
13. Article "Galera," *Encyclopedia universal*, Vol. XXV; AGS, *Guerra*, leg. 416; AA Cartagena, *Rentas*, 1696.

Toledo and Madrid. Even in this region they were relatively scarce as late as 1755, and only in the mid-nineteenth century did the use of the large wagon spread as roads gradually improved.[14]

There are few references to specific cargoes to support an estimate of the capacity of the eighteenth-century cart. Those which are available are given in Table 6. The last item in the table is

Table 6. *Cart and wagon capacities (in U.S. pounds)*[a]

Cargo	Type of cart	Load weight
Salt[b]	*Carreta*	250 lb. (10 *arrobas*)
Salt[c]	*Carreta*	500-700 lb. (3.5 *fanegas*)
Firewood[d]	*Carreta*	900 lb. (36 *arrobas*)
Mercury[e]	*Carreta*	800-1,000 lb. (32-40 *arrobas*)
Military supplies[f]	*Galera,* 8 mules	3,000 lb. (120 *arrobas*)

a. The original figures were in *arrobas* or *fanegas*. One *arroba* = 25 pounds (U.S.), 1 *fanega* = 1.5 bushels.

b. AHN, *Con.*, leg. 230-6. This figure is inexplicably low.

c. AA Navarredonda, *Libro de Acuerdos*, 1755. One bushel of pure salt would weigh 167 pounds (*Handbook of Chemistry and Physics*). The use of bulk measures such as the *fanega* indicates that the salt was probably granulated. Hence, a bushel would weigh considerably less, perhaps about 100 pounds per bushel. If so, the cargo must have weighed 500-700 pounds.

d. Matilla, *Minas de Almadén*, p. 160.

e. Ibid.

f. AGS, *Guerra*, leg. 416.

probably not typical of *galeras* used commercially, since it specifies eight mules, whereas the gate-toll records of Cartagena show no *galeras* with more than six.[15] The second, third, and fourth examples are in rough agreement.. Moreover, they fit with the toll schedules at Andujar in Andalucía, which rated a two-wheeled cart at five times the capacity of a small pack animal, or 500 to 1,000 pounds.[16] Thus, the ordinary oxcart had a maximum weight capacity of about 1,000 pounds, although when bulkier goods were in-

14. AA Murcia, leg. 2795, census of vehicles of 1755; Martín Galindo, *Arrieros maragatos*, p. 27; Angel Cabo Alonso, "La Armuña y su evolución económica," *Estudios Geográficos*, núms. 58, 59 (1955), pp. 385-86.

15. AA Cartagena, *Rentas*, 1696.　　　　　16. AHN, *Con.*, leg. 2867-19.

volved, the cargo was correspondingly lighter and the weight of an average load was considerably less than the maximum.

Although some of the carters of southeastern Castile used mules with their wagons and carts, the ox was the standard draft animal in all of north and central Spain, and as such gave carting some very distinctive characteristics. While many of the oxen (*bueyes*) were raised by the carters themselves, it was also customary to replace worn-out oxen as the cart trains moved through Castile in the spring. A major source of young oxen (*novillos*) was the Cantabrian mountain valleys. The breeders brought the young oxen out of the mountains in the spring as part of the widespread trade be-tween the North and the Castilian plain.[17] The young oxen first traveled with the spare animals which always accompanied a cart train until they became accustomed to the daily routine. The new animals were then paired off with old and steady oxen while they were broken to hauling. On the basis of one train manager's ac-count, about one ox in seven was replaced each year.[18]

Use of oxen forced the carters to stop frequently and locate pasture where the animals could graze and ruminate properly. Hence, pasturage along the roads became extremely important. The oxen were slow moving and docile appearing, but they were easily irritated if not adequately fed and rested. This fact caused trouble when carters had to enter large towns where the oxen were forced by various delays to stay on their feet longer than normal.[19] The use of oxen also imposed upon the mountaineer carters a distinctive annual migration pattern, with the oxen often pastured during the winter in places distant from the carters' homes.

B. *Seasonal patterns in transport*

The transportation system was tied to the weather pattern of Castile. December and January were cold and rainy, making un-tended eighteenth-century roads muddy and difficult to use. At the same time, snow in the mountains closed the passes connecting the

17. AHN, *Con.*, legs. 2093-10; 51197-44; José Luis Martín Galindo, "Arcaismo y modernidad en la explotación agraria de Valdeburón (León)," *Estudios Geográficos, núm.* 83 (1961), pp. 189-93.
18. AHN, *Con.*, leg. 2229-31; AHN, *Con., Libros de Gobierno*, 1784, fols. 766-774.
19. AHN, *Con., Libros de Gobierno*, 1784, fol. 774.

major regions. August, September, and October were hot and dry, making pasturage scarce along the roads. Agricultural activities also influenced transport, especially by pack animal, since in January and February large numbers of men and animals were needed for ploughing and sowing. June and July in Old and New Castile were the months of the grain harvest, and the autumn months brought the olive harvest in the South. At such times, even relatively professionalized transporters had to help in the fields with their animals.

1. *Seasonal patterns and the muleteers.* Virtually all muleteers were connected with agriculture and were transporters only on a seasonal basis, using such animals as were temporarily not needed on the farm. Only the *ordinarios* who provided regular services between towns were perhaps separated from agriculture. In a few cases, the most notable being the muleteers of western León, specialized transporter-traders operated wide-ranging family enterprises, but even these carriers still owned land and maintained homesteads on which farming was an important activity for the family as a whole. In a poor and sparsely populated country, there was probably little point in such a muleteer's specializing in transport to the extent of breaking away from agriculture completely.[20] There were, in fact, positive advantages to maintaining a farm. The use of livestock for both farming and transport created a complementary situation in even a fairly sophisticated transport enterprise. The farm produced and supported the animals needed for transport, while the animals provided seasonally needed power, a way of marketing any surplus farm production, and fertilizer for the soil.

In a small number of cases, transporting may have been more important than farming to the muleteer, but in most cases it was transport that was the secondary activity. The actual amount of transporting time varied from town to town and individual to individual, and there was little correlation between the amount of time spent on the road, the range of activity, and the type of cargo carried. The *Catastro* used three different techniques for indicating such part-time transporting. In many instances the replies indicate the number of months or days per year devoted to transport. In

20. For additional detail, see Domínguez Ortiz, *El siglo XVIII*, pp. 55-76; Vicens Vives, *Historia*, IV, 8-16.

such cases eight months per year was the maximum. Frequently the number of trips made each year is listed, often without indication of destination. In many cases variations in activity are indicated by listing the relative earning power of individual pack animals in a town. In all cases the wide ranges in the amount of time, number of trips, or earning power per animal indicate that transport was generally a part-time occupation undertaken as other activities permitted. Frequently a lesser amount of transport activity coincided with largely local trade or transport of basic necessities. No generalization is possible, however, since there are detailed examples of individuals who transported as little as fifteen days a year, but made the round trip between Cuenca and Bilbao in that time.[21]

The seasonal and casual nature of pack-animal transport is emphasized by an extreme example: the Castilian peasant who worked as a migrant farm laborer at harvest time. He traveled to distant provinces, carrying commodities which he knew were in demand at his destination, and did the same thing on his trip home. In the province of Cuenca, two towns alone counted over a hundred residents who, with mules, in some cases rented, went off to Andalucía for the fall and winter to work in the olive harvest. They returned for the first ploughing in January, their animals loaded with olives and olive oil to sell in their home province. In another case several residents took their animals to the province of Toledo where they worked for two months taking harvested olives to market, supplying transport while the local residents were engaged in the harvest itself. The possibility that such migrant activity is included in other parts of the *Catastro* makes it uncertain just how widespread this type of activity may have been.[22] In general, the great mass of muleteers were farmers or farm workers who engaged in transport from two weeks to eight months of the year.

21. Examples showing the number of trips include: AGS, *Catastro*, libs. 76—Cuenca: Alcalá del Rio Jucar; 335—León: Taliba de Arriba y de Abajo; 369—León: Llanes; 629—Toro: various towns; 546—Segovia: El Escorrial; 135—Extremadura: Alberca: 18—Burgos: Cantabrana; 7—Ávila: Piedralaves. For variations in earnings: Cabo Alonso, pp. 121-22; AGS, *Catastro*, libs. 367—León: Langres; 384—León: Villafranca; 457—Madrid: Val de Santo Domingo. For examples indicating time per year: libs. 100—Cuenca: Castellote; 647 and 651—Valladolid: various towns; 110—Cuenca: Vindel; 137—Extremadura: Casas de Palmero; 44—Burgos: Hervosa; 275—Granada: Alquije; 9—Avila: Cebreros.

22. *Ibid.*, libs. 97—Cuenca: Zaorejas; 99—Cuenca: Alustante.

2. *Seasonal patterns and the carters.* Some of the Castilian carters were peasant-transporters with seasonal patterns very similar to those of the muleteers. These part-time carters were described in the *Catastro* as working as transporters one to four months each year, or else as making a specified number of trips per year to deliver some local product. The largest part of the seasonal carters worked to make and deliver charcoal, the main heating and cooking fuel of the towns of Castile. In many wooded districts the inhabitants used part of their free time to make the charcoal, and at some point during the year when the roads were passable and the draft animals idle, they carried the charcoal to market, often traveling long distances.[23] This seasonal carting was also important to other wood-products industries ranging from firewood through wood for furniture to ceiling beams and planks.[24]

The same seasonal pattern can be observed among some of the peasant-carters of Old Castile. The residents of many towns of the provinces of León, Toro, and Burgos spent about three months each year bringing grain and wine to their home towns to supplement local production. In a few cases this activity was more specialized since some carters, although working only a few weeks, hired themselves out as general transporters. Occasionally one finds an exception to the seasonal pattern, as in the mountains of the province of Burgos. Many forest residents made two or three trips to Burgos or Logroño during the winter months, delivering wool and charcoal with their farm carts.[25]

The professional, long-haul carters of the Spanish interior had developed a unique pattern of seasonal migration which freed them from the limitations of the farming cycle and took advantage of the enforced idleness of the rainy winter months. They freed themselves from seasonal demands for manpower by combining their carts into

23. *Ibid.*, libs. 348—León: Rodrigatos; 510—Salamanca: Alba de Yelte, Aldeaguela; 511—Salamanca: Martiago; 512—Salamanca: Sepulcro Hilario; 537—Segovia: Festilla, San Cristobal; 473—La Mancha: Fuente el Fresno.

24. *Ibid.*, libs. 12—Burgos: Cañicosa; 511—Salamanca: Puebla de Azaba; 527—Salamanca: Hoyos del Espino; 537—Segovia: Festilla, San Cristobal; 561—Sevilla: Constantina; 7—Ávila: Piedralaves; AGS, *Catastro, Comprobaciones*, leg. 1616-4: Constantina.

25. AGS, *Catastro*, libs. 43—Burgos: Cotillos, Puente, Salzeda, Trasabuela; 44—Burgos: Hervas; 45—Burgos: Cilleruelo; 83—Cuenca: Fuentes; 145—Extremadura: Montijo; 336—León: Vega de Boñar; 423—Toro: Abiada, Aldueso, Arconada; 510—Salamanca: Alberquería; Tudela, p. 357.

large cart trains which could be managed by small professional crews. The carters of the Gredos Mountains south of Ávila even hired migratory labor to cut the lumber which was the principal product of their home district.[26] To keep the cart trains on the road as long as possible, the carters went to great lengths to take advantage of the rainy season. Farm oxen were normally wintered at home in the mountain villages where the carters lived. Winter fodder in such areas was limited, and the animals were kept alive on short rations until spring, when they could recover as the new grass came up. Carting oxen, however, had to be in good condition as soon as the roads dried, not emaciated by months of near starvation. This was especially important because once the carting season started, pasture along the roads steadily became scarcer and the condition of the animals tended to deteriorate.[27]

The solution was to winter the animals in the southern and western valleys, often hundreds of miles from the carters' homes. The oxen were settled into rented winter pastures in late November. The Sorian carters wintered their animals in such diverse provinces as Zamora, Extremadura, Toledo, and La Mancha; those around Ávila used pastures in Extremadura; while the carters of Cuenca province wintered in Valencia or Andalucía (See Map 14).[28]

Pastures were sometimes rented by individuals, but more often by several carters contracting collectively for a given piece of grazing land. The carters sharing a pasture often came from several towns in the home province, and there are examples of contracts involving two to nine participants. Some of the contracts were renewed year after year for over a century with no break in the continuity of the agreement.[29] Such sharing of pastures was not universal, and some small operators with as few as twenty oxen made their own

26. AGS, *Catastro*, lib. 525—Salamanca: Navarredonda. For a general discussion of such migratory labor, see Antonio Mejide Pardo, *La Emigración gallega intrapeninsular en el siglo XVIII* (Madrid: C.S.I.C., 1960).

27. AHN, *Hac.*, lib. 8038, fols. 340-80. This is the decision, with numerous precedents cited by both parties, in a crucial case concerning grazing privileges for the carters while in transit. Included is testimony describing their activities.

28. AHN, *Con.*, leg. 1608-3; AGS, *Catastro*, lib. 14—Burgos: Ontoria del Pinar; Tudela, p. 357; Adela Gil Crespo, "La Evolución económica de Requena y su comarca," *Estudios Geográficos*, núm. 50 (1953), p. 59.

29. AHN, *Con.*, legs. 395-9; 1608-1; 51197-11, 13, 27, 32, 43, 48, 52, 54, 60.

arrangements for pastures or else shared contracts with non-carters such as members of the Mesta of sheep owners.[30] Rental agreements were often of several years' duration, and not only included the price and the permitted livestock capacity, but also provided for access to water, limited rights to cut wood, the use of buildings on the land by the guards who stayed with the oxen, and exemptions from local tithes or *diezmos*. Payment was usually made half on entry and half on departure, but occasionally in thirds, the first third on signing the contract. Terms sometimes included provisions for the landowner's previous commitments to other renters, admission of the owner's milk cows, and extra charges for hunting and fishing rights.[31]

Rental contracts imposed strict limits on the shareholder who was unable to use the capacity to which he had committed himself. He could sublet his share to another carter, but could not introduce sheep or other types of livestock. The capacity of a pasture was carefully divided among the participants, and a carter who exceeded his limit was quickly hauled into court. Shares in such contracts were transferable, and a shareholder could sell his portion outright to an outside party, who then became bound by all the terms of the original contract. It was possible for a carter to participate regularly in rental contracts beyond his own needs in order to sublet to smaller operators at a profit, as one widow from San Leonardo did for many years.[32]

The carters' winter migration is illustrated by Map 14, which is based on a number of legal disputes over the use of pastures. There is no assurance that important pasture areas have not been left out, since some carting towns were not mentioned in these documents, but the pattern is clear. Winter pastures were often located at great distances from home, and always in valley areas. These generally coincide with the regions of greatest transport activity illustrated in Chapter II. The carters themselves explained the concentration near Toledo and Ciudad Real in testimony dated 1701. They claimed that a winter location between Seville and Madrid allowed them to make five or six carting trips a year, whereas they

30. *Ibid.*, legs. 2103-10; 2736-10.
31. *Ibid.*, leg. 51197-6, 13, 43, 48, 52; ACS, *Catastro*, lib. 495—Palencia: Valverde; Tudela, p. 375.
32. *Archivo Paroquial de Palacios de la Sierra* (Burgos), *Libro de Pleitos*, 1804, 1808; AHN, *Con.*, legs 2736-10; 51197-32, 54, 60.

could only make three or four if pastured in any other region.[33]

The scarcity of pasture during the summer occasionally caused carters to rent special summer pastures as well. A rather vague royal decree of 1702 located these in "Extremadura, Andalucía, and Old Castile."[34] Only two late eighteenth-century examples of such summer pasture turned up, near Zamora and Medina del Campo in Old Castile,[35] and summer pastures do not appear to have been common. The tendency of carters to stop two and three days in exceptionally good (and free) roadside pastures suggests that this may have been a way of avoiding the need to rent summer grazing.[36]

The carters thus escaped the periodic limitations of local agriculture and took advantage of the winter months by improving the condition of their animals with adequate winter grazing. This allowed them to remain on the roads from March until late November every year.

3. Some implications of seasonal patterns. The seasonal patterns which affected transportation had three important and direct implications for the supply of transport services. There was a great variation in the seasonal availability of transport of all sorts. The winter months seriously reduced the supply of transporters of all kinds, including the professional carters. The availability of muleteers and part-time carters fluctuated with the demand for labor on the land from which most of them obtained a great part of their sustenance. These shortages came during the winter months of December and January, the planting period from late January through March, and the harvest months of June and early July. The patterns came earlier in the South than in the North, but were basically the same all over Castile. This seasonality is demonstrated by road and gate toll records which list revenues by month, the best documented examples being Córdoba and Seville. In those towns the lowest figures are for January, February, and March, and the highest figures, often more than double the winter ones, came in April, May, and August through November. A pronounced dip in revenues was usual in June and early July.[37]

33. AHN, *Con.*, leg. 395-9.
34. AHN, CRC, *Tomo* II, doc. 68.   35. AHN, *Con.*, leg. 51197-6, 53.
36. *Ibid.*, leg. 2229-31; AHN, *Hac.*, lib. 8038, fols. 350-80.
37. For the city of Córdoba, monthly figures for 1753-58, 1763-65, 1766-68, and 1779

Such an irregular supply of transportation was adequate for the needs of a subsistence economy but inefficient and unsuitable for more advanced productive activity. Any processing plant or factory represents a capital installation which must operate as much of the year as possible to achieve maximum efficiency. To operate thus requires a steady and dependable supply of transportation to provide raw materials and dispose of the product.

This regular transportation the muleteers could not provide. The alternative was to build up large stockpiles of raw material while transport was available and to accumulate large inventories of the finished product when it was not. Both processes, by tying up considerable quantities of capital for long periods, reduced the potential profit. That some of the difficulties of the seasonal problem could be avoided by hiring the long-haul, professional ox-carters may help explain the government's tendency to use carters more frequently than muleteers. So long as the government did not monopolize their services, economic growth such as has been ascribed to the Santander area could take place.

Implicit in the carters' seasonal pattern, however, was a second set of problems. The government relied heavily on the carters, particularly for bringing supplies to Madrid. These demands inevitably increased as the population of the country and its capital grew. A substantial increase in population generally creates pressure to convert grazing land to arable wherever possible. Since the carters depended heavily on grazing land to maintain and expand their services, they found it increasingly difficult to meet the growing demand for dependable transportation. The force of population pressure, which increased the demand for transport services, simultaneously limited the principal source of professional transport by destroying the grazing upon which it was based.

This long-term trend was aggravated by the recurrent droughts which brought large, erratic increases in the demand for long-distance transport simply to keep Madrid from starvation. Because the same droughts which destroyed the crops ruined the roadside grazing which the carters needed every day, the ability of the carters to

are in AA Córdoba, *Sección* 5, *Serie* 40, *Caja* 26, docs. 23, 29, 30, 31, 33, 36, 37. For the city of Seville, years 1768-99, 1802, 1804, and 1806 are in AA Sevilla, *Sección* II (*Contaduría*), *carpetas* 243, 244, 245, 285, 286, 287, 288, 290, 291, 292, 326, and 327.

service the economy suffered a net reduction just when transportation demands became abnormally large.[38] As a result, even a moderate subsistence crisis could deprive the industrial sector of transport for the larger part of a year.

Seasonality in transport had a third major implication, outlined here and explored further in Chapter V: it was most unlikely that the peasant-transporters of the countryside could have been drawn into anything like full-time transportation. These muleteers, constituting all but a small part of the transport pool, carried on a substantial interregional trade in wheat, olive oil, wine, and charcoal. This trade, however, was demanded by the marginal nature of agriculture and the regional specialization which was an unconscious attempt to increase over-all productivity. It was made possible by the peasant's long periods of idleness.

These periods of idleness permitted the transport of low-value, bulky commodities because of a cost advantage not present in the situation of the full-time professional transporter. During the off seasons the peasants were idle, and at such times the opportunity cost of transporting was extremely low. Men and animals must be fed all year around, and if even a part of this cost of maintenance in the idle seasons, as well as the direct out-of-pocket expenses, could be defrayed by transporting, the peasant's economic position was improved. Basically he was supported by farming, and even though by transporting he could not earn enough to make a "profit" or even cover all of his maintenance costs, he was supplementing his income. Thus the fact that transport remained for most muleteers a secondary activity was the factor which allowed fairly extensive transfers of subsistence goods.

These transfers were essential to the countryside because of the regional specialization forced upon Castile by the poverty of her agrarian resources. Many areas which produced surpluses of wine or olive oil, for example, were dependent on grain brought from other regions for even a minimal level of subsistence. Frequently, therefore, the peasant engaged in transport because his personal situation, reflecting local needs, made the opportunity cost of engaging in transport not merely low, but negative. Survival required that he dispose of his wine or charcoal or olive oil in order to ob-

38. AHN, *Hac.*, lib. 8038, fol. 351.

tain grain. In many cases his town government contracted for such provisions for the whole community and hired him to do the carrying. It was still a matter of survival.[39]

Drawing such peasant-transporters into specialized transport activity would have separated them from agriculture. The prices offered for the transport services thus provided had to be substantially higher than for the same services in the context of the subsistence economy. The peasant would have lost his primary means of subsistence and the farms would have lost man and animal power at crucial times. Moreover, if the peasants had left their traditional transport patterns, the distribution of many essential commodities would have broken down. Finally, the total demand for transportation varied greatly from year to year, and the peasant who gave up farming completely when transport was in great demand faced unemployment in years when the demand slackened.

For these reasons most of the muleteer activity observed in Castile could not have been channeled easily toward transport services suited to the needs of more productive or "modern" economic activity. Muleteer transport was suited to and fitted into the market-resource-technology complex of traditional Castile. Economic conditions permitted a low money price for such transport within that complex, and those conditions did not exist for the transporter when he left it. Moreover, the traditional complex itself would have been badly damaged by the withdrawal of such transport for other purposes. The relatively large volume of low-cost transport provided by the muleteer-peasants was really available for only a limited range of activities and for certain months of the year.

39. For a discussion of the phenomenon in the context of the sixteenth century in Castile, see da Silva, pp. 1-57. The emphasis on subsistence exchanges was criticized by Jovellanos in the 1790's as an obstacle to an effective national market in grain. Gaspar de Jovellanos, "Informe de la Sociedad Económica de Madrid . . . en el Expediente de Ley Agraria," in *Biblioteca de Autores Españoles*, L, 113-14.

Chapter four. *The supply of transport services, part two: the transporter at work*

A. *The individual enterprise*

The average size of the individual carter or muleteer enterprise was very small, reflecting the fact that most transport was provided by the peasant-transporter of the countryside. The average was probably lowest among the muleteers, although there were some large pack-transport businesses. Table 7 lists the average numbers of animals per muleteer in the middle of the eighteenth century, showing that an average of three was common in Old Castile and four in New Castile and Andalucía. In most cases the higher provincial figures come from the plains provinces of Toro, Valladolid, Extremadura, La Mancha, Córdoba, and Seville. The low averages provide additional support for the assertion that most muleteers were farmers using their work animals for transport during the slack periods in the agrarian cycle. This is supported by the testimony of peasants who traveled hundreds of miles, but frequently used only one or two pack animals.[1]

The only important examples of large-scale enterprise among muleteers include the *arrieros maragatos* of León, the *cabañiles* of Southeastern Castile, and two isolated operators in Málaga and Cádiz. The muleteer enterprise in Málaga had a royal license to carry tobacco and operated two pack trains with a total of thirty-four animals. The business in Cádiz had a legal monopoly on transport within the city and employed four supervisors, several drivers, and an unspecified number of mules.[2]

The *cabañiles* were mule-train operators who used strings of about a hundred animals and worked the year around as bulk car-

1. AHN, Con., leg. 2123-3.
2. AHN, *Con.*, leg. 1242; AGS, *Catastro, Comprobaciones*, leg. 1644-1: Cádiz.

riers. With one exception these individuals confined their activities to the southeast quarter of the peninsula, from Cartagena as far inland as Toledo and Madrid. No detailed descriptions of these carriers are available, but it appears that they employed several drivers with each mule-train and were important in the grain supply of Madrid, and especially of Granada. Table 8 lists the thirty-one such

Table 7. *Animals per muleteer in Castile*[a]

Region	Province	Number of individuals owning pack animals[a]	Average number of animals
Old Castile	Ávila	374	3.14
	Burgos	844	3.25
	León	801	3.13
	Palencia	61	3.48
	Salamanca	287	1.85
	Segovia	107	3.05
	Soria	91	3.05
	Toro	40	4.95
	Valladolid	91	4.68
	Zamora	—[b]	
New Castile	Cuenca	967	3.59
	Extremadura	738	4.12
	Guadalajara	63	3.06
	Madrid	33	4.00
	La Mancha	452	3.19
	Murcia	—[b]	
	Toledo	428	3.52
Andalucía	Córdoba	320	4.04
	Granada	910	2.41
	Jaén	47	3.47
	Seville[c]	449	4.88

a. Based on replies to the *Catastro* of 1750-52 from 388 towns. AGS, *Catastro*, libs. 1-670.

b. No examples found.

c. Includes six towns from the *Comprobaciones* of the *Catastro*, made in 1765.

d. Provincial totals include only those muleteers making clear statements regarding the numbers of animals they owned.

carriers encountered in the sources. Allowing for the important gap for Murcia, there were probably no more than forty such *cabañiles*, with perhaps four thousand mules. As will be demonstrated later, this amounts to 2 or 3 per cent of the pack mules in the country. Legally and functionally, the *cabañiles* were grouped with the professional carters, benefiting from the same privileges.

Table 8. *Large-scale transporters:* Cabañiles (*1752*)

Province	Number of individuals	Number of animals
Córdoba[a]	1	100
Cuenca[b]	5	550
Granada[c]	19	1,570
La Mancha[d]	5	523
Murcia[e]	—	—
Salamanca[f]	1	200
Totals	31	2,943

a. Córdoba: AGS, *Catastro*, lib. 125—Baena (1).

b. Cuenca: *ibid.*, libs. 76—Almodóvar del Pinar (2); 80—Campillo de Altobuey (3).

c. Granada: *ibid.*, lib. 290—Granada (19).

d. La Mancha: *ibid.*, libs. 471—Peñas de San Pedro (4); 473—Villanueva de los Infantes (1).

e. Various data suggest that a number of *cabañiles* were active in Murcia, but the *Catastro* replies gave no details, and no estimate as to how many such transporters existed can be made.

f. Salamanca: *ibid.*, lib. 499—Salamanca (1).

The second group of relatively large scale, specialized pack-transporters was the *arrieros maragatos* of the western part of the province of León.[3] Among the *maragatos* were several fair-sized family operations which owned ten to twenty-five mules and hired one to five drivers to help with the mule train. As early as the middle of the sixteenth century these muleteers were transporting fish and other goods from the north coast to the annual fairs at Medina del Campo, La Bañeza, Villalón, and Medina del Rio Seco. By the end of the eighteenth century, members of this community could be

3. The details which follow concerning the *maragatos* come from Martín Galindo, *Arrieros maragatos*, pp. 9-10, 11, 15, 21-23; AGS, *Catastro*, lib. 1—Ávila.

seen in such distant places as La Coruña, Barcelona, Valencia, and Madrid.

Even these operations, however, were never completely divorced from the soil. The muleteers continued to be legally classified as farmers (*labradores*), and their families continued to work farms which also served as centers for transport activity. The whole family enterprise was centered on a large *patio* with living accommodations along two sides. The courtyard had two entries, an elaborate one facing the street and a more ordinary one opening on the fields. In one corner was a large two-story kitchen. Nearby was a platform for loading and unloading merchandise, and sometimes a small interior yard with a warehouse and hoist. Along one side of the main *patio* were the sheds and stables of the farming operations. The homesteads were often quite substantial, and their ruins remain even today the largest buildings in the former muleteer towns of León.

The *maragatos* were unique among the muleteers in that they were relatively specialized as transporters, and their enterprises were, in effect, small family firms. The businesses continued to exist after the death of the head of the family, and they were sometimes held in trust for minors, operated by women, or run by priests or monasteries. The uniqueness of the *maragatos* went beyond this, since they also formed a distinct ethnic pocket in the country around the town of Astorga. They are described by George Borrow as "a singular and distinct caste, with their own customs, never intermarrying outside the group, and wearing moorish-like dress."[4] They were fiercely proud of their integrity as transporters, and their reputation allowed them to charge premium prices for their services. Most of their operations were quite small, and there were no more than 150 to 200 active transporters in the community, with 400 to 500 mules. They thus formed a very small part of the total pool of transport services.

Although a much higher proportion of the carters were relatively specialized, the bulk of carting also was done by very small operators. The carters were most thoroughly professionalized in the area between Burgos and Soria, but even there the number of carts per owner was not great. A survey of 9 towns in the area shows

4. George Borrow, *The Bible in Spain* (New York: G. P. Putnam's Sons, 1899), pp. 321-23. Borrow's comments actually date from 1835-1837.

9 individuals with over 25 carts, compared with 37 who owned from 11 to 25 carts and 372 persons with 1 to 10.[5] This same ownership pattern existed among the carters of the Navarredonda district in the mountains south of Ávila. The 5 towns involved counted only a handful of residents with more than 10 carts.[6] The small scale of ownership closely parallels that of the migratory sheep-raisers of the Mesta. As much as two-thirds of a typical flock (*rebaña*) of 1,000 sheep belonged to owners with less than 120 animals.[7]

The partial surveys above are verified by the data from the *Catastro* which are presented in Table 9. The over-all average is about three carts per owner, but the variation between provincial averages is much greater than among the muleteers. This reflects the relative specialization achieved by the carters of certain regions in the provinces of Burgos, Soria, Salamanca, Cuenca, Toledo, Córdoba, and Seville. In the provinces with relatively low averages, carting was generally of the same casual and seasonal nature as most muleteer transport.

There are frequent references to relatively large carting concerns in the late eighteenth century, and the number of large firms may have been increasing. The random examples of large enterprises encountered in the sources are presented in Table 10. There is no proof of an increase in the number of large operations, but there are some indications of increased specialization and a concentration of services at Madrid. A number of provincial carters established themselves or relatives in Madrid, probably to be nearer the source of government contracts.[8] The largest enterprise encountered was owned by a resident of Madrid, and at least two other such companies were definitely domiciled in Madrid. In addition, the Duke of Medinaceli maintained at least one train of thirty carts which regularly carried the produce of his estates to the capital.[9] Other

5. Tudela, pp. 383-84.

6. Adela Gil Crespo, "La Mesta de carreteros del reino," *Anales de la Asociación para el Progreso de las Ciencias*, XXII (1957), 227.

7. Julius Klein, *The Mesta, 1273-1836* (Cambridge, Mass.: Harvard University Press, 1920), p. 47.

8. Examples include three natives of Colmenar de Oreja, near Toledo, residing in Madrid in 1798, one from Villaverde and another from Aldea del Pinar. The last two towns are in the province of Soria. See AHN, *Con.*, legs. 2288-22; 51197-12, 30.

9. *Ibid.*, legs. 1608-1; 1111-11, pt. 3; AA Murcia, leg. 2795; A Medinaceli, *Estado de Medinaceli*, leg. 60-82, 83.

evidence for a concentration of carters in Madrid comes from records of the city administration. In 1784, when the hours for entry and departure of carts were changed, fifteen residents were routinely notified.[10] Such urban-based carriers were completely specialized and free of all seasonal limitations except the winter migration.

10. AHN, *Con.*, *Libros de Gobierno*, 1784, fols. 742-44.

Table 9. *Average cart holdings, by province*[a]

Region	Province	Number of individuals[b]	Average number of carts
Old Castile	Ávila	2	3
	Burgos	531	4.96
	León	—[c]	
	Palencia	—[c]	
	Salamanca	328	2.34
	Segovia	98	1.71
	Soria	295	7.33
	Toro	—[c]	
	Valladolid	28	2.14
	Zamora	—[c]	
New Castile	Cuenca[d]	10	35.5
	Extremadura[e]	1	1
	Guadalajara	111	1.50
	La Mancha	116	1.43
	Madrid	—[c]	
	Toledo	151	3.12
	Murcia	—[c]	
Andalucía	Córdoba	20	4.10
	Granada	113	1.49
	Jaén	3	1
	Seville	438	2.13

a. AGS, *Catastro*, libs. 1-670. See Appendix A.

b. These are not complete provincial totals, but simply the numbers of individuals for whom detailed information was available.

c. No examples found.

d. Cuenca: This figure is dominated by the town of Almodóvar del Pinar, which had 7 owners with a total of about 350 carts.

e. The *Catastro* replies for the province of Extremadura are exceptionally unclear about carters.

The large carting operations were clearly family businesses similar to those of the Leonese muleteers. Such firms could be owned jointly by relatives, held in trust for a minor, and were often permanently owned and controlled by women. As a prime example, the largest enterprise encountered, the Madrid firm with four *cuadrillas* of carts, was owned jointly by two sisters for several years. Similarly, women owned and operated fair-sized carting firms for long periods in the provinces of Soria and Cuenca.[11] The transition from small-

11. AHN, *Con.*, leg. 51197-9, 61.

Table 10. *Large carting enterprises*

Number of carts owned	Year
35	1530[a]
30	1738[b]
50	1752[c]
40	"after 1750"[d]
31	1754[e]
20	1755[f]
26	
42	1762[g]
72	
23	"about 1765"[h]
30	
36	1770[i]
21	1783[j]
120	1788-93[k]

a. ARCG, 3-1496-8.

b. A Medinaceli, *Estado de Medinaceli*, leg. 60-83.

c. AGS, *Catastro*, lib. 76—Cuenca: Almodóvar del Pinar. The source lists 7 owners for the town, with 1,000 draft animals between them. At 3 oxen per cart, these 7 holdings represent about 350 carts, or 50 carts per owner.

d. Gil Crespo, "Mesta de carreteros," p. 227.

e. AHN, *Con.*, leg. 211-3.

f. AA Murcia, leg. 2795.

g. AGS, *Catastro, Comprobaciones*, leg. 1615.

h. AHN, *Con.*, leg. 1111-11, pt. 3.

i. Ibid., leg. 1733-24.

j. Ibid., leg. 2657-27. The source lists 3 owners with a total of 63 carts, or 21 carts per owner.

k. Ibid., leg. 1608-1. The source gives "four *carreterías*." A *carretería* was a unit of about 30 carts, so the total number of carts was probably about 120.

scale carter to carting firm was fairly easy, since the actual operation of the carts was in either case in the hands of professional train captains and crews and participation by the owner was optional. It was through the professional manager and a form of short-term partnership that the small holdings of individual carters were consolidated to obtain the economies which came from operation with larger units.

B. *Collective enterprise among the carters*

Although most owners had less than 5 carts, the carts traveled in caravans of 20 to 30 or more vehicles. This was a widely recognized unit and was called a *cuadrilla* or *carretería*. Such cart trains were occasionally the property of a single individual, but more often they represented partnerships involving several owners. The partnership often included one or two fairly larger owners, each with 10 to 30 carts, and one to four or more smaller operators.[12] The largest train recorded in the sources had 60 carts, but most fell between 20 and 30.[13]

In addition to the 30 carts, a typical train included about 90 oxen, 6 or 7 men, 1 or 2 watchdogs, 1 or 2 horses or mules, a number of burros, and occasionally a pair of milk cows. The best description of an actual train is provided by accounts in the Medinaceli archives. The Duke's cart train used 7 men, a horse, a dog, and varied from 26 to 30 carts and from 66 to 77 oxen.[14]

The cart train was run by a professional captain or manager called the *mayoral* or *capataz*, who supervised the operations of the train.[15] He traveled with the train, going ahead on horseback to contract for cargoes, to make arrangements for loading, unloading, and pasture, and to purchase provisions. He also kept the accounts of the partnership. Sometimes the train captain owned the train he

12. *Ibid.*, legs. 1733-24; 211-3; 2868-25.
13. The actual number of carts in a train varied considerably, with examples in the documents as small as 3 carts and as large as 60. Of 27 examples of cart trains noted in 12 sources, 3 had less than 15 carts, 14 had between 16 and 25 carts, 6 had between 26 and 35, while 4 cart trains had more than 35 carts. AHN, *Con.*, leg. 2868-25 lists 10 examples.
14. Tudela, p. 355; AGS, *Catastro*, lib. 14—Burgos: Ontoria del Pinar; A Medinaceli, *Estado de Medinaceli*, leg. 60-83.
15. AHN, *Con.*, leg. 2657-27.

managed, but more often he owned only a few of the carts, and most often he owned none and was working only as a professional manager.[16]

The crew of the train counted five or six men besides the manager. This included an *aperador* who combined the jobs of foreman and cartwright and was responsible for the condition of the carts. Frequently he had an assistant, or *aperador ayudante*. These two saw to the maintenance of the carts and harnesses, obtained wood for new parts, made repairs, etc. As foreman, the *aperador* supervised the yoking of the oxen as the train set out and the making of camp at the end of the day. The livestock was in the charge of a herder called the *pastorero, monadero,* or *boyero*. When the carts were moving he herded along the spare oxen and other animals. At night and during the mid-day rest he watched the grazing oxen, cleaned the watering place, and helped catch and yoke the oxen. Most trains were also accompanied by two to four laborers or *gañanes,* and often by an errand boy or *ayudante gañan*. These men helped with the maintenance of the carts, herding and yoking the oxen, loading and unloading the cargo, and acted as drivers on the road.[17] The crew members were often all from the same town, but it was just as common for them to be from towns scattered all over the carting district. They often owned one or two carts which accompanied the train. Those who owned no carts supplemented their incomes by buying and selling trade goods which they brought in the carts as baggage.[18]

The cooperative nature of these carting partnerships is illustrated by an account dated 1807 and submitted by the train manager to one of the partners (*aparceros*).[19] Such accounts were made at the end of each carting season. The revenues of the year's operation were first totaled. From this were subtracted the general expenses of road tolls, pasturage, food for the crew, and wages. The remaining revenues were divided by the number of carts in the train and

16. For a description, see Tudela, p. 355; for examples: AHN, *Con.,* legs. 1111-11, pt. 1; 2659-27; 51197-50, 61.

17. Described by Tudela, pp. 356-58; supported by AHN, *Con.,* legs. 1111-11, pt. 1; 51197-51; AGS, *Catastro,* lib. 137—Extremadura: Cáceres.

18. Tudela, p. 359; AHN, *Con.,* leg. 1111-11, pts. 2 and 3; AGS, *Catastro,* lib. 14—Burgos: Ontoria del Pinar.

19. Tudela, pp. 385-87. Supporting details, dated 1752, are in AGS, *Catastro, ibid.*

assigned to the partners on the basis of the number of carts contributed. From this subtotal the manager subtracted such costs as the replacing of oxen and harnesses for the individual owner. In the example being described the manager also acted as the partner's agent and delivered part of the owner's profits to a relative in Madrid.

The costs of the crew and the profit (or risk of a loss) on the cargo were thus shared by all of the partners, while each paid individually for the maintenance of his own equipment. These partnerships lasted only for a given transport season, after which the carts and animals were turned back to the owner. The documents suggest, however, that custom and acquaintance provided a greater degree of continuity than can be inferred from the accounting procedures.

Through the professionally managed cart train, the cart owner was able to continue farming and/or wood-cutting at home while receiving income from carts and oxen which he sent out every year. The carts and oxen were freed from the seasonal demands of agriculture and crews kept to a minimum, reducing operating costs and the drain of manpower from local agriculture.

C. *Contracts and types of service*

Details about the arrangements between transporters and their customers proved scarce, except in the case of transport hired by the government. Few private transport contracts were found; investigations in notorial archives failed to uncover any, and the documents of the trade consulates (*consulados*) of Burgos and Bilbao say nothing about transport by land.[20] Henri Lapeyre's book on the Ruíz family describes the problems of land transport in sixteenth-century Castile, but does not supply any detail as to how it was arranged.[21] Direct examination of the Ruíz accounts in Valladolid and the books of merchants of sixteenth-century Burgos

20. Abbott Payson Usher, *The Early History of Deposit Banking in Mediterranean Europe* (Cambridge, Mass.: Harvard University Press, 1943), p. 55; Robert Sidney Smith, *The Spanish Guild Merchant: History of the Consulado, 1200-1700* (Durham, N. C.: Duke University Press, 1940), pp. 41-43, 67.

21. Henri Lapeyre, *Une Famille de marchands, les Ruíz: Contribution à l'étude du commerce entre la France et l'Espagne au temps de Philippe II* (Paris, 1955), pp. 176-77.

yielded entries for payment for transport, but again no details.[22]

The only really detailed contract encountered was found among the Medinaceli papers, and is probably not very typical because of its elaborate detail. Dated 1737, the contract was made by the manager of one of the Duke's estates, who was arranging the transfer of barley from one estate to another. The contract specified the number of animals which would be provided, the price per *fanega* per league, placed all risks upon the carriers while in possession of the goods, and allowed for 1 per cent damage and shrinkage en route. The contract provided for fodder in the amount of one *fanega* of barley per twelve animals as a supplement to the fee.[23]

More typical of transport agreements, in all probability, was one which was signed in 1759, in which the carrier, a muleteer, simply agreed to deliver wine from La Mancha to Madrid at a specified total price per unit. The carrier presumably based this figure on the price of wine in La Mancha plus a margin to pay for the transport. If such agreements were common, it would explain why the cost of transport appears only rarely in account books. The wine in this case would surely have been entered in the customers' accounts without any reference to transport.[24] A rather ambiguous description of such arrangements from La Mancha suggests that the local carriers obtained cargoes from the landowners and were forced to post bond in the form of their real property to guarantee that the cargo would reach its destination.[25]

No examples of transport contracts between the professional carters and private customers came to light. It seems likely, however, that written contracts were used, in view of the relatively large amounts of goods and money involved. Moreover, there is evidence that such contracts were used between the carters and the wool merchants as early as the fifteenth century.[26] The use of such contracts in the eighteenth century was almost a necessity in view of the number of agents which might be involved. The managers of the cart trains often acted for the owners in making such agree-

22. AHP Valladolid, *Sección Ruíz*; *Archivo de la Deputación Provincial de Burgos, Cuentas del siglo XVI*.
23. A Medinaceli, *Estado de Medinaceli*, leg. 71-12, dated Nov. 1, 1737.
24. AHP Madrid, lib. 19408, Oct., 1759.
25. AGS, *Catastro*, lib. 473—La Mancha: Viso del Marques.
26. AGS, *Sello*, 1491, doc. 189.

ments, but in some cases the owner did so himself. In the district of Navarredonda, the town council appointed special commissioners to seek out customers.[27] By 1804 the carters of the Soria-Burgos area were also arranging transport contracts by means of such commissioners.[28]

Contracts with the government, including the salt supply, grain supply, Madrid charcoal supply, navy, army, treasury, the mercury monopoly, and royal construction projects, were made on a printed form which the transporter carried and which served as a form of transport license (*guía*). This form was the same if issued by a government agency or by a supply contractor.[29] The form had blank spaces for the transporter's name, the commodity and quantity, destination, time limit, and price per unit, with a standard clause outlining penalties for late delivery and granting exemptions from road tolls and grazing fees while on government business. The blanks were filled in appropriately when the goods were picked up. The *guía* was then presented on delivery, the cargo was measured, and payment made after suitable deductions if the quantity delivered did not match the quantity on the form. The carrier was required to present this form when so requested by any government official while on route.[30] Such contracts could be transferred from one carrier to another by means of a simple oral statement in front of a government official.[31]

Under normal circumstances the price of transport in these government contracts was set by negotiation and probably corresponded with the market price at the time. Frequently the contracts were negotiated while the carters were still in the winter pastures.[32] The carters felt free to haggle over price while negotiating with the salt-tax administration and charcoal suppliers, but showed no signs of being as independent as they had been in the seventeenth century when some of them refused army contracts in the midst of the Portuguese revolution of 1641.[33] In extreme situations, as in the

27. AA Navarredonda, *Libro de Acuerdos*, 1747, 1757.
28. AHN, *Con.*, leg. 2607.
29. *Ibid.*, legs. 923-31; 1184-20; 1733-24.
30. Examples and descriptions available in *ibid.*, legs. 1184-20; 2229-31; 11452; 51197-42; AGS, *Guerra*, leg. 416.
31. AHN, *Con.*, leg. 1733-24.
32. *Ibid.*, leg. 49240; AA Navarredonda, *Libro de Acuerdos*, 1747.
33. AA Navarredonda, *Libro de Actas*, 1641; *Libro de Acuerdos*, 1749, 1757.

grain shortages of 1753 and 1804, the government attempted to dictate the price of transport, but in the latter case the crown ended by raising the price offered in an attempt to attract additional carriers.[34]

It appears that in general the carters worked with written contracts modeled after those of the government, but that most muleteers used oral agreements. The simple form of the few contracts found and the stable patterns of demand for transport, plus frequent illiteracy, made such written instruments superfluous. The charcoal, salt, grain, wood, and wool came from the same areas year after year and were generally available for carrying at the same time every year. Thus, although even the professional carters insisted that they did not have fixed routes, transportation had a basic regularity which minimized the need for complex business arrangements.[35] It is likely that most casual pack-transport agreements were oral and simple.

Although the business arrangements of most transporters cannot be documented clearly, it is possible to identify distinct types of activity among the pack-animal transporters and the seasonal carters. The two most important of these were the transporter-trader and the transporter-for-hire. The distinction between them is not defined in the sources but was frequently employed in the *Catastro*, and, once spelled out, it seems painfully obvious.[36] The transporter-trader was known as a *tratante* or *traficante*, while the transporter-for-hire was variously called *trajinero, trajinante, cosario,* or *conductor*.

When the activities of a *trajinero* or *trajinante* are described, he is always depicted as carrying goods in which he has no equity. The descriptions are clearest for the province of La Mancha, and the sense of the terms as used there applies to other areas.[37] Most of the seasonal or casual peasant-carters also fall into this category, although they were given many descriptive names. These carters often carried heavy or bulky goods in or near their home towns.

34. AA Murcia, leg. 2795; AHN, *Con.*, legs. 48328; 2607-2.
35. AHN, *Hac.*, lib. 2038, fol. 350.
36. AGS, *Catastro*, libs. 4—Avila: Gordo; 56—Burgos: Torres, Moneo; 116—Cuenca: Roda; 467—La Mancha: Bonillo; 563—Sevilla: Teba; 560—Sevilla: Alcalá de Guadaira.
37. *Ibid.*, lib. 473—La Mancha: Villanueva de los Infantes, Fuente el Fresno; AHN, *Con.*, leg. 1004-23.

Some seasonal carters from Old Castile went farther afield to bring home grain and wine which their local governments had purchased.[38] The terms *cosario* and *conductor* were regional variations in terminology typical of Andalucía. The activities of such individuals matches those of *trajineros*.[39]

A number of relatively specialized carters-for-hire are listed in the *Catastro* for the provinces of Andalucía. Called *carreteros cosarios*, these carters were more thoroughly involved in transport than most seasonal carriers, but were not counted among the carters entitled to the privileges and protection of the royal government.[40] They engaged in general hauling between the numerous large towns of the South, often traveling considerable distances within the region. Except for the really large cities such as Córdoba and Seville, however, there were never more than one or two *cosarios* in a given town.[41]

In contrast to the transporter-for-hire, the transporter-trader usually bought the cargo he carried, or at least part of it, for resale. Three different types of transporter-trader existed, each providing a slightly different kind of service. One of these was the *traficante*, a carrier who bought, transported, and sold some basic commodity such as wine, grain, charcoal, or building tiles. Such persons rarely carried mixed cargoes.[42] The transporter-trader who was called a *tratante*, however, dealt in a wider range of more expensive goods, including olive oil, pots and pans, rice, fish, clothes, soap, and fruit. Often he carried mixed cargoes including small quantities of several such items.[43] The term *tratante* was also applied to a third type of transporter-trader who specialized in buying and marketing certain commodities produced in very small quantities, often as by-products of farming. These carriers handled such goods as special

38. AGS, *Catastro*, libs. 13—Burgos: Mamolar; 275—Granada: Almería; 336—León: Cerecedo; 466—La Mancha: Almadén; 491—Palencia: Lares, Resoba; 526—Toro: Toro.
39. *Ibid.*, lib. 19—Poza; AHN, *Con.*, leg. 1242-19; AHN, *Con.*, *Libros de Gobierno*, 1634, fol. 269.
40. *Ibid.*, libs. 560—Sevilla: Pedrera; 276—Granada: Alamín de la Torre; AA Jeréz de la Frontera, *Libro del Catastro*.
41. *Ibid.*, *Comprobaciones*, leg. 1643-1: Carmona.
42. *Ibid.*, libs. 136—Extremadura: Barcarrota; 358—León: Encinedo, Pedredo, Prado Rey; AA Jeréz de la Frontera, *Libro del Catastro*.
43. *Ibid.*, libs. 39—Burgos: San Pelayo de Arezo; 64—Burgos: Bezares; 76—Cuenca: Alcalá del Rio Jucar; 134—Extremadura: Zarza la Mayor; 138—Extremadura: Cilleros; 336—León: Boñar; 361—León: Santa María del Páramo.

grades of wool, sausage, bacon, saffron, hardware, wax, and hides. In many cases the carrier himself made the commodity involved.[44]

Another kind of specialized service was provided by the *arriero ordinario*. These were muleteers who lived in local or provincial centers and made regular trips to certain cities to purchase goods specially ordered by members of the home community. Such a carrier, often transporting parcels and letters for set fees, dealt in no specific commodities, but provided a professional service. Many smaller towns had one such *ordinario* who regularly visited a nearby provincial capital for spices, hardware, delicacies, etc., while many provincial capitals in the South and West had *ordinarios* who went to Madrid or one of the seaports. The volume of this trade was very slight but the system provided a widespread mechanism for distributing small quantities of many goods. The *ordinario* system was most elaborate in Andalucía, and was also fairly well developed in western Spain. It appeared infrequently in the central areas around Ávila, Segovia, and La Mancha, and was not used in the East and North.[45]

Whether professional or casual, carriers not only specialized in certain types of services, but also in their range of activity. Some confined themselves to purely local activities, rarely sleeping away from home; others operated between adjacent economic regions, while a few transported across the entire country. In the first category, most local carriers appear to have been simple transporters for hire, bringing in the wine, grain, charcoal, and pottery produced in the district. Some, however, acted as transporter-traders dealing in cloth, eggs, game, etc. On the whole, this was a highly diffused type of economic activity which defies careful description. It was this grass-roots carrying capacity which the crown sought to mobilize on occasion through the military baggage service.

Falling between the local carriers and the more specialized transporters who traveled cross-country was a broad class of peasant-

44. *Ibid.*, libs. 71—Burgos: Cuenca del Campo, Villanueva del Campo; 85—Cuenca: El Almarcha; 145—Extremadura: Seradilla; 525—Salamanca: Candelario.

45. *Ibid.*, libs. 1—Ávila: Arevalo; 135—Extremadura: Alberca; 141—Extremadura: Gata; 147—Extremadura: Plasencia; 466—La Mancha: Almagro, 499—Salamanca; 537—Segovia; 560—Sevilla: Antequera, Archidona, Bornos, Ardales; 561—Sevilla; Castaño, Campillo, Cabezas de San Juan; 563—Sevilla: Rota, Salteras, San Lucar la Mayor; AA Jeréz de la Frontera, *Libro del Catastro*. For Castile in general see AHN, *Con.*, leg. 1813-2.

transporters who engaged in regional and interregional trade. These were the numerous part-time muleteers who year after year carried the products of one region to the next. They are the transporters who made possible, for example, the elaborate pattern of exchanges between the plain of Old Castile and the surrounding mountain and coastal areas. Working in transport from two weeks to six months a year, most in this category operated within a radius of fifty to seventy-five miles, although some combined this with an annual round trip to Madrid or a major seaport. Whether working for hire or as traders, these muleteers dealt in a limited range of basic commodities and played an important role in integrating the subsistence economies of the various regions of the peninsula. Their activities made possible the remarkable parallels in regional price movements noted by Earl Hamilton. By far the largest part of the transportation described in the *Catastro* fits into this category.

Finally, there was the fairly small body of transporters which operated over really long distances, crossing several provinces and economic regions in their activities. This included the long-haul carters, the *cabañiles*, and some of the transporter-traders, including the *maragatos* of León and a number of similar carriers scattered throughout the country.

The professional carters, working mostly for the government, generally made from three to six long trips each year, often traveling a thousand miles during a carting season. Although they did not keep to fixed schedules, these carriers followed fairly regular patterns. Those of the Soria-Burgos area ranged from Soria to Santander to Salamanca to Madrid; the carters of Cuenca and Murcia traveled between Valencia, Cartagena, Seville, Toledo, and Madrid, while those from the province of Ávila ranged between Avila, Salamanca, Extremadura, Seville, and Madrid. The *cabañiles*, with their trains of one hundred and more mules, worked in similar fashion, ranging from Cartagena to Granada to Seville, and to Madrid.[46]

For the most part, the private demand for long-distance transport was met by the transporter-traders sometimes referred to as

46. AGS, *Catastro*, libs. 499—Salamanca; 275—Granada; 473—La Mancha: Villanueva de los Infantes; 76—Cuenca: Almodóvar del Pinar.

arrieros de recua because of their strings of mules largely devoted to transport. Many of these muleteers engaged in transport up to eight months a year, but almost all had some ties with agriculture. Probably the larger part of this long-distance trade was carried on by muleteers who considered agriculture as their main activity. The activities of the Leonese *maragatos*, who ranged over much of Spain, have already been mentioned, but it is possible to cite other examples, many of them less preoccupied with transportation.

The peasant-transporters of La Mancha were especially active in this long distance trade, those of some towns concentrating on bringing fruit, olive oil, and fish from the coasts to the interior, alternating with trips to Granada for linens, sugar, and hides.[47] Others from the same province visited the seaports and dealt in blankets, mattresses, thread, cacao, sugar, cinnamon, cloves, and wool, or else carried tobacco into Old Castile.[48] One muleteer, with thirty-four animals, traded regularly between Málaga and Seville, visiting Antequera, Osuna, and probably Jerez, combining his own activities with a government contract to carry tobacco.[49] In the province of Cuenca, peasant-carriers provided the link between Valencia, Cuenca, and Andalucía, exchanging rice and fruit for wheat and olive oil.[50] In the North, muleteers from the province of Segovia distributed tobacco from Madrid to Valladolid, Palencia, Zamora and Salamanca.[51] Others from the northern part of the province of Burgos regularly traveled between Bilbao and Madrid to supply the capital with fish and imported goods and thus paralleled the activities of the *maragatos* to the west.[52] Another group of muleteers from the area north of the city of Salamanca dealt in wheat, fish, and imports, ranging between Ciudad Rodrigo, Bilbao, and Madrid. By the end of the eighteenth century, members of this particular group were to be seen as far away as La Coruña, Barcelona, and Valencia.[53] The greatest annual mileage was registered by a group of transporters from the province of Extremadura. Some

47. *Ibid.*, lib. 473—La Mancha: Villanueva de los Infantes, Viso del Marques.
48. AHN, *Con.*, leg. 2123-3.   49. *Ibid.*, leg. 1243-19.
50. AGS, *Catastro*, lib. 116—Cuenca: Puebla de San Salvador.
51. AHN, *Con.*, leg. 1813-2.
52. AGS, *Catastro*, libs. 17—Burgos: Betretea; 19—Burgos: Ozabejas, Poza; 348—León: Matanza; Martín Galindo, *Arrieros maragatos*.
53. Cabo Alonso, pp. 121-22, 389.

of them covered the six hundred miles between Bilbao and Seville five and six times a year.[54]

A small part of these long-range muleteers, not more than a few hundred, were like those of León and were heavily committed to transport. Most, however, made only a limited number of trips and many, especially the peasants of La Mancha, might be classed as itinerant peddlers. Very few in any case worked with more than four or five animals.

*   *   *

The bulk of the transporters did not make much use of detailed, written agreements in their business. This was possible because most muleteers, although active only seasonally, worked within the subsistence economy, provided a particular type of service, and followed regular patterns of travel. This is only to be expected, since in a relatively poor and static society, the transport patterns were highly predictable. Those demands which were not strictly tied to subsistence were small and were serviced by the *arrieros ordinarios* or the *traficantes* who handled miscellaneous manufactures, luxuries, and imports. Some of the latter were relatively specialized, but many were little more than peddlers. Most of the more professional carriers were involved with the transport of these relatively expensive cargoes, but in general both transporter-traders and transporters-for-hire can be found in local, interregional, and long-distance carrying. The principal exception to all of these generalizations is the long-haul carters who did some private carrying, but spent most of their time working for the government. The scale of this government work was suggested in Chapter II. The terms under which the carters tried to meet this demand are very complicated and require a separate chapter.

D. *The daily routine*

The seasonal transport activity of most muleteers was so casual that no distinctive routine developed among them. In the few cases where a single muleteer owned more than a handful of animals,

54. AGS, *Catastro*, libs., 137—Extremadura: Costuera; 140—Extremadura: Don Benito.

they were handled with the help of hired men, the Leonese muleteers using one man to every five animals. The only details about travel customs among the muleteers comes from a dispute of 1799, which involves a complaint about the carriers of La Mancha, whose small pack animals were herded along the roads like flocks of sheep. The plaintiff asked that these muleteers be required to use the same highway techniques as the carriers in the North, where the animals were arranged in a line, each trained to follow the one to which it was tied.[55]

The cart trains of the professional carters had a more elaborate routine. The oxen not only had to rest all night, if possible in open pasture, but also needed about three hours of rest at midday in order to graze, rest, and digest their food. At noon, therefore, the carters stopped, turned the oxen loose for two or three hours, and prepared their noon meal. They then traveled until sunset, when the cart train stopped in an area selected by the train captain. The carts were parked in a circle, or *rodeandala*, for the night. The oxen were watered again and allowed to graze while the evening meal was eaten, the equipment repaired, and supplies obtained from the nearest town. Under pressure from local users of the common pastures where carting oxen grazed, the carters usually rounded up the animals and bedded them down inside the circle of carts, although they preferred to let the oxen graze all night. In a particularly good pasture, if the grazing had been poor for some time, an overnight stay could stretch to four or five days, much to the disgust of local residents who had to pasture their own cattle on the same ground. Although such stays were rationalized away by the carters, it is clear that they provided a way to maintain the oxen without renting summer pastures. This daily need for pasture was a primary concern of the carters, and in areas where it was scarce, they often stopped early or pushed on till late depending on what was available. If the noon stop was delayed, a mid-afternoon rest was likely to last through the night.[56]

The daily routine of two stages of travel broken by an afternoon

55. AHN, *Con.*, leg. 1813-2.
56. The best single source on the daily routine of the carters is AHN, *Hac.*, lib. 8038, fols. 340-80. Additional details came from AHN, *Con.*, legs. 2093-10; 2229-31; 51197-44; Tudela, p. 381.

rest was modified when a cart train approached Madrid. Entering the gates of the city, passing the toll bar, delivering goods in the narrow streets, unloading, and leaving forced the oxen to spend an unusually long time yoked and standing. It was therefore preferable to stop near Madrid at midday and pasture the oxen until early the next morning. The carters then entered early and tried to get the oxen out again in time to return to pasture for the next night. Carts carrying foodstuffs, charcoal, and wood generally entered as early as possible because delivery was tedious, while trains bring building supplies such as tiles, brick, stone, and cement waited until mid-morning to enter.[57]

On the open road the carts traveled in single file. Since there were not enough men to lead each team of oxen, the animals were trained to follow a lead cart. This kept the size of the crew small, but created problems when the carters had to enter a city. The oxen, irritable from lack of rest and grazing, tended to bolt from the line if something blocked their view of the lead cart. This happened when a carriage tried to cut through the train, or when men teased the oxen. In 1784, after several complaints of damage by oxen, the Sala de Alcaldes y Corte ordered that the system of lead carts be abandoned within the city. The new regulation required the carters to hire men at the city gates to lead each cart.[58]

While visiting smaller cities, a cart train often put up in a *casa de carretería*, or carters' inn, a large building with a courtyard and stables on the ground floor. The second floor contained the kitchen and dining facilities and a grain and general stores room, while the third floor consisted of many small sleeping rooms.[59] A similar establishment still exists in Granada, dating from Moorish times and once used for the charcoal supply. Another was seen still in use by farmers around Valladolid who came to that city to sell their produce.

Lest the reader form too exalted an idea of the sophistication of the carting business, it is worth while to repeat the reaction of an early nineteenth-century Englishman upon meeting a number of cart trains on the road. Traveling from Seville to Badajoz, Richard

57. AHN, *Con.*, leg. 923-31, fols. 49-51.
58. AHN, *Con.*, *Libros de Gobierno*, 1784, fols. 760-74.
59. Tudela, pp. 380-81.

Ford saw ". . . few travelers save the migratory caravans which bring corn down from Salamanca and take back salt from Cádiz. Nothing can be more savage or nomadic; the carts, oxen, men, and dogs are all on a par, but their nightly bivouacs by the sides of the roads, in the glen and underwood, are very picturesque."[60]

The most important thing to emphasize about the daily routine of the carters is the obvious dependence on roadside grazing. In the long run this created the same problems as the winter pastures for the carters and for the government which relied on their services. Carters traditionally pastured their oxen on the common pastures of whatever town they were near. This represented a severe drain on the resources of towns unfortunate enough to be located near well-traveled routes. This in turn reinforced the carters' acceptance of the existing primitive road system, for the simple reason that it provided numerous alternative routes across the country and increased the available pasture. A single well-paved highway would not have benefited such carriers, if only because the roadside grazing would have quickly been used up. As it was, the carters were most active in mid-summer and autumn when grass in Spain is scarcest, and thus the needs of their oxen ran into conflict with the requirements of the livestock of local residents. This conflict worsened toward the end of the century as the population in the countryside increased steadily. For a time the carters and the government were able to control this with an elaborate system of privileges and protection, but when the government lost its sense of direction, and perhaps before, the land hunger became too strong to be controlled by an eighteenth-century bureaucracy.

60. Ford, I, 479.

Maps

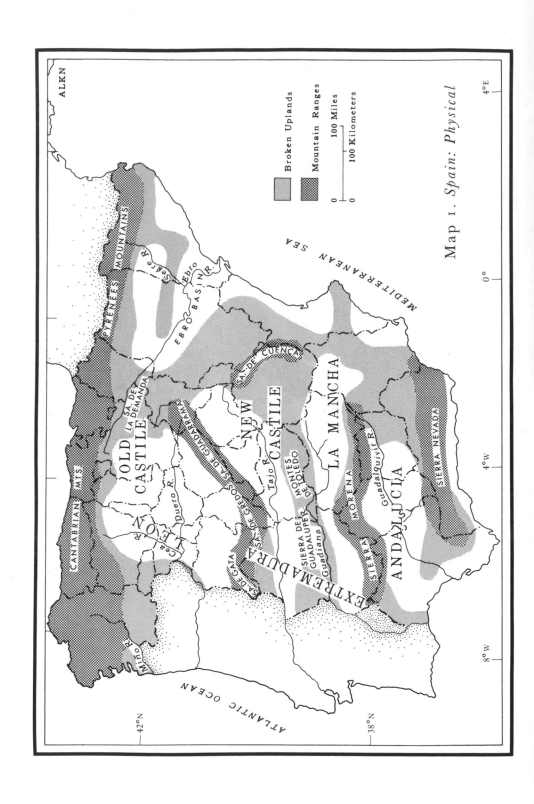

Map 1. *Spain: Physical*

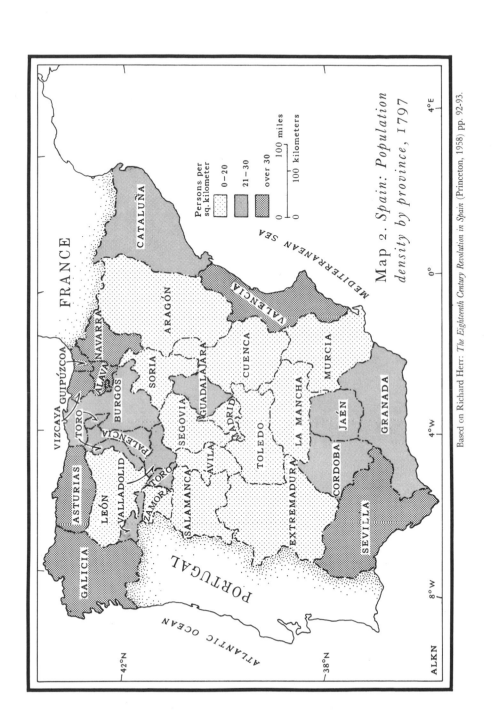

Map 2. Spain: Population density by province, 1797

Persons per sq. kilometer

0–20

21–30

over 30

100 miles

100 kilometers

FRANCE

CATALUÑA

VIZCAYA GUIPÚZCOA

NAVARRA

ALAVA

ARAGÓN

VALENCIA

ASTURIAS

TORO

BURGOS

SORIA

GUADALAJARA

CUENCA

MURCIA

GALICIA

LEÓN

PALENCIA

VALLADOLID

ZAMORA

TORO

SEGOVIA

AVILA

MADRID

TOLEDO

LA MANCHA

JAÉN

GRANADA

SALAMANCA

EXTREMADURA

CORDOBA

SEVILLA

PORTUGAL

ATLANTIC OCEAN

MEDITERRANEAN SEA

42°N

38°N

8°W

4°W

0°

4°E

ALKN

Based on Richard Herr: *The Eighteenth Century Revolution in Spain* (Princeton, 1958) pp. 92–93.

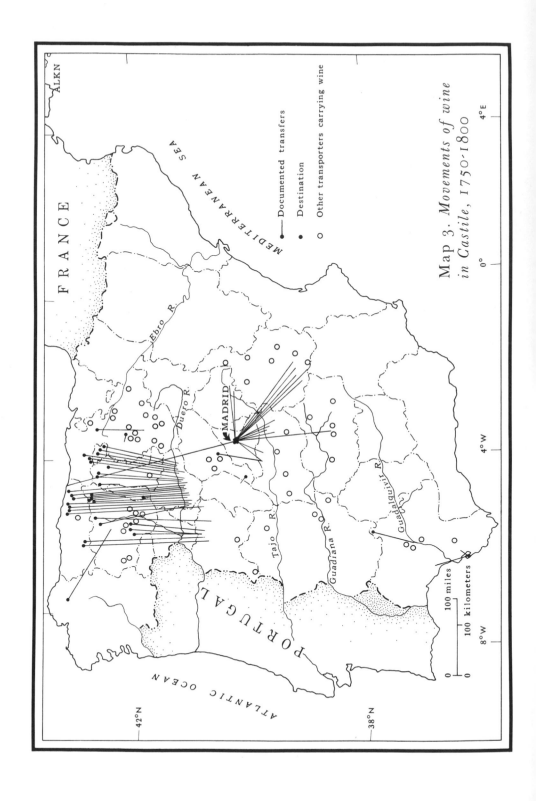

Map 3. *Movements of wine in Castile, 1750-1800*

Documented transfers
Destination
Other transporters carrying wine

FRANCE

PORTUGAL

MADRID

ALKN

MEDITERRANEAN SEA

ATLANTIC OCEAN

Ebro R.

Duero R.

Tajo R.

Guadiana R.

Guadalquivir R.

42°N

38°N

8°W

4°W

0°

4°E

100 miles
100 kilometers

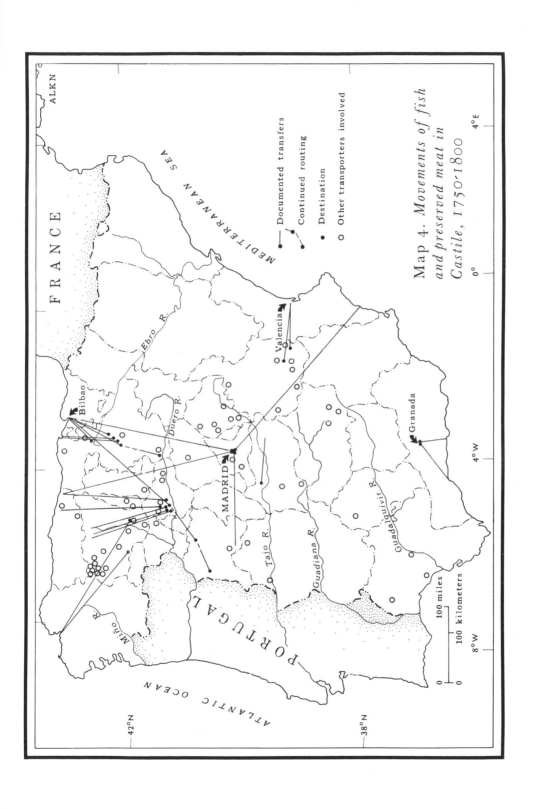

Map 4. *Movements of fish and preserved meat in Castile, 1750-1800*

Documented transfers
Continued routing
Destination
Other transporters involved

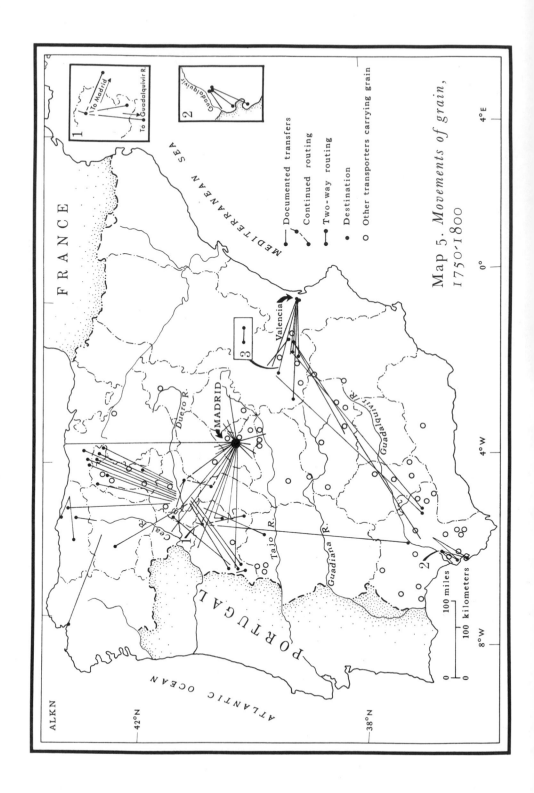

Map 5. *Movements of grain,*
1750-1800

Documented transfers
Continued routing
Two-way routing
Destination
Other transporters carrying grain

MEDITERRANEAN SEA

FRANCE

PORTUGAL

ATLANTIC OCEAN

MADRID

Valencia

Duero R.

Tajo R.

Guadiana R.

Guadalquivir R.

Cea R.

To Madrid
To Guadalquivir R.
Guadalquivir R.

1

2

3

ALKN

42°N

38°N

8°W

4°W

0°

4°E

100 miles
100 kilometers

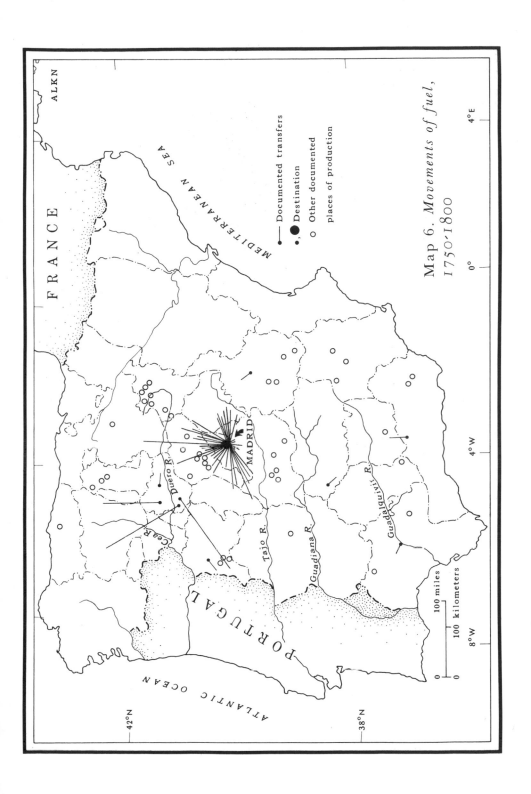

Map 6. *Movements of fuel,
1750-1800*

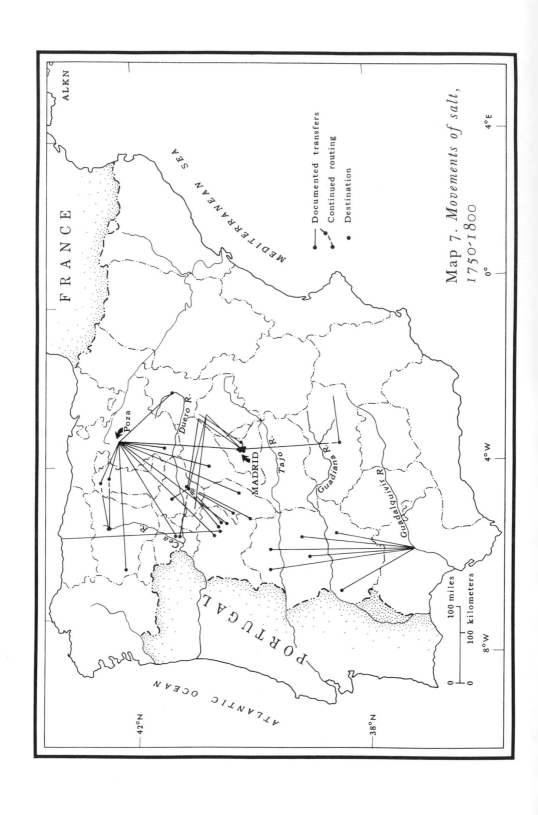

Map 7. *Movements of salt, 1750–1800*

Documented transfers
Continued routing
Destination

FRANCE

ALKN

MEDITERRANEAN SEA

Poza

Duero R.

MADRID

Tajo R.

Guadiana R.

Guadalquivir R.

Cea R.

PORTUGAL

ATLANTIC OCEAN

42° N

38° N

8° W

4° W

0°

4° E

100 miles
100 kilometers
0
0

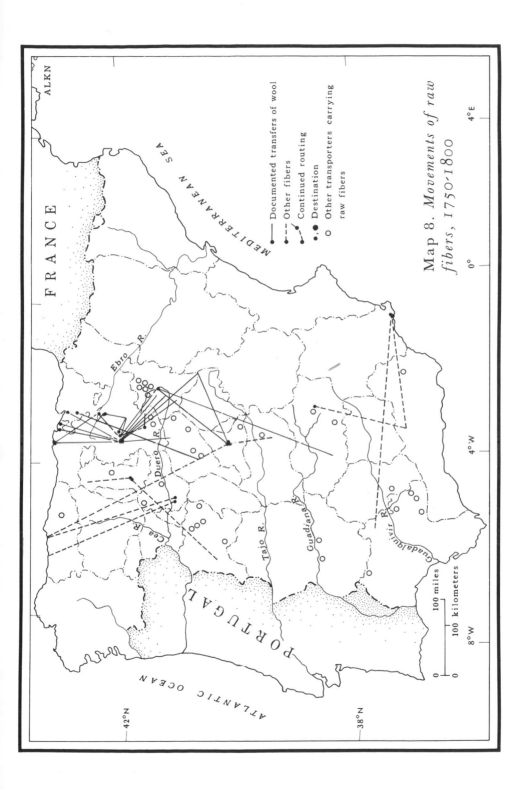

Map 8. *Movements of raw
fibers, 1750-1800*

Documented transfers of wool
Other fibers
Continued routing
Destination
Other transporters carrying
raw fibers

FRANCE

ALKN

MEDITERRANEAN SEA

Ebro R.

Duero R.

Cea R.

Tajo R.

Guadiana R.

Guadalquivir R.

PORTUGAL

ATLANTIC OCEAN

42°N

38°N

8°W

4°W

0°

4°E

100 miles
100 kilometers
0

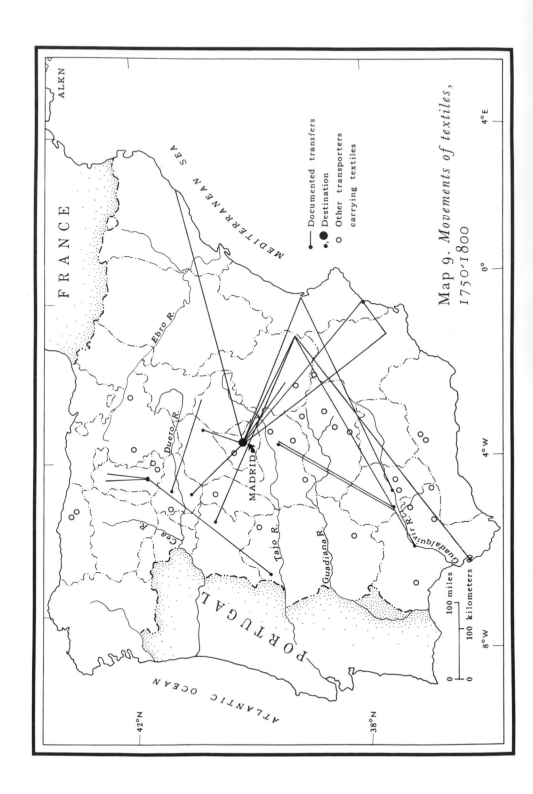

FRANCE

ALKN

MEDITERRANEAN SEAS

Ebro R.

Duero R.

MADRID

Cea R.

Tajo R.

Guadiana R.

Guadalquivir R.

PORTUGAL

ATLANTIC OCEAN

42°N

38°N

8°W

4°W

0°

4°E

— Documented transfers
● Destination
○ Other transporters
  carrying textiles

Map 9. *Movements of textiles,
1750–1800*

100 miles
100 kilometers
0

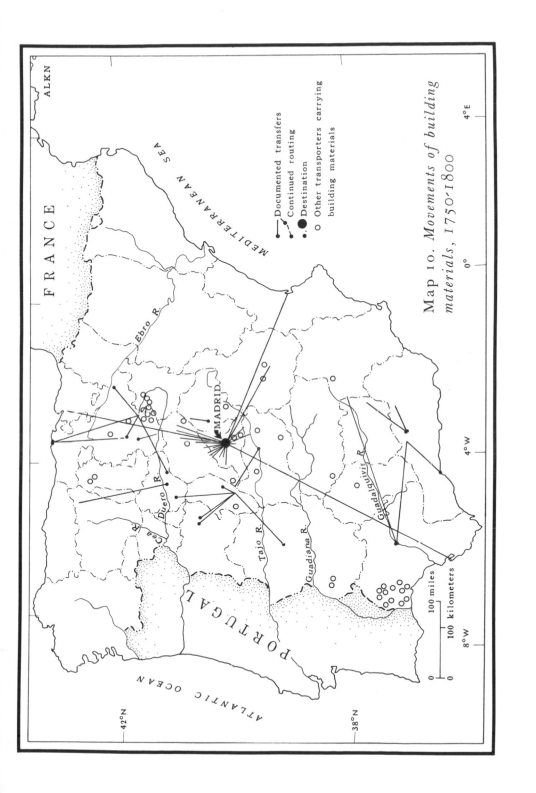

Map 10. *Movements of building materials, 1750–1800*

ALKN

FRANCE

MEDITERRANEAN SEA

ATLANTIC OCEAN

PORTUGAL

MADRID

Ebro R.

Duero R.

Tajo R.

Guadiana R.

Guadalquivir R.

42°N

38°N

8°W

4°W

0°

4°E

Documented transfers
Continued routing
Destination
Other transporters carrying
building materials

0   100 miles
0   100 kilometers

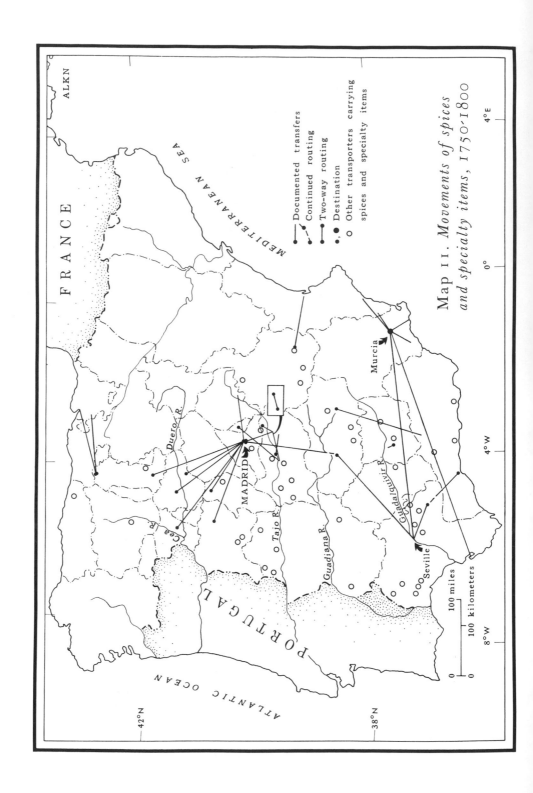

MAP 11. Movements of spices and specialty items, 1750-1800

Documented transfers
Continued routing
Two-way routing
Destination
Other transporters carrying
spices and specialty items

FRANCE

ALKN

MEDITERRANEAN SEAS

PORTUGAL

ATLANTIC OCEAN

Duero R.

Cea R.

MADRID

Tajo R.

Guadiana R.

Guadalquivir R.

Murcia

Seville

100 miles
100 kilometers

42°N

38°N

8°W

4°W

0°

4°E

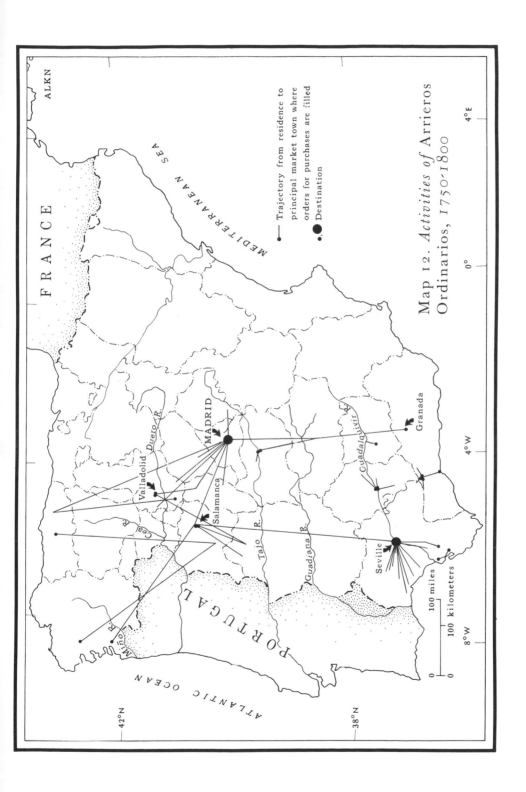

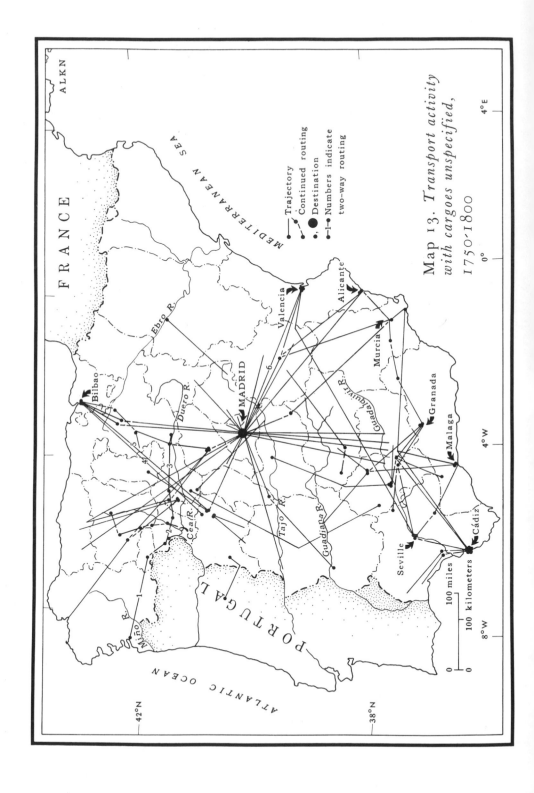

Map 13. *Transport activity with cargoes unspecified, 1750–1800*

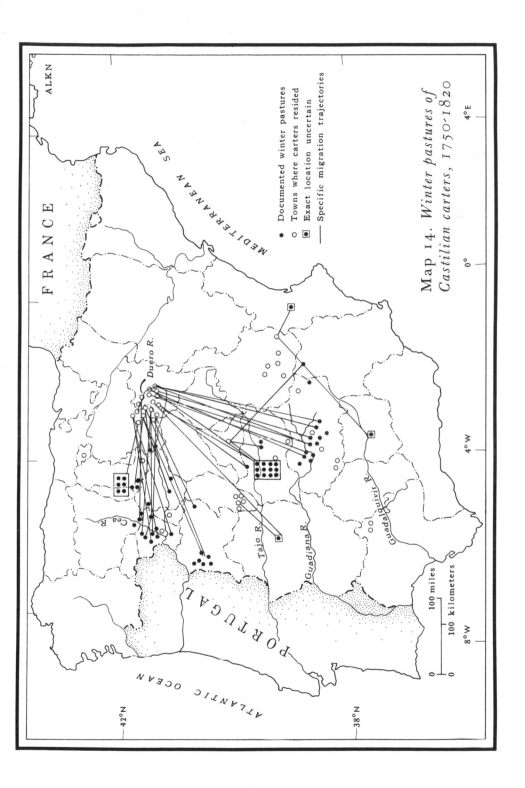

Map 14. *Winter pastures of Castilian carters, 1750-1820*

Documented winter pastures
Towns where carters resided
Exact location uncertain
Specific migration trajectories

FRANCE

ALKN

MEDITERRANEAN SEA

PORTUGAL

ATLANTIC OCEAN

Duero R.

Cea R.

Tajo R.

Guadiana R.

Guadalquivir R.

42°N

38°N

8°W

4°W

0°

4°E

100 miles
100 kilometers
0

Chapter five. *Supply, demand, and the price of transport*

A. *Transport prices*

In preceding sections three critical conclusions were reached regarding the supply of transportation, conclusions based on deductions supported by a variety of sources. It has been suggested (1) that within the subsistence economy of the countryside, transportation was relatively inexpensive because of the low opportunity costs of transporting which confronted seasonally idle peasant-farmers, (2) that this relatively large volume of transport services was not readily available for more specialized, non-subsistence activities, except at a relatively high price, and (3) that the carters who provided all but a fraction of such specialized services were increasingly unable to meet the demands being generated. To support the logic of these conclusions it would be desirable to offer data on the price of transportation which show that there was indeed a price differential between specialized and subsistence transportation; that the price of cart transportation rose rapidly, indicating a shortage of supply; and that the price of subsistence transportation did not rise at the same rate, indicating that there was a real imperfection in the market for transport services. It would also be desirable to show that the price of specialized transport had a great enough impact on the price of the goods transported to affect seriously the marketability of such goods if transport was not subsidized.

An effort was made to develop a body of data on the price of transport services, but the task proved easier to describe than to accomplish. Examination of account books from a number of monasteries bore out Earl J. Hamilton's assertion that in most cases the cost of transport was included in the final price of a delivered commodity.[1] Often, where details were provided, the entries for trans-

1. Earl J. Hamilton, *War and Prices in Spain, 1651-1800* (Cambridge, Mass.: Harvard University Press, 1947), pp. 109-110.

port costs were too irregular to be of any use. Also, for the purposes of this study, a reference to transport costs had to include the quantity of cargo, the total or per unit cost of transportation, and the point of origin of the shipment. Only rarely were all of these details recorded, the origin being the item most frequently omitted.

Table 11. *Cost of transporting grain to Ciudad Rodrigo, 1764-1785*

Year	Number of examples	Marevedis per fanega per league
1764	2	5.4— 6.8
1765	3	8.0—11.1
1766	2	4.6— 9.2
1767	None	—
1768	4	6.8—11.5
1769	2	9.1— 9.6
1770	None	—
1771	1	8.3
1772	1	9.2
1773	1	9.2
1774	2	7.9— 9.2
1775	None	—
1776	None	—
1777	2	6.9— 8.0
1778	1	9.2
1779	3	8.5—10.2
1780	1	8.9
1781	1	9.2
1782	2	8.4— 8.6
1783	1	8.0
1784	2	8.0— 8.8
1785	1	10.3

SOURCE: AHN, *Cleros*, lib. 10541. The examples involved the transport of grain from three towns near Ciudad Rodrigo to the monastery in the city: Bañovarez (*ca.* 50 km.), Olmedo (*ca.* 47 km.), and Lumbrales (*ca.* 49 km.). Costs are given in the accounts as lump sums for transporting a given quantity of grain from the town in question. They were divided by the number of *fanegas* in the shipment and then by the estimated number of leagues covered. There is room for error at this point since there is no way of knowing what conception of the distances involved the participants may have had. The most standard eighteenth-century league in Old Castile has been used.

Of the sources examined, only one monastery, that of the Trin-
itarios in Ciudad Rodrigo, provided all of the necessary details on
transport costs for any length of time during the eighteenth century.
This produced data for the years 1764-1787 which reflect the price
of transportation in the province of Salamanca and the fringes of
bordering Ávila and Extremadura. From this source two series, both
of which are little more than a few examples of prices, were constructed. One of these, presented as Table 11, includes thirty-two
examples of prices paid for the shipment of grain to Ciudad Rodrigo from the three nearby towns of Bañovarez, Olmedo, and Lumbrales. The cost of each shipment was divided by the number of

Table 12. *Cost of transport from Cadalso to Ciudad Rodrigo, 1765-
1788*

Sub-period	Number of examples	Average cost in marevedis *per* arroba
1765-1772	38	68
1773-mid-1786	52	76.5
mid-1786-1788	11	85

SOURCE: AHN, *Cleros*, lib. 10541.

units (*fanegas*) of grain listed, and this figure was divided by the
distance in leagues in order to obtain a figure comparable with
those in the governmental sources given below. The other series,
covering the years 1765-1788, includes 101 examples of wine and
olive oil traveling from the town of Cadalso to Ciudad Rodrigo.
Analysis of these figures showed three subperiods with clearly dis-
cernible average prices, which are shown in Table 12. From the
context of these Ciudad Rodrigo examples, it is clear that they
represent the kind of subsistence commodity transfers which have
been suggested as typical of most pack-animal transport.

If it was difficult to document the price of pack transport, it was
even harder to do so for the price of more specialized or professional transport. The only examples found came from governmental
sources connected with the supply of Madrid and are dated 1773

and 1787. In both years poor crops had raised the demand for transport to supply the city, so the prices may have been higher than usual. The figures are presented in Table 13.

Taken collectively but without other types of evidence, the data presented concerning prices hardly support much generalization. There are not enough quotations for each year, and they show only certain isolated situations. On the other hand, these data can be interpreted as illustrating or suggesting certain points, and the suggestions coincide very well with conclusions regarding the supply of transport based on other sources.

In comparing Table 11 on the cost of transporting grain to Ciudad Rodrigo with Table 13 on the cost of transporting grain to Madrid, it appears that the monastery never paid more than 11.5 *marevedis* per *fanega* per league (M/F/L), and that the price was usually around 9 or 10 M/F/L. The difference between this and the prices the government paid for pack-animal services it used in supplying Madrid (15-20.5 M/F/L in 1773, 18-21 M/F/L in 1787) is striking, and supports the contention that only a relatively high price could attract peasant-transporters for such specialized work. In the government examples, especially the leg of the trip from Navas de San Antonio to Madrid, the work was highly specialized and unattractive. It involved haulage of grain owned by the government over rough terrain with no possibilities for a back-haul cargo from Madrid. In the case of the Ciudad Rodrigo examples, the grain was surplus production moving to the regional market where it was sold. In Ciudad Rodrigo it was possible, according to other entries in the accounts, to obtain wine and olive oil brought by peasant-transporters from the southern slopes of the Sierra de Gata, which were deficient in grain. The transport fees could be low because transportation earnings needed to cover only part of operating costs and because the carrier had a vital interest in the exchange of goods itself. By contrast, the government examples were ones in which the only consideration for the transporters was the price to be received for providing the service.

It can be argued, therefore, that a significant differential had to develop in order to attract men and animals away from agriculture-transport activity to full-time transportation. This postulated lack of substitutability between specialized transport and subsistence economy transport should be supported by figures which show that the price of the former rose rapidly in comparison with transport costs in the subsistence economy. The examples of such prices suggest this was happening. For the years 1765-1788, some 101 examples of cargoes of wine and olive oil are listed as traveling the fifty-seven kilometers (8.6 leagues) from Cadalso to Ciudad Rodrigo. The examples show three distinct sub-periods with different average prices for transport. (Table 12). The increase in the average price amounts

Table 13. *Prices paid by the government for transporting grain to Madrid, 1773 and 1787*

Year	Type of transport	Route	Marevedis per fanega per league[a]
1773	Muleteers	Peñaranda-Navas de San Antonio-Madrid	17
		Peñaranda-Navas de San Antonio only	15
		Navas de San Antonio-Madrid	
		(March)	17 3/4
		(April)	20 1/2
	Carters	Peñaranda-Navas de San Antonio-Madrid	10
		Peñaranda-Navas de San Antonio only	12
1787	Both types	Various points in Old Castile to Madrid	
		(August)	18-21
		(September)	18-20
		(October)	18-20
		(November)	19-20
		(December)	19

a. 34 *marevedis* = 1 *real de vellón*, 1 *fanega* = 1.5 bushels, 1 league *(legua)* = 6.6 kilometers or about 4 miles. An unskilled laborer in Madrid earned 140 *marevedis* per day in 1773 and 157 *marevedis* per day in 1787. A two-pound loaf of bread cost 42 *marevedis* in 1773 and 48 *marevedis* in 1787. Hamilton, *War and Prices*, pp. 252-53, 270.
SOURCES: 1773: AHN, *Con.*, leg. 49240; 1787: *Consejos*, leg. 11452.

to 25 per cent of the average for the first sub-period (1765-1772). This correlates quite well with Hamilton's quinquennial averages of the index numbers of commodity prices in Old Castile-León for the period. Based on the years 1771-1780, these averages rose from 97.6 in 1766-1770 to 119.5 in 1786-1790.[2] In this case, at least, there was no unusual increase in the cost of transport in the countryside.

It would be most desirable to have a similar series of quotations for the price of professional cart transport, but all that can be offered are two figures derived from Table 11. These indicate that in 1773 the crown paid 10 to 12 M/F/L for such transport, and in 1787 paid 18 to 21 M/F/L. Economic conditions (grain shortage in Madrid) were similar in both years. The inference which these figures allow is that while the cost of transport in the rural economy rose about 25 per cent along with the general price level, the cost of carting increased about 90 per cent. This in turn suggests that there was not much transfer from one segment of the market for transport services to the other, and also that the carting industry was not able to expand readily in response to the demands with which it was confronted.

In the late 1780's fees such as the government had to pay for transport mounted quickly when the cargo had to be carried an appreciable distance. The relatively high price required to obtain transport services for work which was unrelated to the subsistence exchange pattern and which offered little chance for a back-haul cargo was bound to be detrimental to economic growth in the interior. In 1787, according to Earl J. Hamilton, the price of wheat in New Castile was 1,853 *marevedis* per *fanega*.[3] Of 40,000 *fanegas* of wheat mentioned in one source for that year, 28,000 were shipped from the town of Adanero. Adanero, however, was no more than a grain collection depot on the southern edge of the plain of Old Castile, and much of the grain came from farther afield, the actual distance averaging thirty leagues.[4] At 20 M/F/L, transport costs from Adanero alone were 420 *marevedis* per *fanega*, and the average figure was about 600 *marevedis* per *fanega*. The latter is 33 per cent of the

2. *Ibid.,* p. 157.
3. *Ibid., Appendix I,* "Commodity Prices in New Castile," p. 252.
4. AHN, *Con.,* leg. 11452.

final price in New Castile, and probably about 50 per cent of the price at the source of supply. Such was the impact of transporting a bulky commodity 120 miles.

A similar example of the impact of transport costs is found in the *Censo* of 1799, which gives the price of wheat in Toledo that year as 2,040 *marevedis* per *fanega*, a figure confirmed by Hamilton's quotation of 2,006 for the same year in New Castile. The *Censo* gave the price of wheat in Salamanca, a wheat-producing area, as only 748 *marevedis* per *fanega*.[5] Even at 1787 transport prices, probably low by 1799, half or more of the differential between regions represented transport costs.[6]

Transport costs of this nature quickly became a significant part of the delivered cost of industrial raw materials, even when the commodity was relatively valuable. An example is provided by raw cotton, which had to be imported from the Mediterranean ports for the royal factory at Ávila. In 1787 in Madrid, cotton cost 9,350 *marevedis* per *arroba*, a unit roughly half of a *fanega* in weight. At 20 M/F/L over the 93 leagues from Valencia to Ávila, transport came to 930 *marevedis* per *arroba*, or about 10 per cent of the delivered price.[7] This was enough to put a plant located on the central plateau at a clear competitive disadvantage compared with coastal industry, especially when the same transport costs repeated in the distribution of the finished product to the scattered markets of Castile.

Thus it is clear that although large numbers of peasant-transporters were available at low fees for servicing the exchange of subsistence goods in the countryside, such carriers could be drawn into more specialized transport work only by fees which represented a substantial part of the cost of delivered raw materials or other goods. The corresponding high price of the finished products restricted them to a very narrow market in the interior. Moreover, the price

5. Hamilton, *War and Prices*, p. 252; *Censo de la riqueza territorial e industrial de España en el año 1799.*

6. In one passage Jovellanos comments that the grain of León was four times as expensive in Asturias, largely because of poor transport. Elsewhere he lists numerous examples of large price differentials in neighboring regions because of the cost of land transport. Jovellanos, "Dos informes," pp. 456-57; "Ley agraria," pp. 128-30.

7. Hamilton, *War and Prices*, p. 252; *Encyclopedia Universal*, article "Trigo" (vol. LXIV), article "Arroba" (vol. VI), article "Fanega" (vol. XXV). The figure 10 per cent is the same quoted from more direct sources by La Force, *Textile Industry*, p. 49.

of carting services was rising more rapidly than prices in general, suggesting a shortage in the supply of this type of transport.

B. *Supply and demand*

In Chapter II at least part of the demand for transport services was quantified, with some indications of the increases in this demand during the last half of the eighteenth century. To demonstrate that a transport crisis was developing in the Spanish interior and complete the description of the supply of transportation, it is necessary to attempt an estimate of the over-all capacity of the transport pool and to determine what part of those services were available outside the subsistence economy. Most of the concrete figures date from the years 1752-1757. It will be necessary to rely on indirect evidence for subsequent decades.

Table 14 lists the numbers of individuals owning either carts or pack animals, regardless of the amount of time spent in transportation each year. Table 15 provides the information needed to determine what share of the transport was provided by professional carters. The latter table requires some clarification. Of the 3,364 "Cart Owners Reported," about a thousand were listed by towns which did not include the number of carts owned by each individual. Since the carting industry averaged three carts per owner, these thousand carters represent about three thousand carts which do not appear under "Carts Reported." Conversely, the 9,437 "Carts Reported" include about 800 carts which were counted by towns not making reference to cart owners. This suggests that about 300 persons who were cart owners are not recorded under "Cart Owners Reported." These two addenda to Table 15 bring the two totals to about 3,700 cart owners and about 12,500 carts active in the transport pool.

Both of the preceding tables were derived from the *Catastro* and require certain qualifications. Some of these are inherent in the *Catastro* itself.[8] The *Catastro* was made by the local representatives of an eighteenth-century bureaucracy and was generally known to be connected with a reform of the tax system. As a result, not only did the tabulators make many errors and omissions through

8. See Appendix A.

accident and design, but the data made available to officials were left
obscure and often incomplete by individuals who hoped to minimize their apparent wealth. These factors inevitably imply that
figures based on the *Catastro* are minimums and must be handled
with care.

Other qualifications derive from the method used in surveying

Table 14. *Owners of carts and pack animals, by province*[a]

Region	Province	Specifically listed in Catastro		Suggested by Catastro data (estimates)	
Old Castile	Ávila	627		55	
	Burgos	2,375		212	
	León	1,755		142	
	Palencia	150		35	
	Salamanca	1,291		106	
	Segovia	2,045		16	
	Soria	1,685		41	
	Toro	390		5	
	Valladolid	470		80	
	Zamora	25		35	
Totals for Old Castile			10,813		727
New Castile	Cuenca	2,300		135	
	Extremadura	2,135		238	
	Guadalajara	811		377	
	La Mancha	852		19	
	Madrid	632		62	
	Toledo	2,500		25	
Totals for New Castile			9,230		856
Andalucía	Córdoba	1,441		—	
	Jaén	461		76	
	Granada	2,377		180	
	Seville	6,599		278	
Totals for Andalucía			10,878		534
Grand Totals			30,921		2,117

a. AGS, *Catastro*, libs. 1-670. See Appendix A.

the *Catastro.* Ideally it would have been proper to read all of the replies to the question relating to transporters. This proved a practical impossibility. In the procedure adopted, the first step was an examination of two or three of the books of replies from each prov-

Table 15. *Cart owners and carts, by province*[a]

Region	Province	Cart owners reported	Carts reported
Old Castile	Ávila	2	6
	Burgos	553	3,006[b]
	León	40	
	Palencia[c]	1	16
	Salamanca	349	916
	Segovia	472	168
	Soria	361	2,161
	Toro[d]		223
	Valladolid	28	60
	Zamora	11	
New Castile	Cuenca[e]	12	515
	Extremadura[f]	24	1
	Guadalajara[g]	111	456
	La Mancha	131	166
	Madrid	24	
	Toledo	263	481
	Murcia	—[h]	
Andalucía	Córdoba	32	140
	Granada	144	168
	Jaén	10	3
	Seville	796	931
Total of examples found		3,364	9,437

a. AGS, *Catastro,* libs. 1-670. See Appendix A.

b. This includes an estimated 250 carts from the town of Vilviestre, which gave only a global earnings figure.

c. Some towns listed only carts, and three suggested carting activity but gave no details.

d. Carts active only in autumn, transporting basic supplies for three months.

e. Includes town of Almodóvar del Pinar, listing 1,000 draft oxen (approximately 350 carts) for 7 owners.

f. Several towns give large values for carting but give no details.

g. Several towns indicate carters visiting Madrid regularly but give no details.

h. No data in the *Catastro.*

ince, noting all references to transport. These details were then compared with the statistical summary books of the *Catastro* in the *Sección del Consejo de Hacienda* of the Archivo Histórico Nacional in Madrid. In this comparison it was determined what economic value was attributed by provincial authorities in each province to three to five transporters. A record was then made of any town wherein the value of all transport activity exceeded this arbitrary minimum. This produced a list of nearly three thousand localities out of the more than ten thousand listed in the *Catastro*. Since examining the replies from the smaller number of towns took an assistant several months, a complete survey would have been impossible.

The procedure outlined obviously left unrecorded the many cases where towns included one, two, or three transporters. In the initial sampling, however, a few of these towns were checked for each province. In addition, for the provinces of Guadalajara and Toledo, the summary books were missing and all replies from those provinces had to be read. A comparison of such parts of the *Catastro* with those only partly surveyed indicates that well over two-thirds of all regular transporters were actually recorded. This included an even greater proportion of persons engaged in transport beyond their immediate locality.

Two regions were omitted from the study. Galicia was left out after examining the summary tables and some of the replies from the area. The region was relatively isolated from Castile in the mid-eighteenth century, and what contacts existed were supplied by transporters from León province. Since it would have taken an additional month to examine the replies from the area, expediency recommended that Gallicia be excluded. More regrettable is the omission of the old province of Murcia, now Murcia and Albacete. This was a thinly populated region, but other documentation suggests that there were several relatively specialized transporters in the province. The *Catastro* books for Murcia, however, contain virtually no useable data.

With these various qualifications in mind, it is reasonable to suggest that in the provinces of the Crown of Castile, excluding Galicia, about 50,000 individuals owned pack animals or carts which were regularly used for transportation at least part of the year.

About 4,000 of these were carters with perhaps 14,000 carts. If the previously suggested average of 3 pack animals per owner is valid, the remaining 46,000 persons represented some 138,000 pack animals. To this we might add the 4,000 mules of the *cabañiles* for a total of 142,000 pack animals in transport at least some of the year. This was probably over half of the mules and donkeys in Castile, since Vincens Vives states that the census returns of the last third of the century show 450,000 such animals in all of Spain.[9] The accuracy of the suggested totals obviously leaves much to be desired, but they certainly represent at least the magnitude of the active transport pool in the 1750's.

Given yet another rough estimate, that most muleteers made four or five trips a year with cargoes, and that the carters averaged five such trips a year, the total supply of transport corresponds fairly well with the known demands from Chapter II. Since the estimates on the numbers of trips per carrier are based upon numerous instances of testimony in the *Catastro*, they have some substance in them. The known demands and the supply of transport in the 1750's are shown together in Table 16.

If the various figures in Table 16 are at all accurate, Madrid in the 1750's absorbed about half of the available pack-animal transport capacity of Castile, simply to bring to the city vital foodstuffs and fuel. In addition, the capital absorbed at least 70 per cent of the professional carting capacity of Castile for the same purposes. By comparison, the demands of the Santander trade were small in volume, but economically important because of the contribution of the wool trade to Spain's balance of payments. Although listed in terms of cartloads of capacity, it is likely that a portion of the Santander trade was actually carried by muleteers traveling to the coast for cargoes of fish and imported goods.

Between 1757 and 1800 the demands which can be documented increased substantially. As indicated in Chapter I, the population of Madrid grew by about 25 per cent, which would raise the transport required for the city to 475,000 pack-animal loads of capacity and 68,000 cartloads. It is likely, moreover, that the actual transport needs grew faster than the population, since the additional supplies had to come from ever greater distances. In the same period the

9. Vicens Vives, *Historia*, IV, 161.

Santander trade grew so that by 1790 it represented some 14,000 cartloads of wool and flour. In addition, it is likely that the demand for transport in the subsistence economy of the countryside also increased. With the spread of farming, the nineteenth-century tendency for large areas to concentrate on single crops was already appearing, and this logically should have required more interregional transfers of basic commodities.

Little data was found to document the response of the transport industry to this growing demand. The scattered price information suggests that the imperfection in the over-all transport market

Table 16. *Transportation: The supply and the demand*

			Supply (1752)
Transport agent	*Trips per year*	*Cartloads of capacity[a]*	*Animal-loads of capacity*
142,000 animals	times 5 =		710,000
or			or
142,000 animals	times 4 =		568,000
14,000 **carts**	times 5 =	70,000 =	280,000
		Total	848,000 to 990,000

				Demands quantifiable
	1750's		*1790's*	
Demanded by	*Cartloads of capacity[a]*	*Animal-loads of capacity*	*Cartloads of capacity[a]*	*Animal-loads of capacity*
Madrid		380,000		475,000[b]
	55,000 =	220,000	68,800[b] =	275,200
Santander	7,000 =	28,000	14,000 =	56,000
	Total	628,000	*Total*	806,200

a. An ordinary cart had the capacity of four pack animals.
b. Estimates achieved by increasing the figures for the 1750's by 25 per cent, the increase recorded for the population of the city.
SOURCES: All of the above figures are drawn from earlier sections of this study.

which separated subsistence from specialized transportation continued to exist. In the countryside supply apparently kept pace with demand, since the prices in the examples offered did no more than keep pace with general price levels.

The carting industry, however, was apparently unable to expand its services as rapidly as the growing demands. Despite government protection and encouragement, the cost of carting services rose much faster than the general price level. Although statistics are lacking, it is evident that a transport crisis was developing. Some of the factors leading to this situation have been discussed. The carters depended on grazing sites along the roads and on winter pasturage, yet access to pastures was becoming increasingly precarious. Ironically, this was due to the same factor which increased the demand for transport: the population rise. The land hunger this generated, and royal policies for satisfying it, led to enclosure of pastures, which was bound to limit the activities of the carters. Yet, with poor roads, rugged terrain, and an imperfect market for transport services, no other alternatives were available. The circumstantial evidence is bolstered by fragmentary price data suggesting that the price of cart transport rose much faster than the general price level and faster than transport prices in the rural economy. Apparently enclosures were imposing rising costs on the carters and reducing their ability to meet the demands being generated. To understand and substantiate further these findings requires a more detailed examination of the carting industry and its relationship with the Spanish crown.

Chapter six. *Transporter associations*

In several parts of eighteenth-century Spain groups of transporters maintained guildlike associations to promote their collective interests and regulate business relations within regional communities of carriers. Some of these associations date back to the late Middle Ages. These groups became convenient channels through which the central government was able to control part of the supply of transport as one facet of the gradual centralization of power in the early modern era. The Crown of Castile first recognized, then patronized, and finally controlled the transporters of some of the associations.

Organizations appeared among only a small part of the transporter population and included only a fraction of the pack-animal transporters. Among the muleteers, in fact, only two, or possibly three, such associations developed, and then only under special circumstances. Among the much smaller number of carters four well-documented organizations appeared, three of which were active in the eighteenth century.

The Transporters' Guild of the city of Valencia was the only example which was clearly part of an urban guild structure. The late eighteenth-century regulations of this guild show it with a guild-hall, several elective officials, a limited membership, and a near monopoly on transport within the city of Valencia and between the city and its seaport. Rates were listed in detail, as were the numbers of men and vehicles required for specific kinds of cargo. There is little to suggest, however, that the authority of the Transporters' Guild of Valencia extended into overland activities.[1]

A similar transporters' guild apparently also existed in Barcelona, with a nominal monopoly over the transport business in the city and from the city throughout Catalonia. This monopoly was

1. AHN, CRC, doc. 465.

broken well before 1750, although the guild attempted to maintain it with legal protests in 1760, 1763, 1769, 1774-1775, 1785, and 1796. These futile disputes tell of rural carriers who brought supplies to Barcelona and took cargoes of merchandise and imports back to the countryside, and of independent transporters who, under the guise of serving specific enterprises, developed regular long-distance services outside the guild's corporate structure.[2]

The rural transporters' associations of the interior differed from the urban-based guilds of Valencia and Barcelona. They were more loosely organized and concerned themselves with different objectives. The city guilds concentrated on maintaining a monopoly, controlling prices, and limiting membership, while the rural groups were more interested in the removal of road tolls and transit restrictions and in the development of a privileged position based on royal patronage.

Only one permanent transporters' association was found among the muleteers of the provinces under the old Crown of Castile. This is not surprising since all but a few hundred of these carriers were peasant-transporters operating in the subsistence economy. They were widely dispersed, transported on a casual, seasonal basis, and were primarily concerned with agriculture. They had no incentive to develop organizations aimed at systematically promoting transportation. If such peasant-transporters had a grievance related to transportation, they sometimes prosecuted it collectively, but only through temporary mechanisms. Thus, although they had no organization, groups of muleteers in La Mancha province twice challenged the accuracy of local wine measures in the late eighteenth century.[3] Similarly, there are several earlier examples in which the muleteers of one town or another went to court to defend their common privileges or toll exemptions.[4] Occasionally local muleteers had enough influence to use their town government as the agent through which such matters were prosecuted.[5]

The one permanent muleteers' association in the interior was that of the *maragatos* of the province of León, sometimes referred to as the *Gremio* (Guild) *de Maragatos*. At least a part of this group

2. Vilar, *Catalogne*, III, 57.   3. *AHN*, Con., legs. 1004-23; 2123-3.
4. ARCG, 3-719-2; 3-1331-9; 3-534-8; 3-1147-1; 3-402-15.
5. ARCG, 3-1370-9.

possessed privileges dated as early as 1364, when the muleteers of Leitariego were exempted from all money taxes and military service. These privileges were cited in 1768 by muleteers of the area when they sought exemption from all road tolls in Castile.[6] Subsequently, in 1776-1777, the Leonese muleteers successfully defended their exemption from the road toll at Mota del Marques in the province of Valladolid, forcing its partial suppression. Two years later, when they were referred to by the court as the *Gremio de Maragatos*, they brought in a suit against the cathedral of Segovia over bridge tolls.[7] In 1797 when the government optimistically decreed the suppression of most road tolls, the *maragatos* followed through with a long complaint listing multiple violations of the new decrees. The crown's response was to issue yet another edict ordering the observance of the previous ones.[8]

These Leonese and Asturian muleteers were clearly well enough organized to carry on a consistent legal effort to avoid payment of road tolls. Since they lived in a number of towns scattered over a considerable area, the prosecution of a series of cases required some kind of permanent organization. The most likely form in this case was a council which customarily met twice a year during the regional festivals. The *maragatos* are described by George Borrow as a distinctive ethnic pocket around the town of Astorga, and Richard Ford gives a similar description, adding that "the whole tribe assembles twice a year at Astorga at the feasts of Corpus and Ascension."[9] No evidence of actual business meetings has been found, despite able work by local historians in municipal and private archives.[10] It is likely, however, that the *maragatos* conducted their collective business regarding transportation at their semi-annual festivals.

Except for this singular example of ethnic cohesion and functional specialization, there is no hint of corporate organization among the pack-animal transporters of Castile. This lack of organization is undoubtedly a reflection of the fact that nearly all such transporters were farmers, or farm workers, and had little in-

6. AHP, Madrid, lib. 19266, fol. 112.
7. AHN, *Con.*, leg. 995, *expedientes* on Valladolid, Segovia.
8. *Ibid.*, leg. 1799-5.
9. Vicens Vives, *Historia*, IV, 161.
10. Cabo Alonso, "La Armuña"; Martín Galindo, *Arrieros maragatos*.

terest in establishing a privileged position as transporters. The Leonese muleteers were relatively specialized transporter-traders of long standing, came from a well-defined region, and possessed a degree of ethnic as well as functional cohesion. They had a real interest in reducing road tolls and other obstacles to trade. It would be surprising if they had no organization for collective action.

At least four regional associations of carters appeared in Castile, three of which were active in the eighteenth century. They included well over half of the long-haul carters of the interior. These corporate groups were spontaneous growths with long histories, but from an early date they operated in a special legal frame of reference. This legal concept, developed under Isabella I, was called the *Cabaña Real de Carreteros* (Royal Association of Carters). In theory the *Cabaña* covered all long-haul carters, but in practice the crown could deal only with those who had their own associations. The *Cabaña Real* was first defined in 1497, and subsequently all carter associations operated as parts thereof.[11]

The earliest of the carter associations was the Brotherhood of Carters of the area between Granada and Murcia. It was probably at the instance of this group that the crown recognized the *Cabaña Real* between 1497 and 1499, endowing those included in its definition with a number of privileges.[12] As early as 1505 "carters of the *Cabaña Real*" were defending their new privileges in court.[13] In 1520 some "carters of the kingdom" brought suit against the justices of eight towns in the Granada area for violating the general privileges of the carters.[14] Another case, dated 1588, was brought against the city of Lorca by the "*cabañiles* and carters."[15] Finally, there is a dispute dated 1600 in which the carters of the town of Huescar, calling themselves "*Hermanos de la Cabaña Real*," sought

11. The full title was the *Cabaña Real de Carreteros, Trajineros, Cabañiles y sus Derramas*. A *trajinero* was a "hauler"; the *cabañiles*, defined elsewhere, were attached in 1629, while the phrase *sus derramas*, literally "its branches," included individuals who entered the long-haul carting business after the privileges were first granted and who remained outside the carter associations. These "branches" included the large carting firms in Madrid in the late eighteenth century. Andres Cornejo, "Cabaña Real," *Diccionario histórico y forense del derecho real de España* (Madrid, 1779); Joaquín Escriche, *Diccionario razonado de legislación y jurisprudencia* (Madrid, 1874), II, 133; AGS, *Cámara de Castilla, exp.* 1831; AHN, *Con.*, legs. 1608-3; 2347-14.
12. NR, lib. 7, tit. 28, *leyes* 1-4; Klein, pp. 22-23.
13. ARCG, 3-1891-19.   14. *Ibid.*, 3-1596-3.
15. *Ibid.*, 3-1390-5.

to have local roads repaired.[16] The use of the word *hermanos* (brothers) is significant, since it most certainly implies that the carters of the area had an established organization. The same word was used by the Soria-Burgos Brotherhood of carters in the late seventeenth century, and a contemporaneous example existed in the Mesta of the sheep herders, the formal title of which was the "Honorable Brotherhood of the Mesta." This parallel terminology makes it easy to accept the existence of a permanent carter organization in southeastern Castile in the sixteenth century. There are no references to carting in the Granada area after 1600, and it is possible that its disappearance was the result of the expulsion of the Moriscos in 1608.

One of the three eighteenth-century carter organizations was located in the area between Cuenca and Murcia, with its center at Almodóvar del Pinar. The information on this group is sketchy. It may not have developed until the late sixteenth century, since in 1553 the carriers of several towns in the area prosecuted a grievance without reference to an organization.[17] The presence of an association can, however, be inferred from a decree of 1613 in which the crown gave official recognition to an attorney whom the carters of "the Bishoprics of Cartagena and Cuenca" had picked to represent them in the court at Murcia.[18] Subsequently these carters appear in the *Catastro* of 1752 as a "Royal Association, of Carters." The form of this organization is unknown, but it was independent of the local government at Almodóvar where it was located, and had a permanent structure since it employed two legal notaries (*escribanos*).[19]

Another such organization existed in the administrative district (*sexmo*) of Navarredonda de la Sierra, a group of five towns in a mountain valley in the southern part of the modern province of Ávila.[20] Long-haul carting was a very old business in this district, and some of its residents participated in the Isabelline wars against

16. *Ibid.*, 3-755-5.   17. *Ibid.*, 3-238-12.
18. AHN, CRC, *Tomo* II, doc. 68; AHN, *Hac.*, lib. 8038, fols. 348, 349.
19. AGS, *Catastro*, lib. 74—Cuenca: Almodóvar del Pinar; Gil Crespo, "Mesta de carreteros," pp. 225-26.
20. Prior to the provincial reorganization of the 1830's, the district was part of the province of Salamanca. The five towns were Navarredonda de la Sierra, Hoyos del Espinar, Santa María de la Vega, La Garganta, and Santa María de Pimpolar.

Granada in the 1480's.[21] The area is also mentioned in a 1599 decree on carting matters.[22]

The local government at Navarredonda was dominated by the carters and was used by them to promote their interests. Hence no strictly private organization appeared, as in Almodóvar del Pinar and in the Soria-Burgos area. When carting matters were discussed, the four outlying towns sent representatives to the meetings of the Navarredonda town council. At these joint sessions the price of transport for the coming year was set, government requests for transportation discussed, and each village assigned a quota of carts to meet the government's demands. The council regularly nominated an attorney (*procurador*) to represent the interests of the district in Madrid. This nomination had to be ratified by the royal judge for carting affairs, but the initiative came from the locality. The joint council paid for the attorney with a special tax of two and one-half *reales* on each working cart and one-half *real* on carts kept at home because of sick owners or animals. These practices were all well established by 1636, the date of the earliest papers in the local archives. They probably date from much earlier and we know that they continued throughout the eighteenth century.

In the 1700's the council began appointing *comisarios* or roving agents. These men investigated complaints about road conditions, illegal tolls, etc., and brought such grievances to the attention of the government in Madrid. These agents were supported in the same way as the attorney who resided in Madrid. With this organization, the Navarredonda carters were able to persist in long legal actions to maintain and expand their privileges. An outstanding example of this was their exemption from military service. The issue arose regularly from about 1660 on, and culminated in a favorable and precedent-setting decision in 1735.[23]

By far the most important of the carters' associations was that

21. AGS, *Sello*, 1490, doc. 159.

22. AHN, *Hac.*, lib. 8038, fols. 345-47; AHN, CRC, *Tomo* II, doc. 68.

23. The data on the Navarredonda carters which follows comes from the four *Libros de Actas* and *Libros de Acuerdos* in the archives of the town council. The books cover much of the seventeenth and eighteenth centuries; the specific years used here are 1636, 1641, 1747, 1749, and 1787. Also used in the archives was a volume labeled *Libro de Privilegios de 1735*, which actually contained documents from both centuries, some postdating the year on the binding. My findings agree in substance with Gil Crespo, "Mesta de carreteros."

of the Soria-Burgos region. During the eighteenth century this was the largest single element of the Castilian carting industry. In the 1750's it counted about five thousand carts, possibly ten times the number controlled by the Navarredonda association. The Soria-Burgos association worked through a representative council and referred to itself as the *"Junta y Hermandad"* (Council and Brotherhood) of the *Cabaña Real de Carreteros*.

The Council consisted of two deputies (*comisarios*) from each of ten towns in the area and was presided over by an elective executive officer called the *alcalde mayor*.[24] In two of the participating towns the deputies were chosen by the town council, but the others were elected by local meetings of carters. Council meetings were called by circular letters sent out by the *alcalde* and were held in his house. When the *alcalde* was away with his carts, he delegated his functions to a substitute.[25] The council apparently did not hold regular meetings, but there are specific references to sessions in 1754, 1787, 1817, 1819, 1826, and 1840.[26] The volume of litigation which the Brotherhood carried on implies that meetings must have been fairly frequent. The executive officer was a permanent official elected by the council, whose authority extended beyond that of a mere presiding officer. After informal consultation with members and deputies, he decided when to call the council meetings and sent out the necessary letters. He also enforced such regulations within the Brotherhood as the council established.[27] During the government of Ferdinand VII, this *alcalde* was subjected to a degree of royal supervision, since there are several cases in which he was ordered to settle disputes between carters and at least one case when he was ordered to stop meddling in disputes with non-carters.[28]

If the town of Palacios de la Sierra was typical, the authority of the Brotherhood's *alcalde* was administered through local "Constables of the *Cabaña Real*," who were supported by special taxes assessed on cart owners and collected by the municipal govern-

24. The towns included were Regumiel, Quintanar de la Sierra, Vilviestre, Palacios de la Sierra, Ontoria del Pinar, San Leonardo, Cañicosa, Salduero, Covaleda, and Duruelo.
25. AHN, *Con.*, leg. 395-9.
26. *Ibid.*, leg. 2868-25; Tudela, pp. 374-76.
27. Tudela, *Ibid.*
28. AHN, *Con.*, leg. 395-9.

ment.[29] The council's legal business was handled by a permanent notary from one of the participating towns.[30]

Although the Soria-Burgos Brotherhood appears relatively late in the sources, by the early eighteenth century it had acquired a position of central importance in the carting industry and in its relationship with the crown. There were carters active in the area as early as the 1480's, when they participated in the wool export trade, but as late as 1578 four towns from the area were suing the city of Burgos without reference to an association or even to the *Cabaña Real* as defined by the crown.[31] The first concrete reference to the Brotherhood is dated 1678 and is appended to a document of 1693 in which an attorney is acting in the name of the "Council and Brotherhood of the Carters of the *Cabaña Real*," who are listed as residents of the Soria-Burgos area.[32] The attorney in question was, in fact, the resident agent whom the Soria-Burgos Brotherhood maintained in Madrid on a permanent basis, perhaps in imitation of the Navarredonda carters.

During the seventeenth century there was also a third attorney for carting affairs in the capital, a *procurador-general* maintained by the crown.[33] This official was paid by the government to represent all of the carters in the *Cabaña Real* as recognized by the crown, rather than to represent only a part of the carting community. The pre-eminence of the Soria-Burgos Brotherhood was recognized at some point in the early eighteenth century when it obtained the right to nominate not only its regional representative, but also the royal official who nominally represented the entire carting industry. By 1754 the Soria-Burgos council was making its third nomination for this key office.[34]

In general, various parts of the transport industry developed associations for collective action. Only within the carting industry, however, were these organizations significant and of direct interest to the government. The carters developed a number of regional

29. AA Palacios de la Sierra, *Ordenanzas* of 1818.
30. AHN, *Con.*, leg. 395-9.
31. AGS, *Sello*, 1488, docs. 27, 160, 341; AA Burgos, doc. 3378.
32. AHN, *Con.*, leg. 395-9.
33. The three posts in question were definitely occupied by three different men in 1693. AHN, CRC, *Tomo* II, doc. 68; AHN, *Hac.*, lib. 8038, fols. 352, 353.
34. AHN, *Con.*, leg. 395-9.

organizations, one of which predominated, but they never achieved a national association like that of the Mesta of the sheepherders, although the necessary components were present. This was probably forestalled by the fact that the crown stepped in with a system of general privileges before the carters could create a national association to make such demands. By the eighteenth century there was a national organization connected with carting, but it was an appendage of the central bureaucracy. Since it satisfied many of the desires of the regional carter organizations, they acquiesced in the situation. Because of this arrangement, carters often used their associations for legal purposes, but just as often entered the courts as individuals without appealing for organized support. Since the eighteenth-century governments favored their interests, individual carters had little trouble getting favorable decisions.[35]

All of the transporter organizations had three important functions. They facilitated the business of transport by setting rates and terms of work, as in Valencia, or by providing commissioners who helped to arrange for shipping contracts, as in Navarredonda and the Burgos-Soria Brotherhood. These associations also regulated relationships within the membership, settling wage disputes, grazing disagreements, etc.

The most important function, however, was "to represent the *Cabaña Real* in all royal and ecclesiastical courts in order to guard and preserve the rights of carting in its traffic, possession of pastures, transit use of pasture, and exemption from conscription."[36] In part because of their importance to the crown, the carters were quite successful in this through much of the seventeenth and eighteenth centuries, obtaining not only generalized privileges, but a special court for carting affairs and a network of local judicial agents to carry the power of that court to the countryside.

The government, however, did not grant these benefits without a purpose and without exacting a price. The presence of regional carter associations meant that by contacting a relatively small number of leaders in the carting community, the crown could mobilize a large block of transport services. The limitations of an eighteenth-century bureaucracy made this a vital consideration. By granting

35. AHP, Madrid, libs. 17343, 17344, 17345, 19409.
36. AHN, *Con.*, leg. 395-9.

privileges to the carter associations, the crown made them dependent on its will. The crown could then demand that the carters give priority to royal demands for transportation, even when other work was more attractive. Within this system of mutual dependence, the government could monopolize carting services.

Chapter seven. *The government and the professional carters*

The government of eighteenth-century Spain subsidized and protected the better organized elements of the transport system. In return for privilege and protection, the crown was more easily able to divert transport services to government purposes. The government's most effective manipulation of the transportation market concentrated upon the specialized long-haul carters. This was because the carters by developing organizations of their own, had simplified the administrative task of dealing with them. The crown, partly for its own purposes, and partly at the instigation of the carters themselves, developed a distinctive set of legal and juridical structures to handle its relations with the carters. In the process the carters' autonomous organizations were increasingly subordinated to a branch of the royal bureaucracy, a typical example of a central government expanding its authority at the cost of local independence.

By the late seventeenth century the carters possessed an impressive array of legal and economic privileges. Some of them dated from the reign of Isabella I, but they reached their greatest scope between 1600 and 1640 and between 1750 and 1800. During the last half of the seventeenth century, most of the privileges remained on the law books, but were curtailed by the courts and by the crown's lack of interest in enforcing them.

The carters' relationship with the government was first defined in 1497 when Isabella created the previously mentioned legal concept known as the *Cabaña Real de Carreteros*. This was done in a charter granted to the regional organization then active in the Granada area.[1] At the same time a number of basic privileges were incorporated into the law codes.[2] In the sixteenth century and the

1. ARCG, 3-3995; Klein, p. 23.
2. NR, lib. 7, tit. 28, *leyes* 1-4; lib. 7, tit. 35, *ley* 2.

early seventeenth century the new laws were loosely interpreted and their scope effectively widened by court decisions in favor of the *Cabaña Real*, the associations within it, and individual carters. The main emphasis of the privileges was on the provision of free pasture for the carters as they traveled and easy access to inexpensive winter grazing. Gradually the privileges came to include matters less immediate to carting, and in the seventeenth century the crown created a special court with jurisdiction over disputes arising from the carters' privileges.

The initial concessions included completely free access to all common pastures in Castile, including access to water and use of the commons for nightly campsites. By 1600 this had been clarified by a detailed listing of the types of land which could be closed to carters.[3] Free use of the commons was supplemented by the right to use enclosed private pastures upon payment of a nominal daily fee. Moreover, once a pasture owner had rented pastures to the carters for winter use, the land could be used for no other purpose until such time as no carter came forward to claim the right to rent it.[4] The privileges quickly came to include the right to cut wood free of taxes or fees if the wood came from communal woodlots and was used for cooking or repairing carts.[5] The carters could also prosecute any town which did not keep the local trails passable for their carts.[6] To forestall feigned ignorance of their privileges by local officials, the carters were authorized to carry printed copies of their privileges bearing the royal council's seal of authorization. In the early seventeenth century the carters obtained two important exemptions from general obligations imposed by the crown: they were exempted from service in both the army and the militia,[7] and towns granted the title "carter communities" were exempted from the *servicio*, a form of direct tax collected by assessing each township a proportion of the total revenue the government sought.[8]

The carters also obtained numerous clarifications of their status.

3. NR, lib. 7, tit. 28, *ley* 3.   4. AHN, CRC, *Tomo* II, doc. 68.
5. NR, lib. 7, tit. 28, *ley* 4.   6. NR, tit. 28, *ley* 1; tit. 35, *ley* 2.
7. AA Navarredonda, *Libro de Privilegios*, 1735; *Libro de Actas*, 1638; Gil Crespo, "Mesta de carreteros," pp. 219-21.
8. AHN, *Hac.*, lib. 8038, fol. 350; AHN, SID, leg. 12; José Luis Sureda Carrión, *La Hacienda castellana y los economistas del siglo XVII* (Madrid: C.S.I.C., 1949), pp. 75-80, 127-63.

These were necessary because their constant travels through many jurisdictions left them open to repeated local exactions. In the earliest privileges the carters were granted free access to all roads and trails used in common by the residents of any locality.[9] When they passed authorized toll points, they were liable for tolls only if there was a clearly marked collection place with a collector on duty.[10] In regions where wood was scarce and valuable, the carters were exempted from arbitrary search and allowed to carry supplies of wood for spare parts while crossing treeless plains.[11] The relationship between the carters and the municipal governments was regulated very early by a decree which required that the laws be interpreted for them on the same basis as for local residents. In the seventeenth century it was necessary to order local authorities to abstain from collecting excise taxes on the consumption of supplies which the carters carried as they crossed jurisdictional boundaries. The courts also ruled that local ordinances concerning pastures, rights of way, and taxation applied to carters only if they had been approved by the royal council (*Consejo de Castilla*) in Madrid.[12] Finally, in 1629, the scope of the *Cabaña Real* itself was expanded slightly to include the *cabañiles*, the long-haul muleteers with pack trains averaging one hundred mules.[13]

To ensure that the privileges of the *Cabaña Real* were upheld, in 1599 the King authorized the creation of a special jurisdiction for carting affairs, with a judge in Madrid who was a member of the royal council.[14] At the same time, the government began providing legal council for the carters, appointing an attorney-general in Madrid in 1599, and attorneys in Granada (1607) and Murcia (1613). The crown also extended royal recognition to the attorneys sent to Madrid by the regional carting organizations on their own initiative.[15] The first of the national carters' judges (*Juez Conserva-*

9. NR, lib. 7, tit. 28, *ley* 1.   10. *Ibid., ley* 2.
11. AHN, *Hac.*, lib. 8038, fol. 349; NR, lib. 7, tit. 28, n. 3 to *leyes* 1-4.
12. AHN, *Hac.*, lib. 8038, fol. 339; AHN, CRC, *Tomo* II, doc. 68; NR, lib. 7, tit. 28, n. 1 to *leyes* 1-4.
13. AHN, *Hac.*, lib. 8038, fol. 348; NR, lib. 7, tit. 28, n. 2 to *leyes* 1-4.
14. NR, lib. 7, tit. 28, *ley* 5; AHN, *Con.*, leg. 1111-11, pt. 1; Escriche, *Diccionario de legislación, article* "Juez Conscrvador."
15. AHN, CRC, *Tomo* II, doc. 68; AHN, *Hac.*, lib. 8038, fols. 345-49, 352-53; NR, lib. 7, tit. 28, n. 1 to *leyes* 1-4; AA Navarredonda, *Libro de Actas*, 1641; Gil Crespo, "Mesta de carreteros," p. 209.

dor) was appointed in 1629 and the office was occupied through most of the seventeenth century.[16]

In general, the crown was very active in its patronage of the carting industry until the middle of the 1640's, but from that time the ability and desire of the government to protect the carters declined rapidly. In the 1650's and 1660's cart trains carrying salt and government supplies were often attacked by local residents,[17] while local officers began to conscript carters into the army and militia.[18] In 1671 the municipalities were authorized to enclose and charge fees for the use of stubble lands which had previously been treated as open commons.[19] The transit grazing rights of the carters were seriously curtailed in 1674, when the use of commons was closely regulated and private pasture owners allowed to refuse rental to passing carters.[20]

The low point of government interest in the carters was apparently reached in the years 1675-1690, since for that period scarcely a single documentary reference to carting came to light. The rise of local interest, suggested by historians such as J. H. Elliott, and by the preceding paragraph, worked against a royally patronized institution.[21] A degree of effective government returned under the Count of Oropesa (1685-1691), but the *Cabaña Real* does not reappear in the sources until the very end of his tenure.

From 1690 to about 1730 the carters and the crown worked sporadically to revive the carters' privileged position. The carters attempted to get reversals of the old court decisions which had narrowed their privileges. The government extended carter privileges in important new ways, and periodically reiterated older ones. The result of this was only a partial improvement, since the carters often lost their appeals and the government frequently neglected or was unable to enforce its decrees.

The government's interest in carting did not imply very effective enforcement before 1730, since the same complaints reappear frequently. The carters' exemption from military service and their

16. AGS, *Cámara de Castilla, exp.* 1831.
17. AHN, *Hac.*, lib. 8038, fols. 338, 339, 352; AHN, CRC, *Tomo* II, doc. 68; NR, lib. 7, tit. 28, n. 6 to *leyes* 1-4.
18. AA Navarredonda, *Libro de Actas*, 1664, 1672.
19. AHN, CRC, *Tomo* II, doc. 68.   20. AHN, *Hac.*, lib. 8038, fols. 339, 340.
21. Elliott, *Imperial Spain*, pp. 357-58.

toll privileges are good examples of this problem. While the exemption from conscription was recognized in Madrid, complaints about its violation were made in 1691, 1694, 1703, and 1704, indicating that foreign and civil war made enforcement difficult, and the issue remained alive until 1735.[22] Similarly, the carters' long-established privileges relative to road tolls were upheld in 1699 in a dispute over the toll at Barbadillo del Mercado, but in the same year were ignored in a case involving the toll at Pancorbo.[23] The general effectiveness of road toll regulation can be judged by a complaint which the carters filed in 1737, citing thirty-five illegal toll points.[24]

Although enforcement was erratic in the early eighteenth century, the *Cabaña Real* did obtain some important restorations of and additions to its privileges. A decree of 1693 marked the breakthrough with a general renewal of the carters' privileges, the first in twenty-five years. To this was appended a list of minor clarifications about local ordinances, local taxes, and the carters' right to bear arms.[25]

Other actions reflect the growing importance of the carters in the supply of Madrid. In 1692 they obtained a judgment against the towns of the district of Alcalá de Henares, straddling the eastern approaches to the capital. The defendants were forced to reopen most of the grazing they had been allowed to enclose in 1671. The following year, 1693, the carters protested that pasture for their oxen was becoming scarce within a radius of ten leagues of Madrid. They claimed that the government was not only ignoring privileges which the carters possessed within five leagues of the city, but was permitting additional enclosures in the area. In response the government authorized the use of additional pastures in the five-league radius on a permanent basis and promised to rescind the enclosure permits. In the same decree the royal council granted a renewal of the emergency general extension of pasture rights such as once had been used in drought years.[26] These moves were followed by a decree of 1702 which re-established the right to rent for transit grazing certain enclosed pastures. The carters had been excluded from this

22. AA Navarredonda, *Libro de Privilegios*, 1735.
23. AA Burgos, docs. 3477, 638.   24. AHN, CRC, *Tomo* II, doc. 68.
25. *Ibid.*
26. *Ibid.*; AHN, *Hac.*, lib. 8038, fols. 352-53.

grazing in 1674. The new decree went a step further and established a maximum rent for their use.[27]

The most important expansion of the carters' privileges came in connection with winter pasturage in the Madrid region, again indicating the growing importance of that city. At least as early as 1660, many cart owners had established themselves as permanent winter tenants in pasture lands in the province of Toledo. This location was convenient because, astride the charcoal and wheat routes from New Castile to Madrid, it permitted the carters to make one and sometimes two extra trips per year. In the last years of the seventeenth century, local interests began to exert pressure to force the carters off these pastures. As a result, in 1701, the new Bourbon government issued a special decree guaranteeing the carters winter pastures for 3,800 oxen within 24 leagues of Madrid. The decree listed 8 specific pastures as reserved for the purpose.[28]

The following year the government made it clear that the new pasture privileges in no way changed the carters' position beyond twenty-four leagues from Madrid and reiterated their right to preference in pasture rentals (a right which had existed since 1590). The government also fixed the annual rental for such grazing at the price which had been charged in 1692. The effectiveness of this last provision was minimal since it was necessary to repeat it in 1716, and by 1750 the rent for such pasture was several times the 1692 figure.[29]

Despite good intentions with respect to the carters, the crown was unable to achieve more than erratic compliance. It engaged in the apparently futile process of reiterating its decrees, renewing all of the carters rights in 1708, 1709, and 1719. Nevertheless, the carters could complain in 1719 that the central government repeatedly had allowed localities to exclude carters from accustomed pastures and that the carters' associations had not even been allowed to send commissioners to investigate the disputes. In the case in question the courts upheld some of the carters' transit grazing rights near Salamanca,[30] and a few years later, in 1723, granted the reopening of stubble lands on the south and east approaches to Ma-

27. AHN, CRC, *Tomo* II, doc. 68.

28. AHN, *Clero*, lib. 707; AHN, *Con.*, legs. 395-9; 1608-1.

29. AHN, *Hac.*, lib. 8038, fols. 353, 354; AGS, *Catastro*, lib. 14—Burgos: Ontoria del Pinar.

30. AHN, *Hac.*, lib. 8038, fols. 343, 345, 347.

drid.[31] In the next five years, however, the carters lost a series of similar appeals for the restoration of transit grazing privileges which had been curtailed by the courts in 1674.[32]

Between 1692 and the late 1720's, therefore, governmental and judicial decisions often favored the carters, but the crown had little luck in getting compliance while the courts were far from consistent in supporting the carters. The year 1728 marked a turning point because it saw the appearance of the first of a series of able native ministers. From 1728 to 1740 the crown was dominated by José Patiño, and under his influence the government began to devote serious attention to the internal problems of the country. The seventy years after 1730 saw more consistent policies in Madrid relative to the carters and also improved support at the local level as the government developed the judge-subdelegate system within the special jurisdiction established for the carters.

In 1730 the earlier limit on fees for the rental of enclosed pastures was renewed,[33] and in the same year the carters won a major suit against the Mesta of the migratory sheep-owners regarding priority in the use of transit grazing land.[34] The next year saw a clarification of the term *trashumante* (migratory) as applied to Mesta sheep and carting oxen. The courts gave the carters the best of two privileges, decreeing that carters had migratory privileges relative to winter pastures, and that town ordinances which excluded migratory sheep from commons grazing were not applicable to migratory oxen used by carters.[35] Additional decisions based on this precedent were handed down in 1751 and 1752 and were later appended to the Spanish law code of 1804-1807 (*Novísima Recopilación*).[36] By the 1750's the carters' rights to free use of town grazing were openly acknowledged by many of the towns in Old Castile in their replies to the *Catastro*.[37] Emergency extensions of these transit grazing rights became an established feature in the eighteenth century. One source indicates that such extensions were made in 1734, 1737, 1750, 1774-1775, 1778, 1793, and 1797-1798.[38]

In 1730 a sixth law was added to those dealing with the *Cabaña*

31. AHN, CRC, *Tomo* II, doc. 68.
33. AHN, CRC, *Tomo* II, doc. 68.
35. AHN, CRC, *Tomo* II, doc. 68.
37. AGS, *Catastro*, libs. 522, 570, 571.
32. AHN, *Hac.*, lib. 8038, fols. 342, 358.
34. Klein, *The Mesta*, p. 22.
36. NR, lib. 7, tit. 28, nn. 6, 7.
38. AHN, *Con.*, legs. 1845-2; 2868-25.

Real, establishing arbitration procedures in cases involving damages by stray carting-oxen. These incidents aften resulted in lengthy litigation over relatively minor matters. Under the new procedure, each party was to select one representative and participate in selecting an impartial third person. These three individuals were to determine the extent of damages and the manner of restitution.[39] There is little evidence that this method of settlement was much used, though the law was reiterated in 1784. Two disputes from 1801 and 1802 indicate that at that time the carters were having trouble getting local authorities to agree to such arbitration.[40]

By the middle of the century the carters' exemption from military service was effectively re-established. A major suit against the army recruiters was won in 1735, and this decision became the guiding precedent in later suits in 1740 and 1752.[41] The continued support of the carters also brought the full restoration of their grazing privileges along the roads. In 1674 and again in 1724 serious restrictions were imposed on the carters, despite some legal successes. Between 1783 and 1787 the matter was fought out once more, and this time the courts removed the restrictions and restored the carters' privileges as they had been in the early seventeenth century. The court even ordered the municipalities involved to repair their local roads.[42]

Internal road tolls and bridge tolls were a chronic source of transport disputes, and it is clear that they were much abused in the eighteenth century. Carters were exempt from such tolls when they carried governmental cargoes, and at other times were exempted if the tolls were not collected in an impartial way with the schedule of charges available on request. These rights were generally upheld by the courts.[43] Under Charles III the government began a gradual attempt to reform such tolls, beginning by asserting that road tolls were justified only if the revenues were used to maintain the road or other facilities necessary to travel. In 1781 the royal council ordered a survey of the road and bridge tolls in the provinces of the

39. NR, lib. 7, tit. 28, *ley* 6.
40. AHN, *Hac.,* lib. 8038, fol. 359; AHN, *Con.,* legs. 2228-22; 2347-14.
41. AA Navarredonda, *Libro de Privilegios,* 1735.
42. AHN, *Hac.,* lib. 8038, fols. 337, 358-62.
43. AA Navarredonda, *Libro de Acuerdos,* 1766; AHN, *Con.,* legs. 549-15; 994, *expediente* on Soria; 51197-1.

Crown of Castile, and in 1782 the principle of maintenance was given the authority of a royal decree. Reports on actual conditions were collected and a few tolls suppressed. Finally, in 1796-1797 two decrees flatly suppressed all road tolls on main highways (*carreteras generales*) except those imposed by the crown for new road projects. Suppressed tolls were capitalized at thirty-three years' yield and the owners were to be paid from the treasury in annual installments. There are some examples of implementation of the decree, but the reform as a whole was beyond the legal, administrative, and financial capacities of the government.[44]

In addition to the more important decisions in favor of the carters, one can cite numerous minor judgments against localities all over Castile, against the city of Madrid, and against other government agencies. The tenor of these decisions is clear. When the carters were obviously in the wrong, they lost. If there was any doubt at all, the courts found in their favor.[45] This did little to soothe the potentially hostile relations between the carters and local residents who resented the carters' heavy drain on local grazing. For the 1790's alone the scattered surviving documents show three cases of assault and battery and two murders.[46]

During the eighteenth century the carters' winter pasturage privileges took two forms. One was the specifically assigned and royally guaranteed pastures within twenty-four leagues of Madrid, the other an over-all preference in renting any pasture land, based on a precedent of 1590. The right to preference was upheld in 1740 when it was decided that the carters could not be evicted even when the land in question changed owners. In the 1780's even the manner of rental was restricted to the carters' advantage. When the town of Luciana in La Mancha sought to rent its lands at auction, the carters maintained their right to rent on the basis of periodic assessments which, in fact, tended to fall behind the market value of the grazing.[47]

44. For a summary of the attempted road toll reforms, see AHN, *Con.*, legs. 994, 995.
45. For examples, dated 1784-1804, see *ibid.*, legs. 1111-1; 2396-1; 1555-2; 1604-13; 2691-28; 2093-10; 2306-23; 2501-10; 2706-15; *Libros de Gobierno*, 1784, fols. 770-74.
46. AHN, *Con.*, legs. 1555-2; 1604-13; 2306-23; 51197-22.
47. *Ibid.*, leg. 1634-29; AHN, CRC, *Tomo* II, doc. 68.

The guarantees to specific pastures near Madrid proved hard to enforce in the face of efforts by owners to switch to more profitable sheep raising or cultivation. The first attack came in 1740 when one of the guaranteed pastures was sold to a convent which then sought to put sheep on the land, and failing that, to raise the rent. Only after fourteen years of litigation did the carters win their point in 1754.[48] In 1760 they came up against a more powerful vested interest when they were evicted from the largest of the guaranteed pastures so that it could be converted into a royal hunting ground. The replacement was a piece of land belonging to an orphanage in Toledo, but the displaced users of this land started a counter-suit which lasted until 1778 and kept the carters from possession until 1775. The case became extremely complex and eventually included an attempt by the Duke of Infantado to switch yet another of the guaranteed pastures to sheep grazing.[49]

Despite favorable decisions, the guaranteed pastures were steadily nibbled away. Of the grazing for 3,800 oxen granted in 1701, there remained by 1788 pasture for less than 2,000 animals. Of the eight pastures in the original grant only two were fully available to carters along with parts of three others. One pasture had been converted to farming, one was reserved for the royal hunt, and the remainder were used by sheep raisers. As of 1793 the carters were seeking to have the guarantee extended to certain pastures just beyond the twenty-four league limit, but were meeting strong resistance from local landowners and users.

An important part of this system of privilege was the special courts which enforced it. Direct legal assistance by the government revived when the attorney-general for the *Cabaña Real* reappeared on the carters' behalf in the 1690's. The first concrete mention of a royal judge for carting matters in the eighteenth century is dated 1719. As the century progressed, this judge, the *Juez Conservador*, came to be the center of an increasingly elaborate system of subjudges who handled most disputes in the first instance. These subjudges (*juezes subdelegados*) were appointed by the *Juez Conservador* on the basis of an authorization in the law of 1599.[50]

The subdelegate system illustrates the haphazard growth of bu-

48. AHN, *Clero*, lib. 707.   49. AHN, *Con.*, leg. 395-9.
50. *Ibid.*, legs. 2102-10; 2093-10; 51197-4, 13, 14, 15, 20.

reaucracy in the eighteenth century. The first reference to a sub-delegate is dated 1723, and they became increasingly common during the last half of the century. By 1800 there were special judges in most provincial capitals and in many other towns. The primary function of these officials was to act as courts of first instance for the carters, with jurisdiction over the territory within ten to twenty leagues of their residences. The courts operated with all of the standard techniques of the Spanish judicial system[51] and enforced rulings from the *Juez Conservador* and the crown in Madrid.[52]

This blend of judicial and police powers was often complicated by the unrelated duties of the men who were appointed as sub-delegates. Often they were local lawyers, and frequently they held other official appointments, including those of *corregidor* (royal administrator at the town level), subjudge for the grain supply, subjudge for the forestry service, regular justice of the peace, district military administrator, soil conservation officer, *alcalde* (chairman) of the town council, and regular judge in the *Chancillería* of Valladolid or Granada. After 1730 all *corregidores* were *ex officio* subdelegates of the carting jurisdiction.[53] When the intendant system was installed at mid-century, all provincial intendants were empowered to act as subjudges for the carters if an issue came before them.[54] Given the nature of the carters' privileges regarding transit, tolls, pastures, water, and woodlots, the possibilities for jurisdictional conflicts between the various offices of a given individual were substantial.

The office of the *Juez Conservador* gradually evolved into a small bureau, known as the protectorate (*protectoría*) of the *Cabaña Real*. It included the judge, the attorney-general, the attorneys sent by regional carter organizations, a lawyer, porters and toll collectors, and various scribes authorized to use the seal of the *Cámara de Castilla*, which was required to give documents official force.[55] As of 1697 this bureau supported itself by collecting a tax of two *reales*

51. AHN, *Hac.*, lib. 8038, fol. 342; AHN, *Con.*, legs. 1604-13; 2306-23; 51197-25.
52. AHN, *Con.*, leg. 51197-39, 44, 48, 51.
53. The *corregidores* were royal officials at the municipal level, and were subordinate to the intendants. *Ibid.*, leg. 51197-61.
54. *Ibid.*, legs. 2334-1; 1555-2; 230-6; 1111-11, pt. 1; 51197-33, 37; Tudela, "La Cabaña real," p. 374.
55. The *Cámara de Castilla* was the legislative subcommittee of the Council of Castile. AHN, *Con.*, *Libros de Gobierno*, 1788, *Tomo* I, fols. 148-50; Tudela, p. 374.

per cart and one-half *real* per pack animal from each transporter on his first entry into Madrid each year. The records of this tax listed the transporters entering, the numbers of carts and animals they used, and gave their home towns. This register must have been a convenient central source of information about transport.[56]

The offices of the more important subdelegates developed in a similar fashion. That in Granada had its subdelegate, an attorney, a lawyer, and the requisite scribes. The office in Murcia had its subdelegate, various scribes, and a constable to enforce its orders.[57] In addition to their judicial duties, these offices were supposed to maintain lists of carts and animals in their jurisdictions, including those who were not legally included in the *Cabaña Real*. References to these lists exist for the provinces of Burgos (1805) Cuenca (late eighteenth century), and Murcia (1753-1755).[58] The last example, in fact, illustrates the use of such lists in the process of requisitioning transport to take grain to Madrid.

The jurisdiction of the *Juez Conservador* and his subdelegates covered every phase of the routine activities of the carters, excepting contracts for transport. Litigation fell into two broad categories, one including disputes between carters and the other covering disagreements with non-carters who sought to infringe upon or limit the carters' privileges. The most prominent source of friction between carters was the custom of sharing winter pastures. Other problems included disputes between owners and managers and between managers and crew members. These cases grew out of disputes between heirs, overgrazing, and misinterpretations of contracts and hiring agreements.[59]

The more important part of the court's activity involved suits between carters and non-carters. The most persistent issue was the carters' right to use all common pastures without paying local fees or taxes. Examples of such disputes can be documented for 1645, 1648, 1668, 1673, 1674, 1719, 1724, 1784, and 1787.[60] The *Juez Conservador* also protected the carters from outside infringements

56. AA Madrid, *Secretaría*, 3-406-63.
57. AHN, *Con.*, leg. 51197-22, 26; Tudela, p. 374.
58. AHN, *Con.*, leg. 2607-2; Gil Crespo, "Requena," p. 57; AA Murcia, leg. 2795.
59. AHN, *Con.*, leg. 51197-5, 12, 16, 19, 24, 30, 32, 46, 49, 52, 60.
60. *Ibid.*, leg. 51197-8, 55, 61; AHN, CRC, *Tomo* II, doc. 68; AHN, *Hac.*, lib. 8038, fols. 338, 339, 350, 356.

on their winter pasture lands, abuses by local residents, and even against damages to their oxen when they strayed into cultivated areas. In the latter situation the court attempted to uphold arbitration proceedings as an alternative to action by the local justices of the peace. It was this court which acted to prevent landowners from evicting carters, forced rental contracts on unwilling landowners, and in some instances assumed jurisdiction in disputes over tithes.[61] The *Juez* also had some supervision over attempts by branches of the government to requisition transport,[62] and he maintained the carters' right to use any road open to local residents.[63]

The jurisdiction of the *Juez Conservador* had definite limits, although in many cases he had the power to decide if disputes actually fell within his domain. He also decided which aspects of more complex disputes belonged within and without the carters' court.[64] In a typical example, a disagreement over the use of a town commons was kept in the carters' jurisdiction, but the resulting assault case was assigned to the regular local courts.[65]

Transportation contracts also remained subject to the ordinary courts, as did a dispute over the pasturing of carting oxen in a carter's home town. Since this involved neither winter nor transit pasture privileges, the carter had to submit to the local court. Similarly, incursions into obviously private pastures were assigned to the local justices.[66] The carters' courts thus had jurisdiction over transit grazing, winter pastures, rights of way, and intra-industry disagreements. By circumventing the regular courts in this manner, the crown greatly increased the carters' chances for impartial or favorable judgments.

The Spanish government thus developed an elaborate system of privileges for the carters. To see that the privileges were respected it created a judicial bureaucracy to enforce them. This bureaucracy served to extend government influence downwards into the private associations of the professional carters. As a result, the carters not only came to rely on government aid, but found it hard to avoid

61. AHN, *Con.*, leg. 51197-12, 21, 27, 28, 34, 40, 41, 51, 53.
62. AHN, CRC, *Tomo* II, doc. 68.
63. AHN, *Con.*, legs. 2177-3; 51197-1, 39, 42.
64. *Ibid.*, legs. 2016-17; 51197-26.   65. *Ibid.*, legs. 1555-2; 2229-31.
66. *Ibid.*, legs. 2229-31; 1936-6; 1733-24.

royal authority. This is the situation which explains why the crown was able to dominate the services of the carting industry.

In general the mechanics of mobilizing these services were quite unsystematic. The government included an array of agencies which independently sought transport as they required it. Authority for demanding the use of carting services rested in the royal council (*Consejo de Castilla*) and was delegated to various governmental bodies and subsequently to contractors working for the crown. If the work was of a type the carters preferred, transport could be obtained by offering the current rates. If the required services were not forthcoming, an administrative official in the relevant locality was authorized to *embargar* (seize or distrain) the needed carts and carters. This was the legal form through which the government asserted the priority written into the carters' privileges. The principle of royal priority involved here dated back to the fifteenth century, when the crown began demanding "baggage service" (*servicio de bagages*) to transport the royal entourage. From very early its terms included the government's obligation to pay a "fair price" for the transportation.[67]

The various uses which government agencies made of the carters are outlined elsewhere, and their demands were generally made without references to each other. The most important of the agencies involved was the *Sala de Alcaldes y Corte*, a subcommittee of the Council of Castile charged with the over-all supply of Madrid. The *Sala* granted and adjudicated certain of the carters' privileges regarding transit pastures within five leagues of the city and winter pastures within twenty-four leagues.[68] The *Sala* relied heavily on the facilities of the carters to ensure adequate supplies. Under Ferdinand VI (1746-1759) the *Sala* experimented with specialized subsidiary agencies such as the Supply Council (*Junta de Abastos*) and a short-lived Commission of the *Cabaña Real*. More enduring was the *Sala's* elaboration of the *Pósito* (Public Granary [of Madrid]).[69] By the 1780's the *Sala* had shifted to large-scale contracts with private organizations, and much of the charcoal, wine, and meat was provided by the *Cinco Gremios Mayores*. The government retained

67. NR, lib. 6, tit. 19, *leyes* 1, 2.
68. AHN, *Con., Libros de Gobierno*, 1804, fol. 1756.
69. AHN, *Códices*, 1272b.

direct control of grain, however, and the organization of the *Pósito* grew steadily.

Towards the end of the century the *Pósito* tentatively began to exploit the potential for rationalizing the use of carting services inherent in the office of the *Juez Conservador*. Since this agency had much information at hand concerning the supply of transport, and also knew the location of the carters' winter pastures, it is not surprising that the *Pósito* began to channel some of its demands through this bureau.[70] This was never done consistently, and some orders for the collection of transport continued to be sent directly to provincial or city officials.[71] Such orders, however, often made use of the information collected by subdelegates. Their lists were used in assigning quotas of carts and animals when coercion was needed to obtain transport. If the crisis was severe, these quotas were extended to include men and animals not normally engaged in professional transportation.[72]

For most purposes there was little coordination of the government's growing demands for transport, with the result that they often conflicted and overlapped. The immediate importance of various government needs differed, and, under pressure of recurrent transport shortages, a rough scale of priorities in the use of carting by the government was evolving towards the end of the century. Use of transport by salt-tax contractors had long had a low priority, and they could neither force carters to leave winter pastures early nor require them to abandon cargoes already contracted in order to handle salt.[73] Wood for naval construction had a higher priority, since the navy could force carters to leave private cargoes, but ship timber in turn had a lower priority than charcoal for Madrid.[74] The highest priority of all went to the transport of grain to Madrid, and it is indicative that it was the Madrid Granary which first made use of the information collected by the *Juez Conservador* to centralize transport requisitions.

*   *   *

There can be no question that the government was seriously concerned with preserving a readily accessible pool of transport

70. Gil Crespo, "Mesta de carreteros," p. 225.
71. AHN, *Con.*, leg. 1232-13.   72. *Ibid.*, legs. 2607-2; 11452.
73. AHN, *Hac.*, lib. 8038, fol. 351.   74. AHN, *Con.*, leg. 1184-20.

services. Carting, because of the nature of its operations and the fact that it had its own organizations, could be subjected more easily to government influence than the muleteers. Moreover, it had certain routine needs which the government could provide, notably access to grazing. These conditions allowed the evolution of a relationship in which the carters were always on call for government needs and received in return government subsidies in the form of access to resources, especially land, which otherwise would have been inaccessible or expensive.

The carters' elaborate guarantees regarding the use of winter pasture lands, however, put them in opposition to towns and individuals owning such land. The increase in the population of Spain which began at mid-century magnified the potential resistence to such privileges since it brought a corresponding demand for conversion of pasture to arable land. At the same time, the export market in wool was increasing, generating an expansion of sedentary sheep raising. This too provided an incentive for landowners to rid themselves of the carters as tenants.

The carters' free access to the resources of the town common lands created permanent friction between the villagers and the carters in at least two ways. In the immediate sense, many townspeople depended on common pastures to support their livestock and provide wood. Pasture is relatively scarce and thin in Castile, and the recurrent arrivals of groups of a hundred hungry oxen was a matter of great concern to local residents. In the long run, the population pressure just mentioned increased the numbers of people wholly or partially dependent on common lands.

To resist such pressures and enforce the privileges of the carters, the government created the system of courts and attorneys with jurisdiction over disputes affecting those privileges. This court was headed by a member of the royal council and had the power to decide just what cases were to be included under its jurisdiction. The special courts could and did reflect government policy in protecting the carters, at least after 1730.

To the extent that the carters' privileges were successfully enforced, the government was forcing owners of pasture land to subsidize the carters. In effect, the crown diverted land resources to the support of a portion of the transport system which was responsive to government needs. The subsidized carting industry was then used to fulfill the general needs of the government in Castile and to supplement the provisioning of Madrid, the administrative center. This last was of crucial importance because of the city's unreliable sources of supply and the subsequent precariousness of public order in the capital.

In thus subsidizing the carters, the crown undoubtedly encouraged the growth of the carting industry, but also diverted the services produced away from the private economy. These services were used instead to supply the steadily growing capital to the point where, in years with poor harvests, Madrid was vitally dependent upon this government-aided transport. Thus the special privileges of the carting industry, applied throughout Castile, represent one of the ways in which the countryside was forced to support an unproductive capital. To put it another way, the privileged position of the carters represented a form of disguised taxation exacted from the countryside and used to support the government and its capital. At the same time, the carting industry became dependent on the government for essential pasture lands and therefore could not escape government demands for its services, even when more attractive alternatives appeared.

This situation curtailed the supply of professional transport available to support economic growth. It could only continue so long as the government could effectively resist the pressures of landowners and users to shift land to what they considered more profitable uses. As government resistance failed, the position of the carters deteriorated. Because of the lack of alternative sources of transport, the incipient transport crisis became a serious economic bottleneck.

Chapter eight. *Transport and the economy, 1750-1850*

Despite the physical obstacles to transport and the scattered population of the Spanish interior, a substantial volume of goods was transported over considerable distances in the eighteenth and early nineteenth centuries. While the size of this trade cannot be estimated with any precision, the number of recognized transporters was about 50,000 in the 1750's. Some 10 per cent of these, mostly carters, were specialized carriers primarily dependent on transporting for their incomes.. The total transport pool involved approximately 142,000 pack animals and 14,000 carts, the latter having the capacity of about 55,000 additional animals.

This transport activity fell into three fairly well defined categories, servicing three distinctive types of commodity transfers. The first of these categories was a class of private transporter-traders which provided the transport needed to distribute small quantities of expensive, low-volume trade goods such as manufactures, imported merchandise, and special consumption items. It is doubtful that there were as many as a thousand such muleteers in all of Castile. In a few areas, such as western León, northern Salamanca, Seville, and Cuenca, there were numbers of professional pack-train carriers with up to twenty-five pack animals. These carriers provided connections between the interior areas and the seaports. In much of Castile, however, the demand for this type of transport was apparently satisfied by a very small number of *ordinarios* visiting the major centers to buy specific commodities on special order. In western Spain the demand for luxury commodities was met almost entirely by the periodic trips of these individuals with their strings of three or four pack animals.

The second major category of transport activity focused on the needs of the central government. Most of the transport services for this business were provided by the long-haul professional carters of the *Cabaña Real*. Owning and operating several thousand oxcarts which averaged five long cargo hauls each year, these transporters carried the salt, ship timber, monetary metals, etc., which the bureaucracy required. More important than these varied activities was the role of the carters in the government's efforts to supplement the supply of Madrid. The carters, under government contract, brought a substantial proportion of the city's basic necessities. As a minor part of their yearly travels, the carters also played a role in the private sector of the economy by contributing to the timber supplies of many cities and especially by carrying wheat, flour, and wool, Castile's major export commodities, from the interior to the seaports.

The third type of transport, by far the most prevalent, involved interregional transfers of basic commodities such as grain, wine, charcoal, and fish. Such transportation was invariably done by part-time transporters whose primary occupation was agriculture. In some cases, this transport work involved disposing of a regional surplus or a special product for cash, but more often it reflected exchanges of commodities based on regional specializations or imposed by nature. The plains of Castile produced wheat and wine, the mountain areas charcoal and wood, the coastal areas fish, fruit, and vegetables. The volume of such regional trade is extremely difficult to measure, but it appears that about four-fifths of the people considered as transporters were involved in carrying such goods. It seems likely, however, in view of the government's concern for the provisioning of Madrid, that these part-time transporters were not able to provide fully for the city's needs. Indeed, the examples of such activity presented suggest that a great deal of this interregional trade involved rural-to-rural transfers, or even a simple seeking out of supplemental supplies of basic commodities for the transporters' home areas.

The boundaries between the three categories were often blurred. Some seasonal carriers transported valuable trade goods. Some specialized pack animal carriers worked for the government, carrying tobacco, salt, and even grain for Madrid. The carters were not, at mid-century, completely dominated by the government. Despite these inconsistencies, the categories are conceptually sound.

Several circumstances helped to determine the volume of transport which developed. The size of Castile, its numerous physical barriers, and its scattered population suggest a substantial degree of local economic isolation. Set against these conditions, however, were the pronounced natural variations between areas, and the irregular productivity of most agricultural areas, which created periodic local deficits in food supplies. These geographic determinants were, of themselves, no guarantee of more than irregular transport activities, and do not completely explain the substantial transport activity observed.

A positive incentive encouraged the part-time peasant-transporter to engage in transportation if he had the animals to do so. The agrarian and weather cycles of Castile combined to leave the peasant with several months in the late summer and the fall during which no productive activity was possible at home. During these idle months the peasant, his family, and his animals continued to eat. For such a person there was virtually no opportunity cost implied in engaging in transport activities. If the peasant recovered the out-of-pocket expenses unique to transporting and only a part of his daily living costs from transport activity, his general economic position was improved thereby. Under such circumstances, transportation could be relatively cheap as compared with professional overland transport, and it was this factor which made possible fairly extensive transfers of bulky commodities in the Spanish interior.

The potential of this large volume of unorganized transport as a source of specialized, professional transport services was limited. Pack animals provided a more flexible form of transportation than oxcarts, but, tied to the farm cycle, they were available only on a very irregular basis. Such services as they provided were generally associated with the transfer of basic commodities which the transporter or his neighbors either produced or consumed directly. Channeling this activity into transportation of a more specialized nature would have entailed administrative problems beyond the capacity of the bureaucracy of eighteenth-century Spain. Moreover, the conversion of such people to specialized transporters would have robbed farming of a large portion of its scarce animal power,[1] de-

1. In the "last third" of the eighteenth century Spain counted only 590,000 mules,

stroyed the cost advantages inherent in the peasants' position as agriculturalists with periods of seasonal idleness, and disrupted the subsistence supply mechanisms of the countryside. These assertions are supported by the observation that the only pack-animal transporters who were really specialized operated either under the same conditions as the professional carters, or as transporter-traders handling low-volume, high-value goods, for which the costs of professional specialized transport remained a small part of the final price. The basic imperfection in the market for transport services which the above suggests is substantiated by the observed difference between transport costs in the countryside and the much higher transport costs incurred by the government when it mobilized specialized transport services.

The critical factor in the supply of professional transport services was the carting industry. The two special circumstances which made possible its extensive operations involved ingenious use of equipment and grazing resources, and a privileged status maintained by the royal government. By organizing small holdings of carts into larger trains with small, professional crews and managers, the expenses of operating the carts were kept to a minimum. At the same time, migration to distant winter pastures enabled the carters to keep their oxen healthy over the winter, while oxen which were wintered on the carters' mountain farms usually were in poor condition by spring. With such pasture arrangements, often coupled with judicious selection of pasture sites, the carters could count on an increased number of payloads during the seasons when the roads were passable.

In addition, carting benefited from a privileged position provided by a government anxious to have a reliable supply of transport at hand. This special status involved specific guarantees of winter pasturage and free access to all common grazing lands in the country. It also made the carters dependent upon the desires and effectiveness of the crown.

The special privileges granted the carters represented a distortion introduced by the government into the transport and trade patterns of the country, and perhaps into the entire economy of

horses, and donkeys in comparison with over 2,000,000 peasant farmers (*labradores*). Vicens Vives, *Historia*, IV, 160.

the Castilian interior. It is unlikely that the carting industry could have become as large as it did without the subsidy the government provided in the form of protected grazing lands. Since this subsidized carting industry was used primarily to supplement the Madrid supply system, it is probable that Madrid would not have become as large as it did without government intervention in the transport system. Government intervention thus used a form of transport subsidy to spread part of the cost of supporting Madrid throughout the country. From the government's viewpoint, this support of Madrid was essential for maintaining public order in the capital. Such intervention, however, made the carters an unreliable source of transport for economic activities more complex than the movement of basic consumption goods.

In the last analysis there were severe inherent limitations in the system of long-haul bulk transport which evolved in the interior of eighteenth-century Spain. The carters were the only significant source of professional transport services specialized enough to carry alternately raw materials, manufactures, exports, or urban supplies as the economy required. As the end of the century approached, the demands for such services grew, yet the potential of the carting industry for expansion was increasingly limited.

The growing need for specialized transport is apparent in various ways. The population of the countryside was rising steadily after about 1750, and with it, total agrarian production. In Castile, however, the increases came from the ploughing of wasteland rather than from the use of improved techniques. Since the newly enclosed land tended to be of poorer quality than the land which had remained in cultivation, and the peasants lacked animals and the fertilizer they produced, the marginal product of new laborers tended to fall.[2] As a result, the rural surpluses which had customarily gravitated toward Madrid were increasingly retained in the economy of the countryside. At the same time, the general increase in population encouraged migration to Madrid and hence a greater demand for food and fuel in that city. The population of Madrid increased some 20 to 25 per cent between 1757 and 1790.[3] Because of the irregularity of Castilian grain output and the growing demands of

2. Carr, *Spain*, pp. 13-14, 23-30.
3. Domínguez Ortiz, *El siglo XVIII*, pp. 55-76.

the subsistence economy, the need for order in the capital required that a greater proportion of the city's supplies be arranged by the government, using the services of professional transporters. An important side effect of this situation was that while in the 1750's the import of grain by sea was an exceptional measure, by the 1780's substantial amounts of wheat were being imported for Madrid almost every year.[4] Since the transport of grain from the seaports effectively doubled the distance and time required to move a given cartload of grain to Madrid, compared with its transit from Old Castile, the number of supply trips each cart could make was correspondingly reduced. In other words, because of loss of transport time and increased empty backhauls, the volume of transport services absorbed by food imports for Madrid tended to be larger than the actual volume of freight involved and larger than the transport space used by similar cargoes under more normal conditions.

The demands for transport to supply Madrid and to fulfill routine governmental needs were augmented by an increase in the demand for transport in the North. While in the 1750's the wool trade required 6,000 to 7,000 cartloads of capacity, by the late 1780's the wool and flour trades required as much as 14,000 cartloads a year.[5]

The inelasticity of the supply of such transport is suggested by the increase in its price from 1773 to 1787, by the fact that the government was perforce evolving an informal system of priorities regarding its use of carting facilities, and by the tendency towards a degree of centralization in coordinating such transport demands. The degree to which the government monopolized the specialized transport of the interior is suggested by the difficulties of Catalan textile manufactures when they sought to send goods to interior markets. They were forced to pay steadily rising prices for Catalan and Valencian transport because none was available in the interior and because there was no return cargo which could be sold profitably in Barcelona. As a result, Catalan goods appear to have penetrated the interior only to the extent that Catalan transporters

4. AHN, *Con.*, legs. 1843-2; 49240; AA Murcia, leg. 2795; Vicens Vives, *Historia*, IV, 160.
5. Palacio Atard, p. 83.

were available.[6] In analytical terms, the demands of the government made the transporters of the interior even more scarce and expensive than those of Catalonia, forcing shippers to pay the prices exacted by the Catalan transporters.

Part of the explanation for the limited growth of the carting industry of the interior comes from the fact that it required large and widely scattered daily and seasonal grazing lands. Castile, a country of poor grasslands, relied on the use of oxen and mules for agriculture as well as transport in the eighteenth century. This created heavy local demands on available grazing with the result that there was a low ceiling on the total number of cart trains which could be operated in the country without arousing local resistance. Carters partially corrected for this by utilizing the numerous interconnecting trails between important centers. This allowed access to a greater number of town commons than a single highway, regardless of its quality. The use of primitive roads had serious drawbacks, however, since they limited the carters to crude vehicles even on level terrain. In the mountains, the roads degenerated into paths which were impassable for any type of cart.

The carting industry was also subject to two types of short-term fluctuations in its ability to provide transport services, one seasonal, the other recurring but unpredictable. The custom of going into winter pastures and the general state of the roads in the wet winter months produced annual seasonal shortages of transport. This yearly shortage was regular and predictable, but nevertheless kept the carters inactive nearly a third of every year. There are some indications of pressure upon the carters to leave winter pastures early.

The more serious short-term problem was that of supplying the growing city of Madrid during the recurrent droughts which have long plagued the Spanish interior. When the rains—and the crops—failed, it was necessary to import grain by sea and to cart it inland to Madrid. As suggested, this doubled the length of haul for such food and reduced the seasonal capacity of each cart, creating an automatic and unavoidable reduction of transport capacity at times of peak demand. Moreover, the droughts which killed the crops also killed the grass along the roads, further limiting the transport system in such crises.

6. Vilar, *Catalogne*, III, 57-58; Vicens Vives, *Manual*, pp. 504-505; Borrow, pp. 290-91.

There is little doubt, moreover, that these crises worsened as the century wore on. Grain had to be brought to Madrid from the sea in varying quantities in 1723, 1734, 1750, 1752-1753, 1763-1764, 1773, 1784-1793, 1800-1805.[7] In 1773, for example, so few transporters appeared at the grain depots, despite their obligations, that it was necessary to use military escorts to assure compliance.[8] By the 1780's even a mild reduction in crop yields required grain imports for Madrid, indicative of the impact of the general population increase on the supply of grain for urban markets. The supply problems of the 1780's were met without complications or starvation, but the crisis of 1800-1805 was more serious.

The year 1804 was symptomatic of the growing bottleneck in overland transportation. To move imported grain to the interior, the government forbade carters from engaging in any other transport, public or private, and raised the price it offered to transporters. It then resorted to requisitioning farm carts and animals in the area around Santander where the grain entered. Finally, in desperation, it was reduced to requisitioning the garden, household, and horse-training carts of the wealthy class in Madrid. This makeshift transport was despatched to Santander to fetch grain. By such methods the government avoided outright starvation in the capital in 1804-1805. Subsequently crops improved, but shortages were still pronounced in 1806 when heavy requisitioning of transport brought new complaints.[9]

The dangers of a breakdown in the supply system are made clear by reference to events in 1811-1812. The disruption of the supply mechanism by the war, plus a short crop, caused some twenty thousand people to die of starvation in Madrid in that winter and spring.[10] The periodic diversions of all transport to supply Madrid were unavoidable and were bound to be detrimental to economic development which depended on regular supplies of transport services.

Behind these short-term limitations in the supply of professional transport was an even more fundamental limitation on cart trans-

7. AHN, *Con.*, legs. 1843-2; 49240; AA Murcia, leg. 2795; Vicens Vives, *Historia*, IV, 160.

8. AHN, *Con.*, leg. 2491-3.   9. *Ibid.*, leg. 49240.

10. Gabriel Lovett, *Napoleon and the Birth of Modern Spain* (New York: New York University Press, 1965), II, 537.

portation. Such transport depended heavily on grazing lands, and ultimately on the will of the government to enforce the privileges of access given the carters. In opposition to this was a steadily growing rural population requiring the enclosure and ploughing of increasing quantities of grazing lands. This enclosure movement was actually encouraged by other facets of government policy designed to create a productive peasantry. Jovellanos, in the 1790's, while demanding more sweeping reform, lauded the government for its internal colonization projects, limited disamortization of royal, municipal, and even church lands, and for its attacks on the Mesta of the migratory sheep raisers, an institution even more vulnerable to enclosure than the carting industry. These policies dated from the 1760's and were considerably accelerated in the last decades of the century.[11] Accompanying this was the gradual spread of Liberal attitudes concerning land ownership, propagated by such luminaries as Jovellanos and Florez Estrada;[12] they maintained that the owner was entitled to choose freely the most profitable use for his land. Under such pressures, the government's policy of support for the *Cabaña Real* implied a contradiction with its enclosure policies. Thus both of the vital mainstays of carting, plentiful pastures and government support, were eroding away, facts which explain the inelasticity of the industry's supply of services.[13]

The government, it is true, attempted to retain pasture areas for the carters in newly enclosed districts, but this proved difficult to enforce, especially after the Napoleonic Wars.[14] The impact of such enclosures at the local level can be measured by developments on a typical estate near Salamanca, where the number of tenant farmers rose from 189 in 1750 to 436 in 1825 and 861 in 1887.[15] On the national level, 1800 to 1860 saw the addition of 4,000,000 hectares to the area cultivated, an increase of 60 per cent in sixty years.[16]

11. Jovellanos, "Ley Agraria," pp. 81, 85. Richard Herr is now completing a major study of the disamortization under Charles IV.

12. See Marcia Dell Davidson, "Three Spanish Economists of the Enlightenment: Campomanes, Jovellanos, Florez Estrada" (Ph.D. dissertation, Duke University, 1962).

13. Vicens Vives, *Historia*, IV, 30-36; Klein, concluding chapters; Joaquín Costa y Martínez, *Colectivismo agrario en España* (Madrid, 1915).

14. AHN, Con., leg. 2868-25; Klein, *loc. cit.*

15. Cabo Alonso, p. 367 ff.

16. Vicens Vives, *Manual*, p. 585; *Historia*, V, 233.

The pressure on the land led to a resurgence of landlord and local interests seeking to convert rented pastures and common lands to more profitable uses such as farming and sedentary sheep raising. The effect of the enclosure movement upon the carting industry even before the Napoleonic era is illustrated by the fate of the winter pastures which had been specifically reserved for cart animals in 1701. Despite prolonged litigation and government support, half of the grazing for 3,800 oxen allotted in 1701 had been lost by the 1790's. Clearly the carting industry was facing a bleak future due to population expansion because of its dependence on open pastures and commons, just at the time when the economy needed more transport facilities. With all of its other difficulties after 1793, the government was unable to resist these trends, and this fact is clearly shown in the decline of the *Cabaña Real*.

During the supply crisis of 1804-1805, the government used the traditional device of opening stubble lands and harvested vineyards to the carters to increase grazing area. When the carters actually sought to use such pasturage, the government was unable to prevent their harassment.[17] Indeed, in the same year the government surrendered its power to force the rental of private pasture to carters in transit by finally recognizing the permanent exemption of such ground from use by carters.[18] In similar crises of the eighteenth century, the carters had always had the right to rent such pastures for an established fee. Later in 1804 the financial plight of the crown forced it to decree an extraordinary levy of 300,000,000 *reales*, the biggest single tax assessment in the history of the country. In traditional fashion, the sum was distributed among the towns and cities to be raised by means of extra taxes (*arbitrios*) on foodstuffs and on the use of otherwise free common pastures. The *Cabaña Real*, which never before had had to pay these special levies, routinely petitioned for exemption, but, for the first time, did not receive it. The only guarantee they got was that they would not be liable for a rate any higher than that paid by local residents.[19] In 1806 the carters managed to get a general reiteration of their priv-

17. AHN, *Con.*, leg. 2868-25.
18. *Ibid.*, leg. 2425-2; NR, lib. 7, tit. 28, *ley* 6, note 13.
19. Santos Sanchez, *Colección de todas las pragmáticas, cédulas, provisiones, circulares, autos acordados, bandos y otras providencias publicadas en el actual reinado del señor Don Carlos IV* (4 vols.; Madrid, 1794, 1797, 1801, 1805), IV, 335.

ileges, but in the same year their total exclusion from private pastures was reaffirmed.[20]

Despite the supposed "restoration" of the Old Regime under Ferdinand VII, the decay of the carters' privileges continued steadily after the defeat of Napoleon. The unsettled conditions of the war period had disrupted the established winter pasture arrangements and had allowed many landowners to change tenants and raise rents, giving rise in the years after 1814 to numerous suits over who had the right to which pastures.[21] In 1815 the crown reaffirmed all of the carters' privileges as of 1808, and there exist a number of cases in which the courts sought to uphold them.[22] This apparently was not very successful since the government had to issue general restatements of privileges, particularly the arbitration privilege, in 1815, 1816, 1817, and 1818.[23] The transit pasturage rights grew difficult to maintain and disputes came from all over the country.[24] While attempting to support the carters in these matters, the government rather inconsistently revoked their exemption from military service in 1816, and in 1817 deprived them of the right to carry arms. [25]

In 1819 two major road tolls reappeared in direct violation of the decrees of 1796 and 1797 which had suppressed them.[26] In the same year the *Juez Conservador* received reports from various subdelegates about the increasing frequency of disputes, the lack of enforcement or support from the courts, and the deteriorating roadways.[27] Even the *Juez Conservador* himself was losing power, since a right-of-way case, which once would have been under his jurisdiction without question, was handed over to the superintendent of roads.[28]

The whole privileged position of the carters received another severe blow when, in 1821, the revolutionary government of 1820-1823 specifically abolished all of the carters' privileges and stated that all pastures were to be used by their owners as they saw fit.[29]

20. AHN, *Con.*, legs. 2868-25; 2501-10; *Libros de Gobierno*, 1815, fol. 1073.
21. AHN, *Con.*, leg. 51197 contains about thirty documents of this type.
22. *Ibid.*, leg. 2868-25; *Libros de Gobierno*, 1815, fol. 1073.
23. AHN, *Con.*, leg. 51197-17, 34, 40, 41, 51.
24. *Ibid.*, leg. 51197-8, 31, 44, 55, 56, 61.
25. *Ibid.*, leg. 51197-35; Tudela, p. 379.   26. AHN, *Con.*, leg. 51197-42.
27. *Ibid.*, leg. 51197-63, 64.   28. *Ibid.*, leg. 51197-50.
29. NR, tit. 7, lib. 28, *ley* 1, n. (a).

The privileges were renewed by Ferdinand VII in 1823,[30] but they retained little vitality. It appears that in the 1820's pastures were being enclosed at a great rate, and the government attempted only to regulate the process, insisting in 1825 that some portion of each pasture be set aside from enclosure for use by the carters. Complaints about lack of compliance continued even though the decree was repeated in 1828. Also in the 1820's more road tolls reappeared, specifically at Fromista, Ayllon, Valeras, and Tordesillas in Old Castile, and at Montalbán in New Castile. These were upheld by the crown as a special form of tax (*arbitrio*) necessary to meet the urgent needs of the government.[31] Thus the government acquiesced in the revival of road tolls under a different name.

Support in Madrid became so lax that in 1833 the *Cabaña Real*, acting through the *alcalde* of the Soria-Burgos Brotherhood, petitioned for the dismissal of the incompetent *Juez Conservador* of the time, nominating a replacement of its own choosing.[32] The final triumph of the Liberal ideal of land ownership over the carters' privileges came in 1836 when the government of the Regency issued a royal order reviving the decree of 1821 which ended all of the carters' special privileges. The last reference to the *Cabaña Real* of the carters dates from 1840-1841, when the carters of the Soria-Burgos area met and reorganized their council into a purely private and regional organization of cart owners.[33] This was the result of an erosion of the carters' position which had begun in the decade before the Napoleonic invasion of Spain.

During the eighteenth century Castilian society and the Spanish government evolved a complex and ingenious system of transport facilities which succeeded reasonably well in meeting the needs of the situation in the interior. There were no significant alternatives to the system which developed. Better roads and more efficient freight wagons might have eased the situation, but because of unfavorable resources and rough terrain, wagon roads would have cost more than in, say, France, and the Spanish crown had less money for such investments than other European countries. What revenue there was had to go to support Spain's wide-ranging commitments

30. AHN, *Con.*, leg. 2868-25.   31. *Ibid.*
32. *Ibid.*, leg. 11867.   33. Tudela, p. 375.

as a major colonial power. Canals, as suggested, were tried but provided an even more expensive and less flexible alternative.

By the end of the century the economy was developing a serious bottleneck in the supply of transport services. As the population grew, it was pressing upon the available resources and exposing the inherent weaknesses of the transportation supply, both by reducing its access to resources and by increasing the demand for transport. The large pool of pack-animal transport could not be mobilized because it was already committed to maintaining the established subsistence economy of the interior. Shifting such transporters to specialized activities on a large scale would have removed the cost advantage of the part-time transporter, taken crucial man and animal power from the agricultural sector, and disrupted the essential interregional exchanges of subsistence commodities. The main source of specialized transport thus continued to be the carting industry. The carters had become dependent on the government for support and the government tended increasingly to monopolize their services for the provisioning of the capital. Because of the growing land hunger, changing attitudes about land ownership, and conflicting government land policies, the carters began losing their vital grazing areas and royal support for their privileges. They were therefore unable to increase their services to meet the demand. The result was diversion of transport to government needs, an increasingly precarious supply situation in Madrid, and rising prices for specialized transport services.

After the turn of the century, when the transportation problem was becoming serious, the government was unable to provide the transporters with an alternative to their declining privileges. Any solution would have required direct financial outlays in the form of subsidies or government-owned pastures. After 1793 the crown was never in a position to undertake such programs. The war against the French Republic, the wars against England, the growing extravagance of the court, and the demands of Napoleon created unprecedented drains on the treasury, while the British navy threatened the vital economic ties with Spanish America. The Napoleonic invasion destroyed the colonial links, and with them went the revenues from the colonies and a large part of the tax base in Spain proper. As a result, the regime of Ferdinand VII was left in abject poverty, while faced with continuing internal disorders.[34]

Since transport is vital to economic growth, the limitations of the traditional transport structure, coupled with the lack of real alternatives, helped to create an absolute ceiling for the level of development in Castile. This ceiling remained present for over fifty years, creating a degree of stagnation and backwardness unmatched in Western Europe. This stagnation can be illustrated in various ways, although it is difficult to assign a specific role to transportation in the situation.

In the background were a number of forces beyond the control of any Spanish policy, such as the massive disruption of the war and the collapse of Spanish colonial and foreign trade. These problems greatly exaggerated the general downward trend of prices of the Kondratieff cycle which reached its low point in the 1840's. Spain experienced a massive fall in prices in which the index of prices in Barcelona (base: 1866-1876 = 100) fell from 224 in 1812 to 103 in 1821, 80 in 1830, and 70 by 1843.[35] This apparently had serious effects on the commercialized parts of agriculture, which began to recover only with protective tariffs in the mid 1820's.

Paralleling the deflationary trend of prices was a generally sluggish pattern of population growth and a distinct regression in the process of urbanization. The population figures for the first half of the century are extremely hazy, but available figures suggest a population of 10,541,000 in 1797, 11,962,767 in 1833, and 15,454,000 in 1857. The average annual increase for the whole sixty years was 0.82 per cent, and for the first thirty-odd years of the century it was probably less than 0.4 per cent, well below the 0.6 per cent per year of 1717-1797. Moreover, the distribution of the population increases was very uneven, with the peripheral areas growing faster than the interior. In 1797 the interior areas of Aragon, Navarre, Old and New Castile, León, and Extremadura accounted for 41.6 per cent of the total population of Spain, while in 1857 this had

34. "The whole of Ferdinand's policy was conditioned . . . by bankruptcy: he devoted an incredible amount of his time to raising small private loans to pay the palace staff and to minor house-keeping economies." Carr, *Spain*, p. 148.

35. Vicens Vives, *Historia*, V, 119-20; *Manual*, p. 666; Juan Sardá, *La política monetaria y las fluctuaciones de la economía española en el siglo XIX* (Madrid: C.S.I.C., 1948).

fallen to 37.4 per cent.[36] The sluggish population figures reflect substantial declines in the birth rate and marital fertility rate between 1768 and 1860, which may in turn reflect the abysmal conditions after 1808.[37]

The pattern of urban regression in the early decades is even more striking if one assembles a few scattered population estimates. Barcelona, with 115,000 people in 1800, counted 83,000 in 1818 and reached its prewar size only in 1832. As of 1850 it still counted only 175,000 people.[38] The fate of Madrid is less clear, but from 167,000 permanent residents in 1800, the population fell to an estimated 150,000 in the mid-1820's, recovered to "about 200,000" about 1840, then expanded to 281,000 as of 1851.[39] Cádiz, after reaching a reputed 100,000 people during the war, fell to less than 56,000 by 1840, well below her eighteenth-century totals. Similarly, Cartagena fell from a reputed 60,000 to 30,000. The smaller interior towns tended to repeat this pattern on a lesser scale.[40] There can be no question that war, trade disruption, and internal disorder dealt a serious blow to urban life in Spain in the first half of the nineteenth century.

With generally falling prices, sluggish population growth, and the set-back to urbanization, it is hardly surprising that the basic structure of the interior economy remained unchanged well into the nineteenth century. Madrid, as the dominant economic center, continued to be essentially a focus of consumption. Central Spain remained a congeries of local, autonomous markets, loosely connected by the pattern of regional peasant-transport described earlier. Primitive local industry in woolens, linens, and pottery continued to operate in a framework of subsistence economy and domestic, seasonal inputs, often until the twentieth century.[41] Despite the disamortization of church and municipal lands and the abolition of private entail, the agriculture of the interior continued in its old patterns of extensive dry farming, producing low yields with small, widely scattered marketable surpluses.[42]

36. Vicens Vives, *Historia*, V, 19-21; *Manual*, 560-61.

37. Massimo Livi-Bacci, "Fertility and Population Growth in Spain in the Eighteenth and Nineteenth Centuries," *Daedalus*, Spring, 1968, pp. 529-30.

38. Antoni Jutglar, *La era industrial en España* (Barcelona: Ed. Nova Terra, 1963), p. 70; Vicens Vives, *Manual*, p. 565.

39. MacKenzie, pp. 105-109; Ford, III, 1075.   40. Ford, I, 315, II, 618.

41. Carr, *Spain*, p. 202.   42. Jutglar, pp. 82-83.

The persistence of this situation interacted with two parallel developments, the continued backwardness of transport and the violent fluctuations of food prices in times of poor harvest. The continuation of the old transport patterns after the dissolution of the carters' association, with strong emphasis on pack-animal carriage, was noted by Barrow in the mid 1830's and by Ford a few years later.[43] The one significant achievement in internal transport, the linking of the Canal de Castilla with the Santander-Reinosa highway, laid the basis for a substantial export trade in wheat and flour to Cuba in the middle decades of the nineteenth century. Until 1866, however, the savings brought by the canal were in large part negated by the long haul through the mountains in carts which Ford described as "coffin looking concerns with solid, creaking wheels."[44] There are signs of some increase in the supply of professional muleteer transport, such as the doubling and trebling of the size of the muleteer towns of León between 1752 and 1877, and a doubling of the number of registered muleteers in certain towns around Salamanca, but these professional muleteers continued to rely on pack animals until the actual introduction of railroads. Only then in desperation did they shift over to mule-drawn wagons in an effort to remain competitive.[45] By the time of the food supply crisis of 1867-1868 the railroads were beginning to figure in wheat transport, but large quantities were still transported long distances by mule and oxcart.[46] Thus the stagnation in the supply of transport may not have been total, but any expansion in the first half of the nineteenth century was within the older economic framework, and little of it brought any reduction in the costs and irregularity of transport services and the oppressive weight of those costs upon internal economic activity.

The effects of this persistent bottleneck in transportation can be seen in the violent fluctuations of prices in periods of poor harvests and in the substantial differentials in price between the pro-

43. Borrow, pp. 290-291; Ford, III, 1362-63.

44. Vicens Vives, *Manual,* p. 611; Ford, III, 1362-63.

45. Martín Galindo, *Arrieros maragatos,* pp. 16-17, 27; Cabo Alonso, p. 121. p. 121.

46. Nicolás Sanchez-Albornoz, "En Espagne, au XIXe siècle: géographie des prix," *Melanges d'histoire economique et sociale en hommage au professor Antony Babel* (Geneva, 1963), II, 201.

ducing and consuming areas. A careful examination of Earl Hamilton's indices of commodity price movements in various regions and of his indices for group prices in New Castile for the eighteenth century shows numerous regional differences in price levels and rates of change in prices.[47] Jovellanos was well aware of this problem in the eighteenth century, noting that the price of Leonese grain was sometimes four times higher in coastal Asturias than at its point of origin, a difference which he explicitly attributed to transportation.[48] A comparison of grain prices in Salamanca as opposed to Madrid for the period 1793-1807 shows a persistent differential of 50 to 80 per cent.[49] As late as 1865-1866, when crops were fairly normal, a similar differential existed between prices in the producing areas (Valladolid, Badajoz, Zaragoza) and the important peripheral cities of Barcelona, Oviedo, and Cádiz.[50] There can be no question that this continuing differential was in large part due to the bottleneck in transporation which crystallized in the late eighteenth century and restricted the movement of grain from producer to consumer.

In times of bad harvest, the inefficiency of transport reversed the price differentials between coast and interior because of the difficulties which it imposed upon the movement of imported grain to interior destinations. During the crisis of 1803-1805 interior towns such as Valladolid and Toro experienced cyclical increases in food prices of as much as 330 per cent between 1800 and 1805, while on the north coast, easily supplied by sea, the increases were about 150 per cent. The same pattern persisted in the crisis of 1867-1868 when interior areas experienced wheat price increases as high as 200 per cent as opposed to 50 to 75 per cent in the major seaports.[51]

It is necessary to emphasize that the stagnation and persistence of old economic patterns in the early nineteenth century did not preclude important changes in the economy of the interior. As men-

47. Hamilton, *War and Prices*, pp. 156, 264-67.
48. Jovellanos, "Dos informes," pp. 456-57.
49. Gonzalo Anés Alvarez, "Las fluctuaciones de los precios del trigo, de la cebada y del aceite en España (1788-1808): un contraste regional," *Moneda y Crédito* (Madrid), núm. 97 (1966), pp. 90-91.
50. Sanchez-Albornoz, "Géographie des prix," figs. 1, 2.
51. Anés Alvarez, pp. 90-91, 121-22; Sanchez-Albornoz, "Géographie des prix," pp. 204-205.

tioned earlier, the middle decades of the century saw radical reform in the market for land, widespread enclosure, and a 60 per
cent increase in the area under cultivation. Vicens Vives sees this
as a continuation of the process begun in the eighteenth century
after a period of retrogression from 1814 to 1835, although he ad-
mits that the expansion may have resumed as early as 1825.[52] In the
1830's not only was land commercialized, but total freedom was
established in transactions involving food, drink, and fuel; thus
some of the obstacles to trade and speculation in those essentially
agrarian commodities were removed.[53]

With the exception of wine production, there are strong indications that this massive increase in output brought relatively
little commercialization of interior agriculture. Between 1800 and
1860, while acreage increased greatly, the per acre yield suffered a
5 to 10 per cent decrease and the per capita output of grain fell
from 371 to 355 kilograms.[54] Carr suggests that much of the agricultural expansion was a speculative phenomenon, in which local
notables bought up disamortized land with a minimal capital investment and then rented it to land-hungry peasants with no tech-
nical abilities other than those of the prevailing primitive methods
of the subsistence economy. The result was in large measure an extension of the patterns of the eighteenth century. To the extent
that agriculture was commercialized, it was on the basis of primitive techniques and transport behind a wall of artificial protection.
The export of wheat and flour to Cuba, which began in the 1780's,
expanded in the nineteenth century on the basis of a monopoly in
Spain's colonial markets which was a direct outgrowth of eighteenth-
century policies. Except in times of severe crisis, the domestic grain
trade became increasingly a monopoly of the interior producers as
they coerced the government into maintaining high tariffs on
agrarian imports from 1825 onwards.[55] Such protection, by minimiz-
ing foreign competition, thus eliminated one source of pressure for
innovation.

The whole process distinctly resembles a phenomenon common
to many backward areas in which local elites, while seeking to ex-

52. Vicens Vives, *Historia*, V, 235.   53. Carr, *Spain*, p. 198.
54. Vicens Vives, *Manual*, p. 585.
55. *Ibid.*, p. 639; Carr, *Spain*, p. 198.

ploit new economic opportunities, also attempt to retain their local powers as landlords, moneylenders, and occupants of the positions of official power, allowing themselves to arrange rules of tenure and credit to their own advantage. Agriculture in such a situation may be commercialized to the extent of using local sovereignty to squeeze a greater marketable surplus from the peasantry. But to change the basic structure so as to offer direct incentives to the peasantry, such as secure tenure or moderate rents and interest rates, in order to stimulate improvement of soil and technique, presented unthinkable risks to the local power structure. The situation, as described by Domínguez Ortiz and Gerald Brenan for both eighteenth- and early twentieth-century Spain, shows remarkable similarities to nineteenth-century China, as described by Southworth and Johnston, and eighteenth-century France as described by Alfred Cobban.[56]

If the local elites of the interior in the nineteenth century were unable or unwilling to bring about structural changes in the rural economy, the same might be said of the economically more advanced elites of the coastal areas. The merchants of Barcelona, the North Coast, and Cádiz had long since become conditioned to look to maritime grain supplies to supplement local production, simply because it was cheaper than grain brought overland from the interior. With the imposition of agrarian tariffs in 1825, they were forced to accept dependence upon the more expensive domestic sources, since at that point they were in no condition to resist tariffs or to channel capital into the rural economy in order to bring about significant changes in production.

The prosperity of the peripheral areas depended upon Spain's foreign trade, and this was a chancy business. Even before the loss of the American empire, the wars with England in 1796-1802 cut off colonial markets and shut down one-third of the Spanish textile industry.[57] The permanent loss of the colonies and the silver and markets which they had provided had a devastating effect upon Spanish trade. In 1798 Spain's foreign trade had a total value of

56. Herman Southworth and Bruce Johnston, eds., *Agricultural Development and Economic Growth* (Ithaca: Cornell University Press, 1967), pp. 86-89; Domínguez Ortiz, *Siglo XVIII*, pp. 281-97; Gerald Brenan, *The Spanish Labyrinth* (Cambridge: The University Press, 1964), pp. 93-102; Alfred Cobban, *The Social Interpretation of the French Revolution* (Cambridge: The University Press, 1965), chaps. iv and v.

57. La Force, *Textile Industry*, p. 16.

around 2,308,000,000 *reales*, about half of it involving the colonies. By 1828 Spain's foreign trade was reduced to 718,400,000 *reales*, about one-fifth of which involved the remnants of her empire. With the total volume of Spanish trade at one-third of its eighteenth-century level as of 1830, it is no wonder that the coastal towns were in obvious decay, and one could hardly expect them to act as a dynamic force in the development of the interior. The peripheral areas had no choice but to submit to the political demands of Madrid and accept the increased food costs which were implied by agrarian tariffs. Thus they were placed in a poor position in the future to re-enter the world market for non-agrarian goods.[58]

There can be no question of the stagnation of Spain in the first decades of the nineteenth century, and there is no lack of obvious reasons for it. The conservatism of interior elites, the collapse of Spanish trade, the loss of the empire, the stagnant population, and the regression of urban life all can be shown to have interacted in a highly regressive fashion at least until 1840. The problem, therefore, is to define the role of the transportation bottleneck which developed when the traditional transport methods failed to provide the necessary services and no applicable alternatives were available.

The problem of transport, in fact, contributes explicitly or implicitly to almost all of the negative factors; contributing to great instability in food prices, failing to integrate the interior and allow the development of greater specialization, and unable to provide the peripheral areas with alternative sources of supply and markets after the debacle which cost Spain her empire.

The costs of this lack of transportation can be suggested by a look at the direct benefits which an improvement in transport offers a given area. The most important of these is the reduction in the share of a commodity's final sale price which must be paid to transporters. As this is reduced the farm price experiences a corresponding increase; thus more income is channeled directly into agriculture. A related fringe benefit comes from the fact that better transport is usually faster and less seasonal, with the result that it reduces the volume of capital tied up in goods undergoing shipment or in stockpiles held as buffers against seasonal lack of transport.[59]

58. Jutglar, p. 83; Vicens Vives, *Historia*, V, 276-80.
59. John W. Mellor, *The Economics of Agricultural Development* (Ithaca: Cor-

The impact of such direct benefits can be striking. As an example, wagon transport in the United States cost thirty to seventy cents per ton-mile in 1800-1819. The combined river-road route from Buffalo to New York City averaged about nineteen cents per ton-mile. With the construction of the Erie Canal, this figure fell to less than one cent per ton-mile, with a corresponding increase in the prices paid to farmers in Buffalo.[60]

In addition to such direct benefits applicable to the existing traffic, a transport improvement usually implies a host of indirect benefits. Higher farm prices mean additional buying power in the countryside, incentives to invest in production either for the distant market or to supply the new local demands, and a whole sequence of multiplier effects which raise the level of economic activity at both ends of the new transport facility.[61]

There is no question that even at existing levels of economic activity important potential benefits of this nature were lost to Spain because of the inability to adapt either old or new transport techniques to changing conditions. It is only necessary to refer to the numerous interregional price differentials mentioned earlier. In Chapter V it was shown that a large share of the substantial interregional differences in two specific instances could be attributed to the high cost of transport. Gonzalo Anés gives the prices of grain in all of the Spanish provinces for the years 1793-1807, demonstrating such differentials in concrete terms. To cite only one example, the price of wheat in Madrid was generally five to fifteen *reales* higher than in Toledo only fifty kilometers away, the price in Madrid varying between fifteen and eighty-seven *reales*.[62] This same differential shows up even more clearly in Antonio Sanchez-Albornoz' prices for 1866, when wheat prices in Valladolid, Badajoz, and

nell University Press, 1966), p. 340; Albert Fishlow, *American Railroads and the Transformation of the Ante-Bellum Economy* (Cambridge, Mass., Harvard University Press, 1965), pp. 22-25, 43-49; Hans A. Adler, "Economic Evaluation of Transport Projects," in *Transport Investment and Economic Development*, ed. Gary Fromm (Washington, D. C.: Brookings Institution, 1965), p. 179.

60. Harvey H. Segal, "Canals and Economic Development," in *Canals and American Economic Development*, ed. Carter Goodrich (New York: Columbia University Press, 1961), p. 227.

61. Fishlow, p. 14; Segal, p. 283; Richard B. Heflebower, "Characteristics of Transport Modes," in *Transport Investment and Economic Development*, p. 35.

62. Anés Alvarez, pp. 91-97.

Zaragoza hovered around fifteen *pesetas*, while in Barcelona, Cádiz, and Oviedo they fluctuated around twenty-three *pesetas*.[63]

With improved transportation, these differentials would have been reduced and the prices in the producing areas substantially increased. In a way, therefore, the poverty of agriculture in the interior was not simply due to uneconomic attitudes and the poverty of resources. In part it was due to the necessity to sacrifice much of potential farm income to transport costs in order to market a commodity at all.

The transportation bottleneck thus played an important role in creating or reinforcing the prolonged stagnation of the interior during the first half of the nineteenth century, encouraging an entrenched and selfish local conservatism which remained powerful throughout the century. The products of the perennially backward interior became increasingly unable to compete with imported agrarian commodities, and the landowning classes insisted on high agrarian tariffs to protect a high-cost agrarian sector. The resulting high food and raw material prices transferred the cost of backwardness to the more progressive areas of the periphery without a corresponding increase in prices paid producers. Manufacturers were therefore priced out of foreign markets and could find few alternative outlets in the static interior. Lacking markets, Spanish industries remained small and inefficient, requiring high industrial tariffs to protect the limited local market.

Thus the ramifications of the transport bottleneck which appeared at the end of the eighteenth century worked for decades to contribute to Spain's most basic economic and political problems. Clearly many factors other than transport contributed to the stagnation of nineteenth-century Spain, but in the interior little headway could be made against them until the transportation bottleneck was broken.

63. Sanchez-Albornoz, "Géographie des prix," figs. 1, 2.

Appendix A. *The* Catastro

The most important single source for Chapters II, III, and V was the so-called *Catastro del Marques de la Ensenada.* The *Catastro* is a detailed economic survey of Castile in the years 1748-1752, made as a preliminary to a proposed reform of the complicated and often unproductive tax system. In place of the existing complex of excise, sales, and nuisance taxes, the crown sought to introduce a single annual tax levied as a fixed percentage of the income or wealth received by every property owner and wage or salary earner. The Spanish used the term *utilidad* or "utility" to designate the generalized income concept. Depending on the context, *utilidad* translates as income, wages, salaries, rent, interest, profit, or value added.

To institute such a sweeping reform it was necessary to have a systematic body of information about the wealth of the nation and the income which the population derived from this wealth. The Spaniards sought to build up a reliable estimate as to the size of this *Utilidad Nacional,* a crude version of the modern concept of national income. This global figure was then compared with the annual costs of the national government. In the final (and futile) calculations, the figures suggested a six per cent tax on the incomes of all individuals and corporate bodies.

The purpose of the *Catastro,* or cadastral survey, was to provide the requisite information about the economy and to serve as a guide for provincial, local, and even individual tax assessments. Every economically active person was asked to answer a questionnaire regarding the size, location, and quality of his lands and his livestock, and his earnings from them and from any part-time activities. Those in service occupations, such as government officials, doctors, transporters, merchants, etc., were to indicate their annual incomes based on the average of the preceding five years. Artisans and manufacturers were to indicate their daily wages and the number of days worked in the average year. Using these replies, each municipality was to compile a detailed set of collective answers to a list of some forty questions intended to cover all income-producing property and activities. Each provincial government then used these municipal replies to compose a set of tables listing types, quality, and earnings from land holdings, livestock holdings, manufacturing activities, service activities, religious property of all types, and property belonging to the Crown of Castile.

Most of this laborious survey was actually carried out, although with widely varying degrees of precision and comprehension, and a surprisingly large proportion of the materials still exist. In the archives of the provincial branches of the Spanish Treasury there may be as many as 10,000 books and bundles of individual replies to the *Catastro*. The municipal replies compiled from these individual responses have survived in the form of 670 bound volumes of manuscript in the *Archivo General de Simancas*. All but four of the more than 100 folio volumes of summary charts from the provinces are available in the *Sección del Consejo de Hacienda* of the *Archivo Histórico Nacional* in Madrid. In addition, the Simancas Archives contain 1,200 *legajos* of materials collected in the 1760's when the government attempted to rectify and up-date the original survey.

For a detailed description of the history and nature of the single-tax project and the *Catastro*, consult Antonio Matilla Tascón, *La unica contribución y el catastro de la Ensenada* (Madrid: Ministerio de Hacienda, 1947). The statistical appendix of this work, unfortunately, suffers from a somewhat uncritical use of the totals provided by the summary books in the *Archivo Histórico Nacional*.

The *Catastro* materials, taken collectively, provide a virtually inexhaustible mine of information about the economic life of the lands under the Crown of Castile in the mid-eighteenth century. One must, however, be very careful about attempting to construct any precise statistics on the basis of such material. The lack of trained personnel in compiling data, general awareness that the *Catastro* was connected with new taxes, and the complexity of the project all contributed to substantial differences in the quality of information from different areas. The problems inherent in this are demonstrated by the results of the *Comprobaciones* of the mid-sixties. Despite obvious prosperity the rectifications of that decade suggested a substantial fall in the *Utilidad Nacional* since 1752! Such difficulties, however, ought not deter one from using this unique and valuable source.

The volume of individual answers was so great, and the material so dispersed, that it proved impossible to make use of them. Examples of these individual replies were examined in places as widely separated as Córdoba and Valladolid, and the impression received was that they dealt primarily with land-holding arrangements and farming incomes. That is not surprising in an overwhelmingly agrarian economy, but since this study dealt with a particular service industry, it meant that the personal replies in the *Catastro* materials could be set aside.

An examination of the summary books at Madrid and the replies from the municipalities at Simancas indicated that with a suitable technique these materials were manageable. A careful reading of the questionnaire and of a number of complete replies from each province indicated that virtually all references to transportation activity appeared under question thirty-two of the municipal replies. In making this preliminary survey, careful note was taken of all details, including the revenue or earnings from various types of transport in each province.

This information from the Simancas collection was then compared with the summary books in the *Archivo Histórico Nacional* in Madrid. Section F of these summaries for each province lists, across the top of the tables, the numerous service occupations encountered in the replies, generally including columns for muleteer and/or carter "utility." The towns of the provinces are listed down the left side of the tables either in alphabetical order or by administrative district. The total "utility" value for each type of service activity is listed after the town name under the appropriate heading. The preliminary information from the Simancas materials was compared with the entries under muleteer and carter "utility," and a minimum "utility" figure established for each province. This minimum was generally equivalent to the listed earnings of three to five local muleteers. Totals below this minimum were ignored in order to simplify the final task by eliminating references to transport activity of a purely local nature or extremely small scale. A list of all towns reporting transport activity with earnings more than the arbitrary minimum was taken from the summary tables for all provinces except Guadalajara and Toledo, since the relevant summary books from those provinces have disappeared.

The precise reference for the summary books in the *Archivo Histórico Nacional* (Madrid) is *Sección del Consejo de Hacienda, libros* 7401-7509. In the course of the study, about half of these books were examined in greater or lesser detail. The product of this survey of the summary books was a list of three to four thousand municipalities which indicated some kind of transport activity above the established minimum. This amounted to about one-fourth of the places actually replying to the *Catastro*. This list was then taken to Simancas, and, with the aid of the alphabetical index to the *Catastro*, the replies to question thirty-two by these towns were read and all references and details relating to transportation were noted. Since the summary books for Guadalajara and Toledo were missing, it was necessary in addition to examine the replies from all towns in order to obtain the information desired. This proved valuable since it also indicated that by eliminating the really small "utility" figures as described above, a relatively small amount of transport activity was left unrecorded.

The task was limited by the exclusion of two areas, Murcia and Galicia. The exclusion of Murcia, including the modern provinces of Murcia and Albacete, was unfortunate since the summary books indicated a considerable amount of transport activity in some Murcian towns on the main route from the Mediterranean coast to Madrid. It was made necessary by the fact that the replies from Murica contained nothing but formulaic phrases referring to documents which are unavailable. The region of Galacia was excluded because it appeared after the preliminary survey that the area was the source of very little transport activity which made contact with the Castilian interior. Since the resources for making the study were limited, it seemed better to concentrate on areas where transportation activity was more extensive. Despite these geographic restrictions, the work of checking the replies and making the preliminary surveys involved the equivalent of about six months of work in the archives. The work was possible only because of the assistance of a remarkably diligent young Spanish woman studying at the University of Valladolid.

All information thus found was summarized in tables made for each province, indicating town, types of activity and cargoes, numbers of individuals, animals and/or carts, "utility" per unit, and total transport "utility" for each town. From these tables it was possible to extract the information included in those tables in the text which indicate the *Catastro* as the source, as well as the bulk of the information which supports the maps illustrating transportation patterns.

Appendix B. *The sources for the maps*

The maps indicating the patterns of transport activity are based upon data drawn from the *Catastro* and supplemented by similar references encountered in various other eighteenth-century sources. About 25 per cent of the raw data on transport movements came from the latter category. The information on winter pastures came almost entirely from references scattered throughout sources other than the *Catastro*. The two types of sources were then combined to produce detailed lists of citations to the sources for each map. The towns providing information are grouped by geographic region (Old Castile—León, New Castile—Extremadura, Andalucía) and by province within each region. Separate columns are provided for the documentary source, the commodity involved, and the origin and/or destination of the cargo. The maps in the text illustrate only those movements described completely by the sources, while the tables include numerous examples of incomplete descriptions of transfers which could not be shown graphically but which fill out the data considerably. In some cases, including leather goods, metals, and olive oil, the completed tables did not show enough fully described transfers to warrant graphic presentation.

In their typescript form, the data documenting the maps occupied forty-one pages of tables. Ideally, these should have been included as an appendix to the text. Unfortunately, despite the generosity of the Rutgers University Research Council in subsidizing publication, financial limitations dictated their exclusion. For the few scholars who may be interested in reviewing this material on internal trade and transportation, copies have been deposited in the Rutgers University Library and may be obtained through the library's Reference Department.

Bibliography

I. Contemporary sources (to 1840)

The most fruitful source for the institutional aspect of transport is the *Archivo Histórico Nacional* in Madrid, especially the *Sección de Consejos*. The *Sección de Cleros* of the AHN yielded some information regarding the cost of transport. The other major source is the *Archivo General de Simancas*, which preserves the 670 volumes of the answers to the *Catastro del Marques de la Ensenada* made in the early 1750's. Details on the *Catastro* are presented in the appendices. The key to using the *Catastro* materials is the 109-volume statistical summary in the *Sección del Consejo de Hacienda* of the AHN. A third governmental collection, useful for the early background of the *Cabaña Real de Carreteros*, is the *Archivo de la Real Chancillería de Granada*.

Attempts were made to use the Provincial Historical Archives, where thousands of notary books are gradually being collected, but these proved disappointing as a source of information about transport. Various private collections were checked, including the Medinaceli Archives (Casa de Piloto, Seville), the Institute of the *Condado* of Valencia de Don Juan (Madrid), the papers of the great Osuna family (AHN, Madrid), the papers of Alba family (Palacio de Liria, Madrid), and those of the Duke of Frias (Castillo de Montemayor, Córdoba). Only the Medinaceli and Osuna collections were very extensive and accessible and the latter held little of interest on the topic.

Municipal archives yielded a number of scattered sources. They are often surprisingly well organized, and where they are not, the officials in charge are often generous about allowing access to the materials. Among the better organized are those of Madrid, Seville, Málaga, Granada, Murcia, Cuenca, Alcalá de Henares, Palencia, and Burgos. Other such archives used or examined were in Córdoba, Jeréz de la Frontera, Cádiz, Cartagena, Albacete, Segovia, Toledo, Ávila, Salamanca, Zamora, Benavente, Tordesillas, Trujillo, Valladolid, and León. Those of Salamanca and Cáceres were in the process of reorganization. Very little documentation has survived in the archives of the very small towns where the carters and muleteers lived. They may preserve one shelf of old materials, as at Navarredonda de la Sierra, or one or two documents, as at Cañicosa, Palacios, and San Leonardo, but most retain nothing from the eighteenth century.

A. *Manuscripts*

1. The *Archivo General de Simancas, Secciones*:
   a) *Cámara de Castilla: expediente* 1831
   b) *Secretaría de Guerra: legajo* 416
   c) *Régistro del Sello*:

Year	Document number
1487	22
1488	27, 160, 341
1489	178
1490	16, 17, 18, 159, 252, 509
1491	189

   d) *Libros del Catastro*: 670 bound volumes of municipal replies to the *Catastro*, over half of which were used in checking replies from several thousand towns. It would serve no purpose to list individually the books used. Please refer to Appendix A and to the entry for the *Archivo Histórico Nacional, Sección del Consejo de Hacienda.*
   e) *Comprobaciones del Catastro: legajos* 1616, 1643, 1644
   f) *Secretaria de Hacienda, Dirección General de Rentas, 2ª Remesa, legajo* 4894

2. The *Archivo Histórico Nacional* (Madrid), *Secciones*:
   a) *Clero: libros* 707, 10541
   b) *Códices, núm.* 1272b
   c) *Colección de Reales Cédulas: documentos* 68, 465
   d) *Consejos Suprimidos, legajos*:

211	1546	1813	2229	2691
230	1555	1843	2264	2706
395	1564	1845	2288	2736
549	1581	1903	2293	2866
923	1604	1936	2306	2867
933	1608	1963	2334	2868
994	1634	1999	2347	9240
995	1666	2016	2396	11452

1004	1669	2043	2425	11457
1040	1677	2062	2491	11867
1111	1700	2093	2501	49240
1184	1703	2102	2607	49248
1232	1733	2123	2654	49328
1242	1780	2177	2657	51197
1243	1799	2228	2670	

Also in the *Sección de Consejos*, the *Libros de Gobierno* of the *Sala de Alcaldes y Corte*, years 1634, 1783, 1784, 1788, 1804, and 1815.

e) *Consejo de Hacienda*:

    (1) *Ordenes Generales de Rentas*, documents 236, 308, 330, 923, and *libro* 8030, folios 330-80

    (2) *Libros Resúmenes del Catastro*: (See Appendix A)

7402	7425	7444	7469	7492
7403	7429	7452	7472	7503
7406	7434	7456	7476	7505
7418	7437	7463	7481	7508
7421	7440	7466	7489	

f) Osuna, *legajo* 1641

g) *Servicio de Información Documental, legajo* 12

3. The *Archivo de la Real Chancillería de Granada: legajos*:

3–238	3–981	3–1318	3–1428
3–402	3–1036	3–1331	3–1496
3–534	3–1097	3–1370	3–1596
3–684	3–1147	3–1390	3–1658
3–719	3–1311	3–1391	3–1659
3–755	3–1312	3–1403	

4. Municipal Archives:

    a) Burgos: documents 638, 3378, 3477, 3478

    b) Cartagena: *Libro de Rentas* for 1696

    c) Córdoba: *Sección* 5, *serie* 40, *caja* 26

    d) Granada: *legajos* 1088, 1876

    e) Jérez de la Frontera: *legajo* 160; *Libro del Catastro*

    f) Madrid: *Contaduría, legajo* 3-191; *Secretaría, legajo* 3-406

    g) Murcia: *legajo* 2795

    h) Navarredonda de la Sierra:

    (1) *Libro de Privilegios*, 1735

    (2) *Libros de Actas*, years 1636, 1638, 1641, 1664, 1672

    (3) *Libros de Acuerdos*, years 1747, 1749, 1755, 1757, 1766, 1788

  i) Palacios de la Sierra, *Ordenanzas* of 1818

  j) Seville, *Sección* II (*Contaduría*), *carpetas*:

243	285	288	292
244	286	290	326
245	287	291	327

5. Other Archives:

  a) *Archivo de la Diputación Provincial de Burgos*: various uncatalogued account books of sixteenth-century merchants

  b) *Archivo del Duque de Medinaceli*: *Sección del Estado de Medinaceli, legajos* 60, 71

  c) *Archivo Histórico Provincial*, Madrid: *Libros de protócolos* 17343, 17344, 17345, 19266, 19409

  d) *Archivo Histórico Provincial*, Valladolid: *Sección Ruíz*, various account books of the sixteenth century

  e) *Archivo Paroquial de Palacios de la Sierra*: *Libro de Pleitos*, years 1804, 1808

B. *Published contemporaneous materials*

Aside from a few travel diaries, little of the contemporaneous economic literature provides much direct insight into the organization of transportation, despite much talk about roads. In general, the items included below are either cited directly in the notes or proved relatively helpful in understanding the economy of the interior.

Actas de las cortes de los antiguos reinados de León y Castilla, 1020-1559. 6 vols. Madrid: Comisión de Gobierno Interior, 1880-89.

Actas de las cortes de Castilla, 1563-1713. Madrid: Comisión de Gobierno Interior. Volumes published sporadically since 1880.

Beckford, William. *The Journal of William Beckford in Portugal and Spain, 1787-88*. London: Rupert Hart-Davis, 1954.

Bertant, François. "Journal de voyage à l'Espagne en 1659," *Revue Hispanique*, XLVII (1919), 315 ff.

Borrow, George. *The Bible in Spain*. New York, 1899. First published ca. 1836.

Bourgoing, Jean François. *Travels in Spain*. Dublin, 1790.

Cabañes, Francisco Xavier de. *Guía general de correos, postas y caminos.* Madrid, 1830.

Calvo y Julian, Vicente. *Discurso político, rústico y legal sobre los labores, ganados y plantios.* Madrid, 1770.

Censo de la riqueza territorial e industrial de España en el año 1799, formado de orden superior. Madrid: Ministerio de Hacienda, 1960.

Clark, Rev. Edward. *Letters concerning the Spanish Nation, 1760-61.* London, 1763.

Colección de documentos inéditos para la historia de España. 113 vols. Madrid, 1842-95.

Cornejo, Andrés. *Diccionario histórico y forense del derecho real de España.* Madrid, 1779.

Dalrymple, Major William. *Travels through Spain and Portugal in 1774 with a Short Account of the Spanish Expedition Against Algiers.* London, 1777.

Diaz de Montalvo, Alonso. *Ordenanzas reales de Castilla, glosadas.* 2 vols. Madrid, 1779.

Escribano, Joseph Mathías. *Itinerario español ó guía de caminos.* Madrid, 1757, 1760, 1767, and 1775.

Escriche, Joaquín. *Diccionario razonado de legislación y jurisprudencia.* 4 vols. Madrid, 1838, 1874.

España dividada en provincias e intendencias—nomenclátor. Madrid, 1789.

Ford, Richard. *Handbook for Spain, 1845.* 3 vols. London: Centaur, 1966. First published in 1845.

Gonzalez, Tomás. *Censo de la Población de . . . la Corona de Castilla en el siglo XVI, con varios apéndices. . . .* Madrid, 1829.

Gonzalez-Palencia Simón, Angela. *Colección de documentos sobre Madrid.* Madrid: Instituto de Estudios Madrileños, 1953.

Itinerario de las carreras de posta, de dentro y fuera del reyno. Madrid, 1761.

Iturburu, Joaquín. *El secretario de los comerciales.* Madrid, 1818.

Jordán de Asso del Rio, Ignacio. *Historia de la economía política de Aragón.* Zaragoza, 1798; republished, Zaragoza: C.S.I.C., 1947.

Jovellanos, Gaspar de. "Dos informes al Señor Superintendente General de Caminos: el uno sobre la carretera principal y el otro sobre dos transversales, desde Castilla a la costa de Asturias," *Biblioteca de Autores Españoles.* Madrid, 1918. L, 456-67.

———. "Informe de la Sociedad Económica de Madrid . . . en el Expediente de Ley Agraria," *Biblioteca de Autores Españoles.* Madrid, 1918. L, 79-138.

Laborde, Alexander, Comte de. "Voyage pittoresque et historique de l'Espagne (1806, 1811, 1812 et 1820)," *Revue Hispanique*, LXIII (1925), 1-572; LXIV (1925), 1-224.

Labrada, José Lucas. *Descripción económica de Galicia*. El Ferrol, 1804.

Larruga y Boneta, Eugenio. *Memorias de las minas, comercio, etc., de España*. 45 vols. Madrid, 1785-1808.

López, Tómas. *Atlas geográfico del reyno de España*. Madrid, 1804.

MacKenzie, Alexander. *A Year in Spain by a Young American*. Boston, 1829.

Miñano, Sebastian de. *Diccionario geográfico-estadístico de España*. Madrid, 1827.

Moreau de Jonnes, Alexander. *Statistique de l'Espagne*. Paris, 1834.

Novísima recopilación de las leyes de España. First published in 6 vols. Madrid, 1805-1807. Edition used: *Códigos españoles, concordados y anotados*. 9 vols. Madrid, 1850. Vols. 7 and 8.

Ponz, Antonio. *Viaje de España*. Madrid: Aguilar, 1947. First published 1785.

Santos Sanchez. *Extracto puntual de todas las pragmáticas, cédulas, provisiones, circulares, autos acordados y otras providencias publicadas en el reinado del señor Don Carlos III*. 3 vols. Madrid, 1792-93.

———. *Colección de todas las pragmáticas, cédulas, provisiones, circulares, autos acordados, bandos y otras providencias publicadas en el actual reinado del señor Don Carlos IV*. 4 vols. Madrid, 1794, 1797, 1801, 1805.

Swineburne, Henry. *Travels through Spain, 1775-76*. London, 1779.

Thickness, Philip. *A Year's Journey through France and a Part of Spain*. London, 1777.

Townsend, Joseph. *A Journey through Spain and Portugal, 1786-1787*. 3 vols. Dublin, 1792.

Twiss, Richard. *Travels through Portugal and Spain*. London, 1775.

Villuga Valenciano, Pedro Juan. *Reportario de todos los caminos de España*. Medina del Campo, 1546; republished, New York, 1902.

Young, Arthur. *Travels in France and a Tour into Spain, 1787, 1788, 1789*. 2 vols. London, 1794.

II. *Modern secondary sources*

The items which follow were selected according to the same criteria as the preceding section. Included are some of the more important bibliographical and archival aids utilized.

Adler, Hans A. "Economic Evaluation of Transport Projects." In *Transport Investment and Economic Development*, ed. Gary Fromm. Washington, D. C.: Brookings Institution, 1965. Pp. 170-95.

Aguado Bleye, Pedro. *Manual de historia de España*. 2 vols. Madrid: Espasa Calpe, 1954.

Aitken, R. "Rutas de trashumancia en la meseta castellana," *Estudios Geográficos, núm.* 51 (1953), 93-138

Alsina de la Torre, Engracia. "Viajes y transportes en tiempo de los Reyes Católicos," *Hispania*, XIV (1954), 365-410.

Altamira, Rafael. *Historia de España*. 4 vols. Madrid, 1929.

Androoni, Leon. "Commerce and Industry in Spain during Ancient and Medieval Times," *Journal of Political Economy*, XXI (1913), 436 ff.

Anés Alvarez, Gonzalo. "Las fluctuaciones de los precios del trigo, de la cebada y del aceite en España (1788-1808) : un contraste regional," *Moneda y Crédito, núm.* 97 (1966), 69-150.

Ansiaux, Maurice. "Histoire économique de la prospérité et de la décadence de l'Espagne au XVIe et au XVIIe siècles," *Revue d'Economie Politique*, VII (1893), 509-66, 1025-59.

Arija Rivares, Emilio. "La minería montañesa en el siglo XVIII," *Economía Montañesa, núm.* 63 (1955), 34-36.

Asociación Nacional de Ganaderos (now Sindicato Nacional de Ganadería). *Descripción de la cañada leonesa, desde Valdeburón a Montemolín*. Madrid, 1856.

———. *Descripción de la cañada segoviana, desde Casabias al Valle de Alcudia*. Madrid, 1856.

———. *Descripción de la cañada soriana desde Yangüas al Valle de Alcudia*. Madrid, 1857.

Aznarez, Juan Francisco. *Estudios de historia jacetana*. Madrid: C.S.I.C., 1960.

Ballesteros y Beretta, Antonio. *Historia de España y su influencia en la historia universal*. 12 vols. 2nd ed. Barcelona: Saluat, 1943.

Barcelo, José Luis. *Historia económica de España*. Madrid: Afrodisio Aguado, 1952.

Barnett, Harold J., and Chandler Morse. *Scarcity and Growth: The Economics of Natural Resource Availability*. Baltimore: Johns Hopkins University Press, 1965.

Barreda, Fernando. *Comercio maritimo entre los Estados Unidos y Santander, 1778-1829*. Santander: Diputacion Provincial, 1950.

Bérindoaque, Henri. *Le mercantilisme en Espagne*. Paris, 1929.

Béthencourt, Antonio. *Patiño en la política de Felipe V*. Valladolid: C.S.I.C., 1954.

Blasco Jiménez, Manuel. *Nomenclátor histórico, geográfico y estadístico-descriptivo de la provincia de Soria.* 1st ed. Soria, 1880.

Blum, Jerome. *Lord and Peasant in Russia from the Ninth to the Nineteenth Century.* New York: Atheneum, 1965.

Bona, Raymond. *Essai sur le problème mercantiliste en Espagne au XVIIᵉ siècle.* Bordeaux, 1911.

Braudel, Fernand. *El Mediterraneo y el mundo mediterraneo en la época de Filipe II.* Trans. Mario Monteforte Toledo and Wenceslao Roces. Mexico City: Fondo de Cultura Económica, 1953. Original French edition, Paris: Armand Colin, 1949.

Brenan, Gerald. *The Spanish Labyrinth.* Cambridge: The University Press, 1964.

Cabo Alonso, Angel. "La Armuña y su evolución económica," *Estudios Geográficos,* núm. 58 (1955), 73-136; núm. 59 (1955), 367-442.

Calderón, Moreno. *Historia jurídica del cultivo y la ganadería en España.* Madrid, 1912.

Callahan, William J. "Crown, Nobility, and Industry in Eighteenth-Century Spain," *International Review of Social History,* 1966, pp. 444-64.

Cameron, Rondo. *France and the Economic Development of Europe, 1800-1914.* 2nd ed. Chicago: Rand McNally & Co., 1965.

Capella, Miguel, and Antonio Matilla Tascón. *Los cinco gremios mayores de Madrid, estudio crítico-histórico.* Madrid: Cámara de Comercio de Madrid, 1957.

Carr, Raymond. "Spain." In Albert Goodwin (ed.), *The European Nobility in the Eighteenth Century.* London: Adam and Charles Black, 1953, pp. 43-59.

———. *Spain, 1808-1939.* London: Oxford University Press, 1966.

Carrera Pujal, Jaime. *Historia de la economía española.* 5 vols. Barcelona: Bosch, 1943-1947.

Casado, Vicente Rodriquez, "Política interior de Carlos III," *Simancas,* I (1950), 123-86.

Casas Torres, J. "Sobre la geografía humana del Valle de Lozoya," *Estudios Geográficos,* núm. 54 (1953), 781-827.

Castillo, Andres V. *Spanish Mercantilism: Gerónimo de Uztariz, Economist.* New York, 1930.

Cobban, Alfred. *The Social Interpretation of the French Revolution.* Cambridge: The University Press, 1965.

Colmeiro, Manuel. *Biblioteca de los economistas españoles de los siglos XVI, XVII, XVIII.* Academia de Ciencias Morales y Políticas, *Memorias,* Vol. I. Madrid, 1861.

———. *Historia de la economía política de España.* 2 vols. Madrid, 1863; republished, Madrid: Taurus, 1965.

Corona, Carlos. *Revolución y reacción en el reinado de Carlos IV.* Madrid: Rialp, 1957.

Costa y Martínez, Joaquín. *Colectivismo agrario en España.* Madrid, 1915.

Danvila y Collado, Manuel. *Reinado de Carlos III.* 6 vols. Madrid, 1896.

Davidson, Marcia Dell. "Three Spanish Economists of the Enlightenment: Campomanes, Jovellanos, Florez Estrada." Ph.D. dissertation, Duke University, 1962.

Davis, Ralph. "English Foreign Trade, 1660-1700," *Economic History Review,* 2nd ser., VII (1954), 150-66.

———. "Merchant Shipping in the Economy of the Late Seventeenth Century," *Economic History Review,* 2nd ser., IX (1956), 59-63.

Deane, Phyllis. *The First Industrial Revolution.* Cambridge: The University Press, 1965.

Defourneaux, Marcelin. "Le Problème de la terre en Andalousie au XVIIIe siècle et les projects de réforme agraire," *Revue Historique,* CCXVII (1957), 42-57.

Desdevises du Dezert, Georges Nicolas. *L'Espagne de l'ancien régime.* 3 vols. Paris, 1897-1904.

———. *Les Institutions de l'Espagne au XVIIIe siècle.* Paris, 1925.

———. "La Société espagnole au XVIIIe siècle," *Revue Hispanique,* LXIV (1925), 225-656.

Domínguez Ortiz, Antonio. "El almirantazgo de los paises septentrionales (creado en Sevilla, 1624) y la política económica de Felipe IV," *Hispania,* VII (1947), 272-90.

———. "La población española a lo largo de la historia," *Boletín de la Real Sociedad Geográfica,* LXXXVI (1950), 250-85.

———. *Política y hacienda de Felipe IV.* Madrid: C.S.I.C., 1960.

———. *La sociedad española en el siglo XVIII.* Madrid: C.S.I.C., 1955.

———. *La sociedad española en el siglo XVII.* Vol. I. Madrid: C.S.I.C., 1963.

Elliott, J. H. "The Decline of Spain," *Past and Present,* No. 20 (1961), 52-75.

———. *Imperial Spain, 1469-1716.* London: Edward Arnold, 1963.

Encyclopedia universal ilustrada europeo-americana. 165 vols. Barcelona-Madrid: Espasa-Calpe, 1924.

"Equivalencias de medidas antiguas al sistema métrico decimal y viceversa," *Almanaque Agricola Ceres* (1955), p. 261.

Escagües de Javierre, Isidro. "La estructura económica del valle de

Duero (un fecundo ejemplo de la interdependencia económica de Vizcaya) ," *Anales de la Asociación Española para el Progreso de las Ciencas*, XXII (1957), 775-830.

Face, Richard D. "The Caravan Merchants and the Fairs of Champagne: A Study in the Techniques of Medieval Commerce." Ph.D. dissertation, University of Wisconsin, 1957.

————. "The Vectuarii in the Overland Commerce between Champagne and Southern Europe," *Economic History Review*, 2nd Ser., XII (1959), 239-46.

Farinelli, Arturo. *Viajes por España y Portugal desde la edad media hasta el siglo XX*. Madrid, 1920. *Suplementos*, Madrid, 1930, 1931.

Fishlow, Albert. *American Railroads and the Transformation of the Ante-Bellum Economy*. Cambridge, Mass: Harvard University Press, 1965.

Fogel, Robert. "The New Economic History: I. Its Findings and Methods," *Economic History Review*, 2nd ser., XIX (1966), 642-56.

Fontana Lazaro, José. "El 'Censo de frutos y manufacturas' de 1799: un análisis crítico," *Moneda y Crédito, núm.* 101 (1967), 54-68.

Fuentes Martiánez, G. *Despoblación y repoblación de España (1482-1920)*. Madrid, 1929.

García Manrique, E. "Utilización del Catastro para un conocimiento mayor de la situación social de nuestros municipios rurales," *Geográfica*, IV-V (Zaragoza, 1957-58), 80-86.

García Ramila, Ismael. *Bibliografía burgalesa*. Burgos: Instituto Fernán Gonzalez, 1961.

García Terrel, Ana María. *Salduero: Estudio de un municipio de los pinares sorianos del Alto Duero*. Zaragoza: C.S.I.C., 1958.

Gil Crespo, Adela. "La evolución económica de Requena y su comarca," *Estudios Geográficos, núm.* 50 (1953), 44-66.

————. "La Mesta de carreteros del reino," *Anales de la Asociación Española para el Progreso de las Ciencias*, XXII (1957), 210-30.

Girard, Albert. "Le Chiffre de la population de l'Espagne," *Revue d'histoire moderne*, 1929, p. 70 ff.

————. "Le Repartition de la population de l'Espagne dans les temps modernes," *Revue d'histoire economique et social*, 1929, pp. 347-62.

Hamilton, Earl J. *American Treasure and the Price Revolution in Spain, 1501-1650*. Cambridge, Mass., 1934.

————. *War and Prices in Spain, 1651-1800*. Cambridge, Mass.: Harvard University Press, 1947.

Harwitz, Mitchell. "Regional Development Policy." In *Transport Invest-*

ment and Economic Development, ed. Gary Fromm, pp. 144-69. Washington, D. C.: Brookings Institution, 1965.

Heflebower, Richard B. "Characteristics of Transport Modes." In *Transport Investment and Economic Development*, ed. Gary Fromm, pp. 30 ff. Washington, D. C.: Brookings Institution, 1965.

Herr, Richard. *The Eighteenth-Century Revolution in Spain.* Princeton, N. J.: Princeton University Press, 1958.

Hopfuer, Hellmuth. "La evolución de las bosques de Castilla la Vieja en tiempos históricos," *Estudios Geográficos, núm.* 56 (1954), 415 ff.

Hume, Martin. *Modern Spain.* London, 1923.

Indice Histórico Español. Trimestrial. Barcelona: Centro de Estudios Históricos Internacionales. Begins in 1953.

Jiménez de Gregorio, Fernando. *Diccionario de los pueblos de la provincia de Toledo hasta finalizar el siglo XVIII.* Vol I: A-M. Toledo: Editorial Católica Toledana, 1962.

——. *Notas para una geografía de la población murciana.* Murcia: Sucesor de Nogues, 1956.

——. *Notas geográficas y históricas de Valdepeñas a finales del siglo XVIII.* Ciudad Real: Instituto de Estudios Manchegos, 1949.

——. "La población en la jara toledana," *Estudios Geográficos, núm.* 55 (1953), 209 ff.

——.*Toledo a mediados del siglo XVIII, economía, sociedad y administración.* Toledo: Rafael Gomez-Menor, 1959.

John, A. H. "Aspects of English Economic Growth in the First Half of the Eighteenth Century," *Economica*, XXVIII (1961), 176-90.

Jutglar, Antoni. *La era industrial en España.* Barcelona: Ed. Nova Terra, 1963.

Kamen, H. "The Decline of Castile: The Last Crisis," *Economic History Review*, 2nd ser., XVII (1964), 63-76.

Klein, Julius. *The Mesta, 1273-1836.* Cambridge, Mass., 1920.

Kleinpenning, M. G. *La región pinariega.* Groningen: Doruk V.R.B., 1962.

Koenigsberger, Helmut G. "Decadence of Shift? Changes in the Civilization of Italy and Europe in the 16th and 17th centuries," *Transactions of the Royal Historical Society*, Ser. V, Vol. X, 1-18.

Konetzke, R. "Entrepreneurial Activities of Spanish and Portuguese Noblemen," *Explorations in Entrepreneurial History*, VI (1955), 115-20.

Labanda Egido, Pedro. *La raza vacuna de trabajo serranía soriana.* Soria: Junto Provincial de Formacion Pecuara, 1950.

La Force, James Clayburne, Jr. *The Development of the Spanish Textile Industry, 1750-1800.* Berkeley: University of California Press, 1965.

———. "Royal Textile Factories in Spain, 1700-1800," *Journal of Economic History,* XXIV (1964), 337-63.

———. "Technological Diffusion in the 18th Century. The Spanish Textile Industry," *Technology and Culture,* V (1964), 322-43.

Lane, Frederick C. *Venetian Ships and Shipbuilders of the Renaissance.* Baltimore: Johns Hopkins University Press, 1934.

Lansing, John B. *Transportation and Economic Policy.* New York: Free Press, 1966.

Lapeyre, Henri. *Une Famille de marchands, les Ruíz: Contribution à l'étude du commerce entre la France et l'Espagne au temps de Philippe II.* Paris: A. Colin, 1955.

Larraz, López, José. *La época del mercantilismo en Castilla, 1500-1700.* Madrid: C.S.I.C., 1943.

Livi-Bacci, Massimo. "Fertility and Population Growth in Spain in the Eighteenth and Nineteenth Centuries," *Daedalus,* 1968, pp. 523-35.

Lopez, R. S. "The Evolution of Land Transport in the Middle Ages," *Past and Present,* No. 9 (1956), 17-29.

López de Ayala, Jerónimo, Conde de Cedillo. *Toledo en el siglo XVI.* Madrid, 1901.

López Gomez, Julia. "El puerto de Alicante," *Estudios Geográficos,* núm. 60 (1955), 511-83.

López Mata, Teofilo. *La Provincia de Burgos en la geografía y en la historia.* Burgos: Hijos de Santiago Rodriguez, 1963.

Lovett, Gabriel. *Napoleon and the Birth of Modern Spain.* 2 vols. New York: New York University Press, 1965.

Madoz, Pascual. *Diccionario geográfico histórico.* 10 vols. Madrid, 1844-50.

Mantañez Mantilla, María. *El correo en la España de las Austrias.* Madrid: C.S.I.C., 1953.

Martín Galindo, José Luis. "Actividades agrícolas y ganaderas en maragatería," *Estudios Geográficos, núm.* 70 (1958), 55-85.

———. "Arcaísmo y modernidad en la explotación agraria de Valdeburón (León)," *Estudios Geográficos, núm.* 83 (1961), 167-222.

———. *Arrieros maragatos en el siglo XVIII.* Valladolid: C.S.I.C., 1956.

———. "Evolución de las actividades agrícolas y ganaderas en maragatería," *Archivos Leoneses,* XI (León, 1957), 110-37.

Martini, Alberto, ed. *Atlas de España.* Barcelona, 1931.

Martorell y Télles Girón, Ricardo. *Aportaciones al estudio de la población de Madrid en el siglo XVII.* Madrid, 1930.

Masía Vilanova, Juan. "Dos épocas históricas en las comunicaciones alicantinas," *Galatea, núm.* 1 (1954), 14-17.

Mateos, María Dolores. *La España del antiguo régimen: estudios históricos.* Ed. Miguel Artola. No. 0, *Salamanca.* Salamanca: Universidad de Salamanca, 1966.

Matilla Tascón, Antonio. *Historia de las minas de Almadén.* Vol. I. Madrid: Ministerio de Hacienda, 1958.

———. *Indice de las órdenes generales de rentas.* Madrid: Ministerio de Hacienda, 1962.

———. "El primer catastro de la villa de Madrid," *Revista de Archivos, Bibliotecas y Museos,* LXIX (1961), 463-530.

———. *La unica contribución y el catastro de la Ensenada.* Madrid: Ministerio de Hacienda, 1947.

Meijide Pardo, Antonio. *La Emigración gallega intrapeninsular en el siglo XVIII.* Madrid: C.S.I.C., 1960.

Mellor, John W. *The Economics of Agricultural Development.* Ithaca: Cornell University Press, 1966.

"Memorias inéditas sobre archivos españoles," *Boletín de la Dirección General de Archivos y Bibliotecas,* No. 30 (July, 1955), unnumbered appendix.

Menéndez Pidal, Gonzalo. *Los Caminos en la historia de España.* Madrid: Instituto de Cultura Hispánica, 1951.

Merino Alvarez, A. *Geografía histórica del territorio de la actual provincia de Murcia.* Madrid, 1915.

Moxo, Salvador de. *La alcabala. Sus orígenes, concepto y naturaleza.* Madrid: C.S.I.C., 1963.

Mounier, André. *Les Faits et la doctrine économique en Espagne sous Philippe V: Geronimo de Uztariz (1670-1732).* Bordeaux, 1919.

Muñoz Pérez, José. "Mapa aduanero del XVIII español," *Estudios Geográficos, núm.* 61 (1955), 747-98.

Myint, Hla. *The Economics of the Developing Countries.* New York: Praeger, 1965.

Nadal, Jorge. *La población española.* Barcelona: Ariel, 1966.

Palacio Atard, Vicente. *El comercio de Castilla y el puerto de Santander en el siglo XVIII.* Madrid: C.S.I.C., 1960.

Parry, J. H. *The Age of Reconnaissance, Discovery, Exploration, and Settlement.* Cleveland: World Publishing Co., 1963.

Perez Bua, Manuel. *Las reformas de Carlos III en el régimen local de España.* Madrid, 1919.

Perez Bustamonte, Ciriaco. "El reinado de Fernando VI en el reformismo espanol del siglo XVIII," *Revista de la Universidad de Madrid,* III (1954), 490-515.

Perez Valera, Isabel. *Ciudad Real en el siglo XVIII.* Madrid: C.S.I.C., 1955.

Pike, Ruth. "Seville in the Sixteenth Century," *Hispanic American Historical Review,* XLI (1961), 1-30.

Planchuelo Portales, Gregorio. "Aportación al conocimiento de la jara toledana, el rio Jébalo," *Estudios Geográficos, núm.* 51 (1955), 241 ff.

——. *Estudio del alto Guadiana y de la altiplanicie del Campo de Montiel.* Madrid: C.S.I.C., 1954.

Plaza Bores, Angel de la. *Archivo General de Simancas: Guía del investigador.* Valladolid: Dirección General de Archivos y Bibliotecas, 1962.

Quintanilla, Mariano. "La fábrica de paños a comienzos del siglo XIX," *Estudios Segovianos,* X (1958-59), 534-46.

Quiros, Francisco. "Puertollano y su cuenca minera," *Estudios Geográficos, núm.* 63 (1956), 207-47.

Redlich, Fritz. " 'New' and Traditional Approaches to Economic History and Their Interdependence," *Journal of Economic History,* XXV (1965), 480-95.

Ringrose, David R. "The Government and the Carters in Spain, 1476-1700," *Economic History Review,* 2nd ser., XXII (1969), 45-57.

Rios y Rios, Angél de. *Memorias sobre las antiguas y modernas comunidades de pastos.* Reinosa, 1915.

Rivero de Andrea, Fernando. *El Catastro en España, Francia, Italia, Bélgica, Holanda y Suiza: Estudio de legislación comparada.* Madrid: Ministerio de Hacienda, 1957.

Rostow, W. W. *The Stages of Economic Growth.* Cambridge: The University Press, 1960.

Sánchez-Albornoz, Nicolás. "En Espagne, au XIXe siècle: geographie des prix." In *Melanges d'histoire economique et sociale en hommage au professor Antony Babel.* 2 vols. Geneva: Universite du Genève, 1963. II, 191-209.

——. *España hace un siglo: una economía dual.* Barcelona: Ediciones Península, 1968.

Sanchez, Alonso, B. *Fuentes de la historia española e hispanoamericana.* 3rd ed. 3 vols. Madrid: C.S.I.C., 1952.

Sanchez Belda, Luis. *Guía del archivo histórico nacional.* Madrid: Junta Técnica de Archivos, Bibliotecas y Museos, 1960.

Sanchez Gavito, Luis. *Vías pecuarias atraves del tiempo.* Madrid: Sindicato Nacional de Ganadería, 1955.

Sardá, Juan. *La política monetaria y las fluctuaciones de la economía española en el siglo XIX.* Madrid: C.S.I.C., 1948.

Sarrailh, Jean. *L'Espagne éclairée.* Paris: Imp. Nationale, 1954. Spanish ed., *La España ilustrada.* Mexico City: Fondo de Cultura Económica, 1957.

——. "Voyageurs français au XVIIIe siècle," *Bulletin Hispanique,* XXXVI (1934), 29-70.

Segal, Harvey H. "Canals and Economic Development." In *Canals and American Economic Development,* ed. Carter Goodrich. New York: Columbia University Press, 1961. Pp. 216-48.

Shafer, Robert Jones. *The Economic Societies in the Spanish World, 1763-1821.* Syracuse: Syracuse University Press, 1958.

Silva, José Gentil da. *En Espagne, développement économique, subsistance, déclin.* Paris: Mouton, 1965.

Singer, Charles, *et al.,* eds. *A History of Technology.* Vol. III: *1500-1750.* Oxford: The Clarendon Press, 1957.

Sintes y Obrador, Francisco. *Guía de los archivos de Madrid.* Madrid: Dirección General de Archivos y Bibliotecas, 1952.

Slicher van Bath, B. H. *The Agrarian History of Western Europe, A.D. 500-1850.* Trans. Olive Ordish. London: Edward Arnold, 1963.

Smith, Robert Sidney. *The Spanish Guild Merchant: A History of the Consulado, 1200-1700.* Durham, N. C.: Duke University Press, 1940.

Soldevila, Ferrán. *Historia de España.* 3 vols. Barcelona: Ariel, 1952, 1953, 1954.

Southworth, Herman M., and Bruce F. Johnston, eds. *Agricultural Development and Economic Growth.* Ithaca: Cornell University Press, 1967.

Sureda, Carrión, José Luis. *La Hacienda castellana y los economistas del siglo XVII.* Madrid: C.S.I.C., 1949.

——. "La Política económica española en el siglo XVIII," *Anales de Economía,* XXI (1962), 10-55.

Terrel y Cuevas, Angel. *De Covaleda y para Covaleda.* Soria, 1912.

Tudela de la Orden, José. "La cabaña real de carreteros," *Homenaje a Don Ramón Carande.* Madrid: Sociedad de Estudios y Publicaciones, 1963. Pp. 349-95.

Uría Riu, Juan. "Tradiciones sobre el origen de la trashumancia de los 'vaquieros' de Asturias y su interpretación," *Estudios Geográficos,* núm. 56 (1955), 321-35.

Usher, Abbott Payson. *Early History of Deposit Banking in Mediterranean Europe.* Cambridge, Mass.: Harvard University Press, 1943.

——. "Spanish American Navigation." In *Facts and Factors in Economic*

History, ed. Edwin F. Gay. Cambridge: Harvard University Press, 1932.

Vicens Vives, Jaime, ed. *Historia de España y America.* 5 vols. Barcelona: Editorial Vicens Vives, 1961.

————, and Jorge Nadal Oller. *Manual de historia económica de España.* Barcelona: Editorial Vicens Vives, 1959, 1964.

Vilar, Pierre. *Catalogne dans l'Espagne Moderne.* 3 vols. Paris: S.E.V.P.E.N., 1965.

————. *Crecimiento y desarrollo: Economia e historia, reflexiones sobre el caso español.* Barcelona: Ediciones Ariel, 1964.

————. "Le temps du Quichote," *Europe,* January, 1956, pp. 3-16.

Ward, S. G. P. *Wellington's Headquarters: A Study of the Administrative Problems in the Peninsula, 1809-1814.* London: Oxford University Press, 1957.

Way, Ruth. *A Geography of Spain and Portugal.* London: Methuen, 1962.

Index

119; government support of, 8, 119; growth of, 42; as a market, 8, 21, 23, 26, 28, 39, 134; population of, 38-39, 90, 124; Public Granary of, 38, 116; royal palace of, 27; as source of goods for trade, 23; supply of, 10, 15, 22, 30, 31, 33, 37-42, 59, 81, 107-108, 116, 121, 122, 124-27; in transport-trade patterns, 8, 23
Madrid (region), pastures in, 108, 112. *See also* Pastures
Málaga, 21, 58
Manufactures, transport of, 24-31
Maps, sources for, 147
Maragatos, 61, 73, 94, 95. *See also* Muleteers
Market centers, importance of, 24
Markets: colonial, xxi, 30; exterior, xxi; interior, xxi, 6-8, 13, 16, 21, 28, 85; Madrid, 8, 134; national, and canals, 16; for transport services, xxiii, xxiv
Matilla Tascón, Antonio, 144
Mayoral, 65
Meat, supply of, 8
Medinaceli, Duke of, 62; archives of, 65, 68
Mercancias. See Commodities transported
Mercury shipment by cart, 36-37
Mesta of the sheepherders, xxiii, 11, 53, 62, 97, 101, 109
Metals and metal products, 12, 26, 31
Migration, seasonal, by carters, 53, 82
Migratory labor. *See* Labor, migrant and seasonal
Military service, carters exemption from, 98, 104, 106-107, 110
Military, transport for, 31-34. *See also* Government
Mining centers, 12, 36-37
Mints, transport for, 31, 36
Mixed cargoes, transfers of, 28
Monastic lands, sale of, 10. *See also* Enclosures
Monadero, 66
Money, supply of, 11
Mountains as geographical barriers, 3-4
Mules, 44-46, 48
Muleteers, xxiii, 34, 44, 49, 58, 60, 61, 73; as *cabañiles*, 105; in *Catastro*, 145; contracts for transport by, 70; daily routine of, 75-76; and farming, 49, 61; increase in numbers, 135; large scale enterprises of, 58; Leonese, 49, 95-96; organization of, 95; seasonal irregularity of activity of, 55, 75, 90; types of services of, 70; use of by government, 35, 37
Municipal lands, sale of, 10. *See also* Enclosures
Murcia (province), 22, 96, 114, 146

Napoleonic Wars, 15, 33, 128
Navarredonda de la Sierra, carters of, 37, 97
Navy, transport for, 19, 34
New Castile, 9, 10, 21, 22
North coast, export trade of, 41
Novísima Recopilación de las Leyes de España (1804-1807), 109

Old Castile, 10, 21, 22, 23, 28
Olive oil, 21
Opportunity costs, transporter, 56, 122, 123
Ordinances, local, 105
Ordinarios. See Arrieros; Muleteers
Oropesa, Count of, 106